Attachment-Focused Family Play Therapy

Attachment-Focused Family Play Therapy presents an essential roadmap for therapists working with traumatized youth.

Exploring trauma and attachment through a neurobiological focus, the book lays out a flexible framework for practitioners treating young clients within the context of their family relationships. Chapters demonstrate how techniques of play and expressive therapy can be integrated into work with different developmental stages, while providing the tools needed to fully incorporate the family into the healing process. The book also provides clinical examples and guidance on the ethical decision-making needed to effectively implement attachment work and facilitate positive change.

Written in an accessible style, *Attachment-Focused Family Play Therapy* is an important resource for mental health professionals who work with traumatized children, adolescents, and adults.

Cathi Spooner, LCSW, RPT/S, is a licensed clincial social worker, registered play therapy supervisor, clinical trauma specialist, and is certified in basic sand therapy. She is the founder of Renewing Hearts Counseling and Consulting and has been providing psychotherapy to children, adolescents, and their families for over 20 years.

"This book takes the mystery out of integrating play therapy with attachment and family-systems theories. It offers therapists a roadmap to understanding the neurobiology of trauma and connects how trauma affects the brain and the ability to self-regulate. This is a well-written book for mental health professionals utilizing attachment-based play therapy with children, adolescents, and families. Cathi Spooner has done an incredible job providing implementable approaches to help clients build and repair attachments."

— *Althea T. Simpson, LCSW, RPT-S, founder and CEO of Unicorn Life Play Therapy*

"If you are a therapist working with traumatized children and their families, you must get this book! Cathi Spooner guides the reader through the entire play therapy process, using case studies, vignettes, and neuroscience to support and explain the nuances of working with this challenging population. This information speaks to new therapists, as well as seasoned clinicians, and does so in a way that is engaging and affirmative. Using up-to-date research, Cathi Spooner's work is a gamechanger for those of us who are seeking to apply trauma-informed and empirically supported methods to help the families with whom we work. I'm grateful for clinicians such as Cathi Spooner who are willing to share their expertise and experience to expand the knowledge base for those working with this population."

— *Norman E. Thibault, PhD, LMFT, president, Association for Training on Trauma and Attachment in Children (ATTACh); founding owner and CEO, Three Points Center*

"Cathi Spooner masterfully integrates and presents academic research and theory using layman's terms in a way that makes for an effortless and enjoyable read! Ms. Spooner's use of creative counseling techniques affords both clinician and client the opportunity to explore challenging experiences through alternative means. This unprecedented approach to trauma and attachment is a much-needed addition in the field of counseling!"

— *Monica Bergandi, M.Ed., resident in counseling, Bright Horizons Counseling LLC*

"Cathi Spooner has embodied the essence of being a trauma-focused therapist in her book. She takes the reader on a journey through trauma, its effect on neurobiology, and the ways in which a therapist can effectively work with families and/or clients who have experienced trauma. The book describes scenarios and references direct therapeutic interventions that are helpful not only to beginners but also the most seasoned clinicians. It would be impossible to treat the whole client without understanding the dynamics of trauma and its biological impact, and the book does just that. This book is a must read, and the information in it is essential for gaining insight and empathy into the client process."

— *Rebecca Cottle-Makhene, LPC-S, registered play therapist supervisor; certified child and adolescent trauma professional (CATP); licensed professional school counselor*

Attachment-Focused Family Play Therapy

An Intervention for Children and Adolescents after Trauma

CATHI SPOONER

Routledge
Taylor & Francis Group

NEW YORK AND LONDON

First published 2021
by Routledge
52 Vanderbilt Avenue, New York, NY 10017

and by Routledge
2 Park Square, Milton Park, Abingdon, Oxon, OX14 4RN

Routledge is an imprint of the Taylor & Francis Group, an informa business

Library of Congress Cataloging-in-Publication Data
Names: Spooner, Cathi, author.
Title: Attachment-focused family play therapy : interventions for
children and adolescents after trauma / Cathi Spooner.
Description: New York, NY : Routledge, 2021. | Includes
bibliographical references and index. | Summary: "Attachment-
Focused Family Play Therapy presents an essential roadmap for
therapists working with traumatized youth. Written in an accessible
style, Attachment-Focused Family Play Therapy is an important
resource for mental health professionals who work with traumatized
children, adolescents, and adults" – Provided by publisher.
Identifiers: LCCN 2020019786 (print) | LCCN 2020019787 (ebook) |
ISBN 9781138935846 (hardback) | ISBN 9781138935853 (paperback) |
ISBN 9781315672847 (ebook)
Subjects: LCSH: Play therapy. | Family therapy. | Arts–Therapeutic
use. | Psychic trauma in children–Treatment. | Attachment behavior
in children.
Classification: LCC RJ505.P6 S66 2021 (print) | LCC RJ505.P6
(ebook) | DDC 618.92/891653–dc23
LC record available at https://lccn.loc.gov/2020019786
LC ebook record available at https://lccn.loc.gov/2020019787

ISBN: 978-1-138-93584-6 (hbk)
ISBN: 978-1-138-93585-3 (pbk)
ISBN: 978-1-315-67284-7 (ebk)

Typeset in Avenir and Dante
by River Editorial Ltd, Devon, UK

Dedication

To my husband and our two sons, you are my inspiration to continue to grow and be the best person that I can possibly be. Thank you for your support and patience while I spent hours in my office writing, especially when I thought I had no more clinical knowledge left in my brain. Thank you for loving me despite my imperfections and the times when I have blown it. To my sons, you are proof that *good enough* parenting can result in one's children becoming amazing people that any parent would be proud to call their children. I love you more than words can ever say.

To my mother, who relentlessly encouraged me to complete this book and regularly told me how proud she is of me. Mom, from you I learned to be fascinated by the psychology of people and have compassion toward others. You are kind and generous in spirit. Thank you for always believing in me.

To Routledge, thank you for your patience during all of my many life transitions while completing this book. Thank you for the opportunity to write this book.

Contents

Preface

I always knew that I wanted to help children. I remember as a little girl that I felt passionate about helping children overcome problems. Even the books I read when I was young were about vulnerable children and how they were able to overcome their difficulties.

Many years later in the 1980s, while working as a self-contained special education teacher for emotionally disturbed children, I was first introduced to play therapy by a school psychologist and a school social worker. The school psychologist and I began conducting weekly therapy groups with the children in my class using fairy tales. The school psychologist had just read the classic book by Bruno Bettelheim (1976), *The Uses of Enchantment: The Meaning and Importance of Fairy Tales,* and we used the principles of the book to conduct play therapy group sessions. The fairy tales we chose to use focused on children overcoming difficulties. Of course, every good fairy tale includes an evil adult that the child or children must defeat, and I was always the one chosen as the evil adult who must be defeated. I played my part with great enthusiasm as the children defeated me. It was magical to watch them feel empowered and enjoy their experience of the group. What I noticed was that my relationships with the children in my class strengthened as we played together, and through the play they were able to gain that valuable sense of empowerment.

Finding this modality of play therapy was the beginning of my professional journey, but it was another 15 years, after I had obtained my clinical social work license, before I discovered where I could actually be trained in play therapy. In those early years of training as a therapist, no one knew much about play therapy or where one could obtain training. I had long ago lost contact with the school psychologist and school social worker I'd worked with as a special education teacher so I could not ask their advice. In graduate school in 1991, I learned about family therapy and instantly fell in love with it as a way to help struggling youth. Then, in 2002, I met a colleague who knew about play and expressive arts therapy and helped me to get the play therapy training I'd been seeking. I learned that play therapy had grown over the intervening years, which was exciting. It started me on my new adventure in play therapy, combining it with family therapy.

By now, as a practicing child and adolescent therapist, it was my firm belief that children need to heal within the context of family whenever possible. Children are dependent on their family for survival as well for their sense of love and belonging. It's a well-established belief within the field of child and adolescent mental health that children whose families engage in the change process with them make better progress in treatment than do those children whose parents simply drop them off to be "fixed" without engaging in the treatment. I was still finding that in the mental health community, most therapists were working primarily with the child and not with the child's family in therapy sessions. Of course, there are times when individual therapy sessions are critical, but the inclusion of the family can significantly improve treatment outcomes for children. Most of the play therapy models I had learned had focused only on individual play therapy, yet most of my training and my clinical experience as a therapist was focused on children and adolescents along with the family.

I also began to learn about *attachment theory* and the impact of trauma on children and adolescents. I found that I was frustrated with the disconnection between using play therapy with children and the limitations of finding a treatment model that integrated families. Children exist in families, and in my experience working with traumatized children I became aware of the impact of trauma on the whole family. Siblings of victims were also impacted. In many families, several children in the family might have experienced trauma, yet they were all receiving individual therapy, not family therapy⊠even though the family attachment relationships were significantly impacted by the trauma. Therapists were simply not integrating family members into the treatment process. Attachment models not only focused just on parent–child dyads, but also many of the attachment models didn't integrate play and expressive arts into the treatment process.

In my practice I began to remedy this situation by developing the treatment model offered in this book, all of which came from my professional desire to have a framework that helped me navigate through difficult family dynamics using a trauma-informed and attachment-focused lens. I'm also a "neurobiology nerd" so I value the importance of having a research-informed basis for treatment with traumatized children and adolescents. Attachment theory grounded in neurobiology allows for a solid clinical foundation to provide ethical treatment to traumatized families. Since all families and individuals are unique, I think it's important to make sure the treatment model is flexible enough to adjust to the needs of the families and the individuals within these families to avoid a "one size fits all" approach to treatment.

I know I work best when I have a framework to help me navigate through the clinical decision-making process when working with families. It's easy to get "lost in the forest" and unable to find our way out unless we have some kind of a "roadmap." I also noticed that the therapists I supervised also felt more confident when they had a framework to help them provide effective therapy. Initially, the problem was that most of my supervisees were reluctant to provide play therapy with the whole family in order to address the unhealthy family dynamics supporting the mental health challenges of the child. In my experience, most of my colleagues also shied away from therapy sessions that included multiple family members. Because of my firm belief in the power of children healing within a family context, I was very persistent with my supervisees and eventually they became willing to try out my inclusive treatment model. They found that they were able to gain a much better understanding of the family relationship patterns and facilitate change when family members were involved in treatment. The best way to address family relationship patterns is to address them in real time within the session, and using video clips in parent coaching sessions helped parents to become more effective therapeutic agents of change for their children.

The Attachment-based Family Play Therapy model is designed to provide that much-needed roadmap for therapists working with traumatized youth to help their young clients heal within the context of their family relationships. This model uses a neurobiology lens for trauma and attachment, and teaches therapists a framework for integrating the therapeutic powers of play, and family members, into the treatment process to address the impact of trauma on relationships with parents and siblings. As a foundationally trained therapist using Dialectical Behavior Therapy (DBT), I love that DBT teaches specific skills to regulate strong emotions. DBT uses acronyms to help remember the skills. When learning DBT, I realized that most of the skills taught I was already using to help me cope with my own life stressors. In the book, packaging the skills in this way and giving them specific names and an acronym helps clients remember them and use them more effectively. The *Family SPACE* and *3 Rs of Relationship* skills are tried and true attachment-based parenting skills based on research. Creating an acronym for these skills also helps therapists teach the skills to parents, and helps parents remember the skills when implementing them at home.

Video is another key component of this treatment model. I love using video to help me learn to improve my skills and help supervisees improve theirs. Seeing something in real time is much more effective than hearing someone verbally describe a situation. The description will always include that person's perception of the event based on their memory of it. Watching a video of the same event provides the opportunity to observe the situation without the filter of someone else's perception and memory. Video is an invaluable tool for learning to improve clinical skills, and helping parents to become powerful therapeutic agents of change within their family. Once parents get over the initial fear of being judged, they usually recognize the value of videotaping the family sessions.

It has been my privilege to work with families and be invited into their worlds to help them in the healing process. I have been blessed by their willingness to trust me, and to be vulnerable with me as they work through often overwhelming challenges. Life is hard for everyone at some point, and it has been an honor to work with my clients since I first began my clinical journey in 1990. The client stories in this book are fictional, but based on real struggles of clients during my professional career. I use the term parents in the book to avoid confusion and maintain consistency. However, families are diverse and caregivers are often grandparents, foster parents, aunts, uncles, and older siblings. The use of the term parents is not meant to diminish their importance. I also use male pronouns when referring to children. This is also meant to avoid confusion and maintain consistency. I'm sure using male pronouns rather than female or other gender neutral pronouns has much to do with the fact that I am a mother of boys, so my frame of reference typically thinks in terms of male pronouns.

It is my hope that therapists reading this book will find it useful to help families overcome the devastation of trauma and embrace resiliency. Therapists have the ability to influence families and communities for generations based on their ability to heal "one family at a time." This is a sacred privilege. This book is my offering to my colleagues to aid them in this sacred work.

About the Author

Cathi Spooner graduated from Virginia Commonwealth University in 1992 with a Master's Degree in Social Work, specializing in working with children and families. She is an experienced national and international trainer and consultant for mental health professionals, working with children, adolescents, and families. She provides training to mental health professionals on the topics of play therapy, sand tray therapy, trauma, and attachment issues at the local, state, national, and international level. She provides clinical consultation to organizations working with youth and families and provides play therapy and clinical licensure supervision.

Cathi has been an active member of the Association for Play Therapy since 2003, is a Registered Play Therapy Supervisor, is certified in Basic Sand Therapy, is a Certified Trauma Specialist, and is foundationally trained in Dialectical Behavior Therapy. She works with children, adolescents, and adults impacted by trauma and attachment issues, depression, anxiety, grief and loss, behavior problems, court-involved youth, homelessness, ADHD, Autism Spectrum disorder, foster care and adoption issues, parental separation, divorce, and school problems. She has worked with children and their families in a variety of capacities including therapeutic recreation, special education for children with emotional and learning difficulties, residential mental health treatment programs, substance abuse treatment, and outpatient psychotherapy.

She and her husband have two grown sons and two dogs, their furry children. Cathi enjoys hiking and the outdoors. She also enjoys using the healing qualities of art and poetry for her own mental health and self-expression. Her family and love of the outdoors help to keep her grounded in life.

Part I

Neurobiology of Trauma, Attachment, Behaviors, and Emotion Regulation

Rationale for an Attachment-based Family Play Therapy Approach Integrating Play and Expressive Arts

This chapter will provide an overview of research and clinical practice with trauma, attachment, and treatment with families. An introduction to the rationale for an attachment focus when working with families will be discussed, as well as the effectiveness of play therapy and the integration of play and expressive arts. Over the last two decades, mental health professionals have increased their knowledge of the neurobiology of relationships and trauma. The increase in the understanding of how our brain plays a role in our behavior and in our relationships has helped therapists become more grounded in research when developing and implementing treatment models with their clients, especially traumatized clients. Play therapy has been utilized by therapists for decades and has been shown to be an effective modality to help children resolve their mental health problems. Integrating parents as well as other family members into the treatment process has been shown to improve outcomes. Attachment therapists have used neurobiology to help guide their work with traumatized and attachment disordered clients. A brief overview of the treatment model for working with traumatized children and their families will be presented to introduce the basic structure and rationale for integrating play therapy and expressive arts—with a focus on neurobiology.

Three Decades of Research on Trauma and Attachment Neurobiology: An Overview

The last three decades of research have given mental health professionals a greater understanding of how the brain is impacted by trauma and attachment. Professionals with a foundational understanding of the neurobiology of trauma and attachment are able to understand the complex nature of the behavior manifested by traumatized youth within their relationships and daily activities. Our brain *wiring* begins its development *in utero* and continues on up into our late twenties and early thirties. It develops sequentially and hierarchically from the least complex functions in our brain stem to the most complex functions in our prefrontal cortex (Perry, Pollard, Blakely, Baker, & Vigilante, 1995). All of our experiences provide the foundation that influences our individually unique neural wiring with all the nuances of those experiences. We remember each event, each sensory input in our lives—the emotions we felt, what we thought, what we saw, what we heard, what we smelled, and what we physically felt.

These *felt experiences* are stored in our memories with all of this information attached to it. (Perry et al., 1995; Shapiro, 2012; Siegel & Hartzell, 2003; Steele & Malchiodi, 2012; Steele & Raider, 2001). Marrone (2014) discusses the connection between autobiographical memory, attachment, and one's current lived experiences. He explains that our memories are integrated into our daily functioning to better understand the connection between our growing up years and our view of the world and ourselves. Memory and trauma will be discussed in more depth in Chapter 3. When working with traumatized children, it's critical that we understand how children perceive the world and their relationships because those memories become the foundation of their reality and the *lens* through which they interact with others. I like to use the analogy of eyeglasses with colored lenses to understand how our experiences influence our view of the world and others. Imagine that you are looking at the world around you wearing glasses with blue lenses—and that those are the only glasses you ever wore to see. Obviously, your perception would be that the world is blue because the lenses you are looking through are blue. Your perception forms your reality and therefore your decision-making and actions are based on your experience of seeing the world as blue. On the other hand, if I wore purple lenses and perceived the world as purple, and we were in the same room together looking at the same people and things,

I would see the world differently than you in some ways because I would see everything as purple and you would see everything as blue. Our different perspectives would be because of our different realities.

As with all things in relationships, we all have similar perceptions of shared experiences with others in our lives which influences our beliefs about ourselves, others, and the world. To expand on the eyeglass analogy here, let's examine the purple lens to increase our understanding of shared perceptions. The color purple is not a primary color. It's a mixture of blue and red. If you are wearing eyeglasses with blue lenses and I am wearing eyeglasses with purple lenses, then we both have a shared experience of blue hues in our perception of the world. Our perception of the world during relational interactions may overlap through our understanding and beliefs. These shared perceptions and beliefs tend to help us understand one another better. For example, siblings raised in a home with domestic violence will share certain perceptions about family life, while also having slightly different nuances of understanding based on age, temperament, observations, and cognitive abilities. These are important aspects of memory and understanding within family systems that therapists will need to explore to better identify relationship patterns.

The research of Allan Schore (Schore, 2000, 2001; Schore & Schore, 2008) provides an understanding about how early caregiver experiences impact the brain of the developing infant and how the infant responds. These interactions with parents determine the perception of the parents' ability to care for them and keep them safe. Siegel and Hartzell (2003) state the relational mind

> emerges as the flow of energy and information occurs within a brain, or between brains. Studies of infants have long revealed the interpersonal nature of our earliest days: attuned, reciprocal, mutual, collaborative, contingent communication describes the fundamental universal process that links infant to parent.
>
> (p. 95)

It's important for therapists to understand that those early pre-verbal experiences influence later development in children. Even though the children do not have language for these early felt experiences, these experiences are still wired in to memory in the child's brain.

Therapists need to recognize that family members may have differing perceptions of a trauma within a family because each family member will have experienced the same trauma event differently. Family members need help in understanding that each member's lens will result in their experiencing the trauma memory differently, which will influence the healing process for each family member. These concepts will be explored in later chapters in order to provide an understanding of trauma behaviors, support the promotion of healthy regulation of emotions, and help these children and their families create healthy attachments during the healing process.

All behavior is a manifestation of neural transmissions that are triggered by an individual's experiences, as well as by their inherited genetic make-up. This can help us better understand trauma behavior. Our brain consists of about 100 billion neurons interconnected through neural pathways, adding up to a length of over 100 million miles in length. (Siegel, 2001). These neural pathways connect and develop various neural systems throughout our bodies (Perry et al., 1995; Siegel, 2001, 2011; Siegel & Hartzell, 2003). These systems are activated by information received from our environment through our senses (sight, sound, smell, touch, taste), as well as our internal systems processing information to create a response based on the specific functions they are designed to activate, such as basic life functions (breathing, heart rate) and more complex functions, such as learning and walking. Brain development is impacted by the interplay among inherited genetics and environmental influences. The environmental experiences of a child will influence brain development and neural integration at each stage of a child's life. For example, the brain development of a 3-year-old child will look different from the brain development of a 10-year-old child because of their experiences and developmental growth.

The impact of trauma varies across a continuum based on a variety of factors, such as age of impact and brain development, inherent resiliency, understanding of the traumatic event, and access to support. The brain of a child experiencing ongoing trauma at 3 years old will develop differently than the brain of a child who has not experienced traumatic events. The brain of a 10-year-old child who has not experienced a traumatic event until that age will be different from a child who has experienced trauma since early childhood. The integration of neural pathways throughout the brain is dependent upon whether or not the child's experiences stimulate the growth of neural pathways or *prune* them if they are not stimulated (Fishbane, 2007; Perry, 2006; Siegel, 2001, 2011).

There are complex networks of neural pathways that transmit information throughout our body that will elicit a response to information received and processed in our brain. Our brain is an amazing organism that is designed to keep us alive and will respond in ways that will do so. If a threat is perceived through information received via our senses, the brain will be alerted to the threat, real or perceived, and activate survival responses, such as the *fight, flight, or freeze* behavior. If I am walking down the street and I see and smell something or someone that looks unsafe, then my fear emotions will be activated and will alert my brain so the threat can be assessed. Stephen Porges (2011) has studied this phenomenon extensively and created what he calls *Polyvagal Theory*. He coined the term *neuroception* to explain the neural system that assesses threat and activates or deactivates fight, flight, or freeze behaviors. A traumatic event will activate the neural systems charged with the purpose of survival.

If trauma is experienced as an ongoing event, the neural adaptation process will continually activate the body's stress response. Prolonged activation of the body's stress response creates maladaptive behaviors that will become hard-wired (Perry et al., 1995), so to speak, creating trauma behaviors that are persistent and maladaptive—to include viewing the world through a trauma lens. Trauma forever changes one's experience of the world and one's neural system. For the traumatized person, this *trauma lens* becomes his or her reality, even if the perception of threat is not an actual threat. This faulty reality then influences his perception of the world as continually unsafe and will activate largely maladaptive behaviors. These maladaptive behaviors can become a barrier to forming healthy relationships with others. According to Porges (2011), when the threat system is activated then a healthy social engagement cannot occur. Understanding the areas of the brain impacted most directly by trauma can help to better understand the behavior of traumatized children and help them learn how to develop and engage in healthy relationship behaviors (Perry, 2006; Weber & Reynolds, 2004).

The focus of the treatment framework offered in this book is designed to help traumatized children learn to engage in relationship behaviors that are healthy, to form secure attachments with their family members, and later on form healthy relationships with others—as well as looking to their attachment figures to help them learn to effectively regulate their emotions. Most treatment models for traumatized children use an attachment framework to support children in learning how to develop healthy social bonds with parents. Trauma can impact whole family systems for generations if change does not occur. Addressing trauma within the family provides a much better outcome for children since children do not exist in a vacuum. Family members need to learn how to talk about the trauma to feel safe again, and to process their experiences. Therapists need to help family members understand the different colored lenses of each family member to successfully bring healing. Children who are able to heal within a family that is also healing are more likely to develop and sustain resiliency. For families who have experienced generational trauma, it will be important for the trauma to be addressed within the family context in order to break the cycle of trauma for future generations.

Family Systems Theory and Attachment Theory

Family Systems Theory focuses on understanding the complex interactions between family members and their communication patterns in order to better understand the behaviors of those family members. It is rooted in Systems Theory, which provides a more general understanding of interactions between entities. Family Systems Theory provides a framework for understanding relationship patterns and how family relationships impact behavior, whereas *Attachment Theory* examines the quality and nuances of the interaction patterns between primary caregiver and child. Family Systems Theory models can either examine relationship patterns over several generations to examine a broader understanding of the child's behavior and/or examine family relationships within the nuclear family only. The broader view allows therapists to better understand how entrenched certain family patterns are within the child's family. For example, take the family in which there is a history of three generations of abuse versus the family in which there are generally well-functioning parents and then the child experiences a traumatic event one time. The severity of the impact of trauma will be mitigated by the resiliency factors of a generally well-functioning family system. In families with a history of trauma, including domestic violence and addiction, over several generations will have more entrenched dysfunction which will create challenges in the healing process.

Children who grow up in families with a generational history of trauma often lack the parental social support needed because their parents have also experienced trauma which has altered their neurobiology and ability to effectively parent their child without intervention. Many of my clients over the years who come from families with generational trauma have difficulty distinguishing between perceived and actual threat, which influences their responses to social situations. For example, 14-year-old Jane lives with her maternal grandmother, Linda, because Jane's mother,

Mary, is in jail for drug charges. Mary grew up in a home with domestic violence and was sexually abused by an uncle and one of her cousins. Mary learned to deal with the abuse by disconnecting from her emotions and seeking solace in unhealthy friendships with drinkers and marijuana users. Mary's mother, Linda, was distracted by her abusive relationship with Mary's father and unable to provide the needed emotional support for Mary. Linda was sexually abused by her father and also learned to block out the memories by emotionally disconnecting. The generational pattern of relationships in this family system has been that relationships are chaotic, hurtful, and abusive. The ability of family members to recognize threats has been compromised and family members have learned to survive rather than thrive.

When Jane went to live with her grandmother, Linda, after Mary was arrested, she was raped at a party by a boy she liked while they were drinking alcohol and smoking marijuana. Jane reported the rape to a friend who told her own mother who eventually told Linda. This information activated Linda's memories of her own sexual abuse which she had learned to dissociate from (as a way to manage the trauma and escape the pain) so that made it difficult for her to support Jane. Instead, Linda tried to minimize the impact of the traumatic experience on Jane so instead of being able to provide emotional support and advocacy for Jane, Linda rationalized the need to "forget about the whole event" so that Jane could "move on" with her life. However, in order for Jane to really heal from her trauma, she as well as her family members will need to address their own experiences so that they can develop a new paradigm of relationships and safety that includes healthy relationship patterns. Family Systems Theory provides a framework for understanding how trauma relationship patterns are played out within the family system and for helping family members to change them.

Attachment Theory explores how the quality of the relationship influences a child's social emotional development, emotion regulation, and ability to form healthy relationships. From a neurobiology standpoint,

> attachment is considered a basic, in-born, biologically adaptive "motivational system" that drives the infant to create a few, selective attachments in his life. These attachments provide a relationship in which the infant will (1) seek proximity to the attachment figure; (2) have a sense of a safe-haven in which when he is upset the attachment figure will soothe his distress; and (3) develop an "internal working model of a secure base"—an internal schema of

the self with the other self-with-attachment-figure that will provide him with a security enabling him to explore the world, have a sense of well-being, and to soothe himself in times of distress in the future.

(Siegel, 2001, p. 69)

Jane learned that she could not use her mother or her grandmother for safety and support as secure attachment figures because they were impacted by their own trauma histories. Early childhood professionals have focused on understanding the quality of the parent–child relationship and its impact on a number of developmental tasks related to social emotional development. The nuances of parent–child interaction patterns are examined to identify what contributes to healthy, resilient children and what results in difficulties for children in these areas. The work of John Bowlby and Mary Ainsworth (Marrone, 2014) provides understanding about the role of attachment on child development. Bowlby (1982) examined the interactions of mothers and their children which has influenced modern-day understanding of child development. Ainsworth expanded on Bowlby's Attachment Theory and identified styles of attachment that have become foundational principles for mental health professionals (Marrone, 2014; Van Rosmalen, van der Horst, & van der Veer, 2016). Through her work with mothers and children, Ainsworth identified three attachment styles: secure, anxious avoidant, and anxious ambivalent. These attachment styles were later expanded by Mary Main and Judith Solomon (Marrone, 2014) to include disorganized attachment to explain how serious attachment issues impact a child's ability to regulate him- or herself using the parent. Mental health professionals and early childhood professionals working with children have learned much about the importance of early social bonds between parents and their children on the social, emotional, cognitive, and physical development of children.

Over the past several decades, researchers have examined the neurobiological roots of attachment, emotion regulation, and the ability of the child to manage behavior within relationships. Modern attachment theorists have explored how the quality of the parent–child relationship influences self-concept, decision-making, emotion regulation, and behavior. Children raised in families with secure attachment patterns are often resilient and able to effectively navigate the ups and downs of healthy relationships and the world in general, largely because they can effectively regulate their emotions. Parents act as co-regulators for a child's emotions and help the child learn to internalize the ability to manage strong emotions. Attachment-based family interventions focus on helping parents to make changes in their interactions with their child. This change in parental behavior is associated with an improvement in their child's behavior (Kindsvatter & Desmond, 2013). Byng-Hall (2008) advocated for the integration of Attachment Theory in family therapy in order to assist family therapists in recognizing attachment issues that arise within family systems. He stated:

> the attachment system is activated when fear or anxiety is present. Reflecting on frightening times also evokes the attachment response in children from preschool age upward so long as they have begun to develop the ability to reflect on their experience.
>
> (Byng-Hall, 2008, pp. 130–131)

Recognizing attachment patterns within family systems when working with traumatized families allows therapists the ability to help the whole family heal, and disrupt generational trauma patterns.

Attachment and the Development of an Integrated Self

Attachment patterns also play a role in a child's development of a felt sense of self. According to Siegel and Hartzell (2003),

> how we come to talk to ourselves is shaped by how others have talked with us. Those who study narrative as a central feature of how we come to define ourselves hold a similar view: we construct the narrative of our lives based on the nature of the interactions we have had with others.
>
> (p. 97)

The interactional communications between parent and child impact the child's experiences of himself and lay the foundation for an emerging mentalization about self and others. For instance, when an infant is teething and experiencing significant discomfort, he will cry and seek to be soothed and comforted by his parent. The child will experience the soft touch of the parent holding him and gently rocking him. He will look into the parent's eyes seeking a smile and gentle gaze that will reassure him that he is cared for and comforted. The voice tone, facial expression, and body language of the parent will communicate to him an invitation to accept comfort. All of this sensory information will be taken in and processed through the body and brain. If the parent is able to remain emotionally regulated and recognize that the child's cries are the result of physical discomfort and not a rejection of the parenting, then the parent will be able to stay engaged and provide the comfort the child is seeking. The parent will feel competent and their mutual experience of this interaction will be rewarding for both parent and child.

When these experiences of mutual satisfaction of intersubjectivity occur routinely between parent and child, then the shared experiences of the interaction within their relationship are reinforced to be mutually positive. The child experiences himself as loved and valued by his parent. A child's sense of self is initially derived from his interactions with his parent and he will interpret his parent's responses to him as an indication of himself (Hughes, 2006). These experiences between child and caregiver lay the foundation for developing a positive sense of self. However, if the child's parent has a history of poor emotional connection and struggles to tolerate emotional distress, then their shared experiences will not be as rewarding. Parents with limited ability to tolerate emotional distress within relationships will find it difficult to regulate their own emotions in order to help their child to regulate his emotional distress. There will be limited ability to experience their shared interactions as mutually satisfactory.

In his book, *The Body Keeps Score*, Bessel Van Der Kolk (2014) describes what he calls the *Mohawk* of self-awareness. Along the midline areas of the brain from the back to the front are neural circuits that process information coming through our senses and emotions that help us to form our conscious awareness and sense of self. According to Van Der Kolk (2014), these areas of the midline of the brain include the posterior and anterior cingulate, medial prefrontal cortex (mPFC), insula, and orbital prefrontal cortex. The posterior cingulate helps us to recognize physical awareness of where we are in relation to physical space. The mPFC helps our brain to better understand what our amygdala is communicating to us. For example, if my amygdala registers potential threat when I am walking down a street and I observe a car approaching me, then my mPFC will help me to discern the level of danger. It will help me to examine the speed of the car and where the car is in relation to me. When my brain is able to engage the mPFC after becoming alerted to possible danger, then I am able to respond to the situation effectively. For many traumatized people, the ability to effectively process threat is impaired which results in the traumatized person responding to situations in a manner that doesn't fit the situation. The insula acts as a relay station between the sensory information coming in through the body and the emotion processing areas of the brain. The orbital prefrontal cortex integrates the sensory information, and the anterior cingulate coordinates our emotions and thinking. These areas of the brain help us to develop a sense of consciousness of ourselves, and of ourselves in relation to what is happening around us.

This connection between the body and our sense of self is an important concept to keep in mind when working with traumatized people. Van Der Kolk (2014) discusses the impact of trauma in the brain, mind, and body. He states:

> the lack of self-awareness in victims of chronic childhood trauma is sometimes so profound that they cannot recognize themselves in the mirror. Brain scans show that this is not the result of mere inattention: The structures in charge of self-recognition may be knocked out along with the structures related to self-experience.
>
> (Van Der Kolk, 2014, p. 94)

In an attempt to block out certain trauma memories and how they are stored in the mind and body, victims of trauma block out the ability to fully experience themselves and life itself. It's the price that's paid to survive, and will ultimately contribute to a fragmented sense of self. An important aspect of trauma work includes helping victims of trauma to integrate a sense of self which will help them to engage in healthier relationships behaviors. In Jane's family, she was not able to experience her mother, Mary, in a safe manner because Mary had learned to emotionally disconnect through her drug use. Mary was not able to create a sense of safety for Jane because Mary could not feel safe. Jane was also not able to use her grandmother, Linda, as a secure attachment figure because Linda also learned to emotionally disconnect. This family's perception of relationships was that relationships were not safe.

If children are not able to enjoy that shared experience of love and acceptance in a safe environment, then their perceptions of themselves as lovable and acceptable will be impaired. They will develop negative beliefs of themselves that will negatively influence their ability to establish and maintain healthy relationships. Jane developed perceptions of herself as inferior and often sought out friendships with peers who felt the same way about themselves, which made them vulnerable to misuse of drugs and alcohol. This was the case with Jane which eventually led to her difficulty recognizing unsafe peers and vulnerability to exposure to sexual assault by a peer, which ultimately reinforced her perception of relationships and the world as unsafe.

Rationale for Integrating Play and Family into the Treatment Process

Research on play and expressive therapies shows successful outcomes in treatment for children. Using the therapeutic aspects of play, art, music, poetry, drama, and dance provides the ability to address mental health issues in nontraditional ways. Halfon, Yilmaz, and Cadvar (2019) studied 40 children in an outpatient clinic setting using a psychodynamic play therapy model that focused on the use of symbolic play and mentalization. High mentalization (discussed in more depth in Chapter 4) increases one's likelihood of improved emotional wellness. The study examined the effectiveness of this type of intervention using adherence to high mentalization treatment on reducing negative affect states such as sadness, anxiety, and fear. The results indicated the children's affect regulation improved using of the symbolic play intervention that focused on targeting mentalizations. Several studies (Leavitt, Morrison, Gardner, & Gallagher, 1996; Schottelkorb, Doumas, & Garcia, 2012; Tornero & Capella, 2017) using play and expressive arts to address trauma found that play and expressive arts intervention models were effective in resolving trauma in children and adolescents. A review of research literature conducted by Post, Phipps, Camp, and Grybush (2019) to examine the effectiveness of Child-Centered Play Therapy (CCPT) in order to reduce mental health issues in marginalized children found it to be effective in resolving their mental health difficulties.

Bratton, Ray, Rhine, and Jones (2005) conducted a meta-analysis review of 93 studies on play therapy treatment. They found that play therapy was an effective treatment approach and that Filial Therapy improved treatment effectiveness. Filial Therapy is a play therapy approach that teaches parents to be therapeutic agents of change in the therapy sessions with their child. A review of 50 years of research on the effectiveness of Filial Therapy conducted by Cornett and Bratton (2015) concluded that Filial Therapy is an effective treatment approach across a variety of populations, family structures, and mental health concerns.

Art therapists have long understood the benefit of integrating the therapeutic elements of art into trauma work with their clients. Research using art therapy interventions found it to be beneficial for depression and anxiety in elderly women (Ciasca et al., 2018), as well as for the reduction of impulsive behaviors in children with ADHD and comorbid intellectual disabilities (Habib & Ali, 2015), and for trauma in refugee youth (Rowe et al., 2017). Steele and Malchiodi (2012) consider the use of expressive arts to be "trauma-informed because of their ability to allow for processing of the traumatic narrative through nonverbal expressions" (p. 13).

Integrating Play and Expressive Therapies with Families

When working with children, I find the most effective way to establish a therapeutic relationship is to play with them. Play is a natural way in which children explore and learn about the world around them and social relationships. In his book, *The Therapeutic Powers of Play*, Charles Schaefer (1993), views play as a natural mode of communication in the same way that talking is to adults. Play is the way in which children can communicate to others what they are exploring and making sense of in their worlds and their relationships. Integrating play into treatment with families allows for children of all developmental stages to have an avenue to express themselves and engage with family members. To really engage children in the change process, therapists need to meet children where they are developmentally. Gaskill and Perry (2014) advocate for the benefit of using play and expressive arts with traumatized children and the importance of integrating play therapy into the treatment of traumatized children. Perry (2006) developed the Neurosequential Model of Therapeutics to assess and inform mental health professionals about the neurological impact of trauma across the continuum of child development. Gaskill and Perry (2014) "have observed that children participating in play therapy appear to take considerably more time to process information and make effective changes in thinking or behaving, compared to adults in conventional therapies" (p. 181). In my experience, trying to have a 7-year-old child explain the inner workings of his emotions and emotional triggers is often an exercise in futility. Children don't have the cognitive capacity to effectively process deep emotional issues to the extent that an adult is capable. Even adults struggle to identify their emotions and emotional triggers, yet we think a child is able to process their emotions through traditional talk therapy. Play and expressive arts can give me as much or even more information about the emotional issues and cognitive distortions plaguing my clients, and more quickly and with less distress, than traditional talk therapy.

Play and expressive arts modalities also aid in the development of therapeutic rapport to create a sense of safety within the treatment process. Using play and expressive arts with adolescents and adults has provided a valuable tool to help me understand the impact of trauma from the client's point of view. Steele and Raider (2001) advocate for the use of play and expressive arts to help children effectively reprocess traumatic memories. They stated trauma is experienced by children on a sensorimotor level without language and stored symbolically into memory. According to Steele and Raider (2001),

> when that memory cannot be linked linguistically in a contextual framework it remains at a symbolic level for which there are no words to describe it. In order to retrieve that memory so it can be "encoded" and given a language and then integrated into consciousness it must be retrieved and externalized in its symbolic perceptual (iconic) form. Drawing helps to accomplish this externalization.
>
> (pp. 33–34)

It's true—a picture is worth a thousand words. Expressive arts modalities such as art, sand tray, music, drama, and poetry allow clients the ability to first use symbolic representation and then use language to give meaning to the symbols (sand tray figures, artwork, sound, etc.) in order to more effectively process the information stored in the memories. Helping traumatized clients to process and resolve traumatic experiences is an emotionally painful process. Using expressive modes of treatment can help them process the traumatic events in a safe manner. Helping them to feel safe and understood is at the heart of the treatment process.

The use of play and expressive arts therapeutically in the treatment process allows children to engage in the change process and the inclusion of parents in the play sessions increases the benefits of treatment. With children and adolescents, trauma impacts the whole family. Families usually include children in different developmental stages. For instance, consider the challenges involved when working with a family consisting of children in elementary school, middle school, or even high school. These families present challenges for therapists because of the different cognitive, social emotional, and physical needs of each child. It's important to be able to engage all family members in the clinical session in order to observe relationship patterns and the dynamics of the family within the session, as well as to facilitate healing within the family. Including the whole family in the session allows therapists to also observe how parents work to meet the attachment needs of each child within the context of the family. It's impossible to meet the attachment needs of all family members perfectly 100% of the time, so our goal as therapists is to help parents work toward overall balance and to help them facilitate and support healthy relationship patterns to create a sense of positive well-being within the family.

Play and expressive therapies provide an avenue to observe and intervene in *real time* with families during clinical sessions. Play can help to facilitate positive interactions between parent and child as well as between siblings to increase mutual enjoyment within the relationship. Affective neuroscientist, Jaak Panksepp (2010) identified the PLAY system as one of the core emotion circuits in the brain (which will be discussed in more depth in Chapter 2). The PLAY system is "the emotion system that produces feelings of joy; although motivation for play is located in the subcortex, it is capable of programming the cortex to become truly social; located in the brain regions rich in opioids and dopamine" (Kestley, 2014, p. 28). Charles Schaefer (1993) identified 14 therapeutic elements of play. He states that "the basic premise of determining therapeutic factors is that the play therapy process contains a limited number of elements that are differentiated from each other by their specific effects on a child" (Schaefer, 1993, p. 5). These therapeutic elements provide the foundation for creating positive change for the child in clinical practice. Play and expressive therapies provide the ability to engage all family members in the change process while meeting the developmental needs of each child. When working with families with children of diverse ages, the play-based activities provide the ability to include fun as well as therapeutic interventions. This foundation will create an environment that can be experienced by each family member as a safe experience in order to facilitate a therapeutic relationship with all family members.

Porges (2011) explored play as it relates to the neuroception circuits. For example, when is play perceived as a threat versus when is play not perceived as a threat? He determined that the neuroception circuits that assess threat allows for the social engagement system to be activated if no threat is determined to be present. Play occurs within the context of social interaction and can only be experienced as mutually enjoyable when no threat has been assessed. According to Porges (2011):

the social engagement system is an integrated system with both a somatomotor component regulating the striated muscles of the face and a visceromotor component regulating the heart via a myelinated vagus. The system is capable of dampening activation of the sympathetic nervous system and the hypothalamic-pituitary-adrenal axis activity. By calming the viscera and regulating facial muscles, this system enables and promotes positive social interactions in safe contexts.

(p. 270)

Play can be perceived as threatening or non-threatening and will impact behavior within the play interaction. How often have mothers told their sons not to wrestle in the house because their play will instantaneously turn into aggression when one of the boys becomes hurt and perceives the other brother as intentionally causing him harm? Play is perceived as non-threatening and safe until one of the children perceives a threat which will activate the threat system. The threat system and safety system cannot be active at the same time. Since play is a natural behavior for children, understanding the relationship between a child's ability to play and feelings of safety provide therapists with valuable information to help repair relationships within the family. It will be important for therapists to be aware of the interactions within the therapy sessions and monitor the interactions among family members to identify signs of possible threat to help family members process those experiences within the session since these are interactions that likely occur at home and sabotage healthy, safe relationship building.

Integrating Attachment-based Treatment and Expressive Therapies

There are several models of attachment-based interventions with children and their caregivers that integrate play into the treatment process, such as *Theraplay, Filial Therapy, Parent Child Interaction Therapy (PCIT)*, and *Child Parent Psychotherapy (CPP)*. Research has provided evidence of the effectiveness of these models to repair attachment relationships and reduce behavioral problems in children. These positive results were found to include child trauma and neglect and in families from a variety of cultures (Foley, Higdon, & White, 2006; Lim & Ogawa, 2014; Ryan & Madsen,

2007; Solis, Meyers, & Varjas, 2004; Taubenheim & Tiano, 2012; Wettig, Coleman, & Geider, 2011). These models use the therapeutic powers of play, but are limited to dyadic parent–child sessions and not the whole family system. Parents are taught to become the therapeutic agents of healing for their children. Each of these models uses a specific program model for implementation to teach parents skills for attunement and structuring under the direction of the therapist. Another dyadic attachment-based model that works with traumatized children is Dyadic Developmental Psychotherapy (DDP). This attachment-based treatment model focuses on working with parents and their child to improve attachment relationships. Becker-Weidman (2006) studied the effectiveness of DDP for children diagnosed with trauma-attachment disorders. The study included 64 children using a control group and an experimental group. Children in the control group received treatment by other providers in the community and children in the experimental group received weekly DDP sessions. The children who received DDP demonstrated positive changes and the control group children did not demonstrate a reduction in their mental health challenges. All of these treatment models have demonstrated that inclusion of parents in the healing process will increase the effectiveness of treatment to help children overcome the negative impact of their traumatic experiences. These models only include parent and child in the sessions. They do not include the whole family.

Families experiencing trauma and attachment difficulties need to heal within the context of their relationships in order to re-experience these relationships in a healthy, safe way. Creating new memories and new perceptions of safety within relationships will allow for healthy attachment patterns to occur. In my own work with families, I use a model based on an understanding of the neurobiology of trauma and attachment, rooted in the fundamental principles of trauma and attachment theories. Using research-based information about trauma and attachment ensures that the interventions will be effective when appropriately implemented. In addition to being grounded in research and theory, I want to use a model that will integrate play and expressive therapies to allow flexibility in the application of the interventions so that the developmental needs of all family members are met. Most of the attachment-based family models do not integrate the entire family and expressive arts and play therapy.

In families, parents must balance the needs of each individual member so that the overall family needs are met. It is quite a balancing act to accomplish. Meeting the attachment needs of each child in the family often feels like an impossible task. Traditional attachment-based treatment models do not allow for the ability to observe how parents are able to manage this juggling act, which I believe is an important piece of the puzzle to better understand how attachment needs are satisfied.

Much of the attachment focused neurobiology research over the past several decades has focused on children and their parents. According to Van Rosmalen et al. (2016), one of the pioneers working with children and families, William Blatz, developed a theory of child development in the 1920s and 1930s called Security Theory.

> In all of his writings, it becomes clear that Blatz strongly felt that a child needed a sense of belonging, and his notion that children need to be able to rely on their parents in order to grow up mentally healthy.
>
> (van Rosmalen et al., p. 5)

In addition to the need for a strong relationship with the parents, Blatz also believed that children need to experience safety in their relationships with other family members, as well as develop social bonds with others outside of the family.

Interpersonal neurobiology research examines how the brain processes information and influences emotions, emotion regulation, behaviors, and relationships. Expanding the focus to include siblings provides a broader view of family systems and their relationships within the treatment process. Sibling relationships influence our understanding about ourselves as much as do our parental relationships, but in different ways. Our siblings teach us about peer relationships; our parents teach us about authority figure relationships.

To better understand this, consider the Jones family in which there are two parents and three children. Both Mr. and Mrs. Jones grew up in families impacted by abuse and addiction, which has influenced their paradigm for parenting and family relationships. While Mr. and Mrs. Jones tried hard to provide a more stable environment for their children than they themselves grew up in, they both struggled with knowing how to manage the aggressive behavior of their middle child, Nick. Nick was often irritable and impulsive. He was easily angered and would become physically aggressive towards his sisters, sometimes to the point of hitting and screaming when he became frustrated. The parents were unable to help their son regulate his emotions and were often overwhelmed by his aggressive behavior. They would vacillate between yelling at him, taking away privileges, or even ignoring his behavior. Nick's sisters experienced Nick as physically aggressive, unsafe, especially because their parents were unable to protect them from Nick's behavior. In this scenario, the sisters would try to protect themselves from Nick and their chronic anger, fear, frustration, and sense of helplessness would sometimes spill over into their relationships with peers. Since Nick was also feeling hopeless and confused by his own behavior, he was not able to use his parents to help him learn how to regulate his difficult emotions in order to engage in healthy relationships with his sisters. This negatively influenced his view of himself as "bad," which caused him to experience significant shame which he'd react to by becoming even more aggressive.

Without strong, wise, and empathic parental oversight and skill to help Nick and his sisters navigate their relationships in a safe and healthy manner, these siblings are unlikely to develop the skills to form healthy social bonds with peers as they grow into adulthood. If therapists only address Nick's behavior, then Nick and his sisters will lose the opportunity to repair their relationships and parents lose the ability to play a role in the healing process with their children. Children need to be able to count on their parents to know how to help their children manage and regulate their strong emotions in order for everyone in the family to feel safe. The framework discussed in this book was developed to include the entire family system. This allows the therapist the opportunity to observe firsthand the interactions between the parents and their children and interactions among the siblings. The ability to observe these interactions allows the therapist to better understand how these relationship patterns may be reinforcing unwanted behaviors and be impeding healthy attachment relationships among family members. Since it's impossible for one therapist to observe all the interactions within a session, the use of videotaping provides the opportunity to capture all the interactions within the session, and then use the video later on to assist parents in recognizing where and how to make effective changes.

Overview of the Treatment Model

The *Attachment-based Family Play Therapy* framework integrates the therapeutic powers of play and expressive therapies to address complex issues within the family system, while also effectively taking into consideration the various developmental needs of family members using a neurobiology framework. Play and expressive therapies help to reduce the resistance that occurs when difficult emotional issues need to be addressed, and increase the ability for families to engage in the change process.

The Attachment-based Family Play Therapy framework consists of four phases of treatment and attachment-based principles for the implementation of the treatment model. These four phases are the *Observational Assessment* phase; *Safety and Engagement* phase; *Realignment* phase; and *Attunement* phase. The four phases of treatment help guide therapists through the treatment decision-making process. During each stage of treatment, therapists will consider the unique family and attachment dynamics within the family system, the developmental needs of family members, and the neurobiology of trauma and attachment issues in order to identify appropriate play and expressive therapy intervention strategies. Application of the treatment framework requires therapists to fully understand the nuances of attachment patterns and the neurobiology of co-regulation in order to identify strengths and deficits within the family relationships, especially between children and parents.

A critical aspect of the treatment model is the therapeutic presence of therapists working with these families which requires the ability to be fully present in order to model secure attachment patterns, and facilitate the healing process within the family. Therefore, the Guiding Principles of this model help therapists understand the underlying philosophy needed to effectively implement this treatment model with families. There are many good attachment-based treatment models to use with traumatized children and their parents. This treatment model was developed to help family relationships among all family members in order for the families to heal and develop resiliency. It is designed to be flexible enough for therapists to use their clinical-decision making skills while also having a framework to help guide them effectively through the treatment process.

References

Becker-Weidman, A. (2006). Treatment for children with trauma-attachment disorders: Dyadic developmental psychotherapy. *Child and Adolescent Social Work Journal, 23*(2), 147–171. doi:10.1111/j.1365-2206.00557.x

Bowlby, J. (1982). *Attachment and loss: Attachment Volume One* (2nd ed.). New York, NY: Basic Books.

Bratton, S. C., Ray, D., Rhine, T., & Jones, L. (2005). The efficacy of play therapy with children: A meta-analytic review of treatment outcomes. *Professional Psychology: Research and Practice, 36*(4), 376–390. doi:10.1037/0735-7028.36.4.376

Byng-Hall, J. (2008). The crucial roles of attachment in family therapy. *Journal of Family Therapy, 30*, 129–146.

Ciasca, E. C., Ferreira, R. C., Santana, C. L. A., Forlenza, O. V., dos Santos, G. D., Brum, P. S., & Nunes, P. V. (2018). Art therapy as an adjuvant treatment for depression in elderly women: A randomized controlled trial. *Brazilian Journal of Psychiatry*, 1–8. doi:10.1590/1516-4446-2017-2250

Cornett, N., & Bratton, S. C. (2015). A golden intervention: 50 years of research on filial therapy. *International Journal of Play Therapy, 24*(3), 119–133. doi:10.1037/a0039088

Fishbane, M. D. (2007). Wired to connect: Neuroscience, relationships and therapy. *Family Process, 46*(3), 395–412.

Foley, Y. C., Higdon, L., & White, J. F. (2006). A qualitative study of filial therapy: Parent's voices. *International Journal of Play Therapy, 15*(1), 37–64.

Gaskill, R. L., & Perry, B. D. (2014). The neurobiological power of play: Using the neurosequential model of therapeutics to guide play in the healing process. In C. A. Malchioti & D. A. Crenshaw (Eds.), *Creative arts and play therapy for attachment problems* (pp. 178–194). New York, NY: Guilford Press.

Habib, H. A., & Ali, U. (2015). Efficacy of art therapy in the reduction of impulsive behaviors of children with ADHD co-morbid intellectual disability. *Pakistan Journal of Psychology, 46*(2), 23–33.

Halfon, S., Yilmaz, M., & Cadvar, A. (2019). Mentalization, session-to-session negative emotion expression, symbolic play, and affect regulation in psychodynamic child psychotherapy. *Psychotherapy*, 1–13. doi:10.1037/pst0000201

Hughes, D. A. (2006). *Building the bonds of attachment: Awakening love in deeply troubled children*. Lanham, MD: Jason Aronson.

Kestley, T. (2014). *The interpersonal neurobiology of play: Brain-building interventions for emotional well-being*. New York, NY: W.W. Norton & Company, Inc.

Kindsvatter, A., & Desmond, K. J. (2013). Addressing parent-child conflict: Attachment-based interventions with parents. *Journal of Counseling & Development, 91*, 105–112.

Leavitt, K. S., Morrison, J. A., Gardner, S. A., & Gallagher, M. M. (1996). Group play therapy for cumulatively traumatized child survivors of familial AIDS. *International Journal of Play Therapy, 5*(1), 1–17.

Lim, S., & Ogawa, Y. (2014). Once I had kids, now I am raising kids: Child-Parent relationship therapy (CPRT) with a Sudanese refugee family – A case study. *International Journal of Play Therapy, 23*(2), 70–89. doi:10.1037/a0036362

Marrone, M. (2014). *Attachment and interaction: From Bowlby to current clinical theory and practice* (2nd ed.). London, UK: Jessica Kingsley Publishing.

Panksepp, J. (2010). Affective neuroscience of the emotional BrainMind: Evolutionary perspectives and implications for understanding depression. *Dialogues in Clinical Neuroscience, 12*(4), 533–545.

Perry, B. D. (2006). Applying principles of neurodevelopment to clinical work with maltreated and traumatized children: The neurosequential model of therapeutics. In N. Boyd Webb (Ed.), *Working with traumatized youth in child welfare* (pp. 27–52). New York, NY: Guilford Press.

Perry, B. D., Pollard, R. A., Blakley, T. I., Baker, W. I., & Vigilante, D. (1995). Childhood trauma, the neurobiology of adaptation, and "use-dependent" development of the brain: How "states" become "traits". *Infant Mental Health Journal, 16*(4), 271–291.

Porges, S. W. (2011). *The polyvagal theory: Neurophysiological foundations of emotions, attachment, communication, self-regulation.* New York, NY: W.W. Norton & Company.

Post, P. B., Phipps, C. B., Camp, A. C., & Grybush, A. L. (2019). The effectiveness of child-centered play therapy among marginalized children. *International Journal of Play Therapy, 28*(2), 88–97. doi:10:1037/pla0000096

Rowe, C., Watson-Ormond, R., English, L., Rubesin, H., Marshall, A., Linton, K., Amolegbe, A., Agnew-Brune, C. & Eng, E. (2017). Evaluating art therapy to heal the effects of trauma among refugee youth: The Burma art therapy program evaluation. *Health Promotion Project, 18*(1), 26–33. doi:10.1177/1524839915626413

Ryan, S. D., & Madsen, M. D. (2007). Filial family play therapy with an adoptive family: A response to preadoptive maltreatment. *International Journal of Play Therapy, 16*(2), 112–132. doi:10.1037/1555-6824.16.2.112

Schaefer, C. (Ed.). (1993). *The Therapeutic Powers of Play.* Northvale, NJ: Jason Aronson, Inc.

Schore, A. N. (2000). Attachment and the regulation of the right brain. *Attachment and Human Development, 2*(1), 23–47.

Schore, A. N. (2001). Effects of a secure attachment relationship on right brain development, affect regulation, and infant mental health. *Infant Mental Health Journal, 22*(1–2), 7–66.

Schore, J. R., & Schore, A. N. (2008). Modern attachment theory: The central role of affect regulation in development and treatment. *Clinical Social Work Journal, 36*, 9–20. doi:10.1007/s10615-007-7

Schottelkorb, A. A., Doumas, D. M., & Garcia, R. (2012). Treatment for childhood refugee trauma: A randomized, controlled trial. *International Journal of Play Therapy, 21*(2), 57–73. doi:10.1037/a0027430

Shapiro, F. (2012). *Getting past your past.* New York, NY: Rodale.

Siegel, D. J. (2001). Toward an interpersonal neurobiology of the developing mind: Attachment relationships, "Mindsight'" and neural integration. *Infant Mental Health Journal, 22*(1–2), 67–94.

Siegel, D. J. (2011). *Mindsight: The new science of personal transformation.* New York, NY: Bantam Books.

Siegel, D. J., & Hartzell, M. (2003). *Parenting from the inside out: How a deeper understanding can help you raise children who thrive.* New York, NY: Jeremy P. Tarcher/Penguin.

Solis, C. M., Meyers, J., & Varjas, K. M. (2004). A qualitative case study of the process and impact of filial therapy with an African American parent. *International Journal of Play Therapy, 13*(2), 99–118.

Steele, W., & Malchiodi, C. A. (2012). *Trauma-informed practices with children and adolescents.* New York, NY: Routledge Taylor & Francis Group.

Steele, W., & Raider, M. (2001). *Structured sensory intervention for traumatized children, adolescents and parents: Strategies to alleviate trauma.* Lewiston, NY: The Edwin Mellen Press.

Taubenheim, A., & Tiano, J. D. (2012). Rationale and modifications for implementing parent-child interaction therapy with rural Appalachian parents. *Rural Mental Health,* Fall/Winter, 16–26.

Tornero, M. D. L. A., & Capella, C. (2017). Change during psychotherapy through sand play tray in children that have been sexually abused. *Frontiers in Psychology, 8*, 1–12. doi:10.3389/fpsyg.2017.00617

Van Der Kolk, B. (2014). *The body keeps score: Brain, mind, and body in the healing of trauma*. New York, NY: Penguin Books.

Van Rosmalen, L., van der Horst, F. C. P., & van der Veer, R. (2016). From secure dependency to attachment: Mary Ainsworth's integration of Blatz's security theory into Bowlby's attachment theory. *History of Psychology, 19*(1), 22–39.

Weber, D. A., & Reynolds, C. R. (2004). Clinical perspectives on neurobiological effects of psychological trauma. *Neuropsychology Review, 14*(2), 115–129.

Wettig, H. H. G., Coleman, A. R., & Geider, F. J. (2011). Evaluating the effectiveness of theraplay in treating shy, socially withdrawn children. *International Journal of Play Therapy, 20*(1), 26–37. doi:10.1037/a0022666

The Neurobiology of   **2**
Trauma, Behavior, and
Co-Regulation

This chapter focuses on understanding the neurobiology behind our emotions and explains how trauma can impact our behavior. An overview of key areas of the brain cites research that specifies how these brain areas may even be physiologically changed by trauma. When working with traumatized families, relationship patterns and the ability to regulate emotions are directed by the neurobiology of each person in the family. Understanding that all behavior is directed by the brain helps therapists determine what interventions to use in order to accomplish the desired changes within the family system. Research from respected experts in the field of interpersonal neurobiology will provide an overview that will serve as the lens through which therapists work with traumatized children and their families. This lens provides the foundation for the attachment-based treatment model proposed in this book.

Humans are social beings and our brain circuitry functions to respond, and engage, based on social information received both internally and externally. The interaction between key areas of the brain in both the limbic and prefrontal cortex regions, create our emotional brain and our social engagement system which facilitates attachment. However, healthy neural connections in these areas of the brain can be impaired due to the impact of trauma, which can interfere with the ability to develop healthy attachments. Our right brain plays a central role in the ability to develop relationships. To understand how the social brain works, we need to understand the brain's three main areas: the *reptilian* or *primitive brain*, the *limbic system*, and the *cortical* areas, especially the *frontal cortex* areas (see Figure 2.1). These three areas are made up of complex networks of neural pathways that connect the vast circuitry within our brain.

Brain evolution

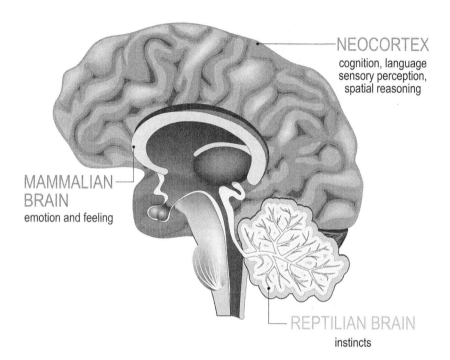

NEOCORTEX
cognition, language
sensory perception,
spatial reasoning

MAMMALIAN
BRAIN
emotion and feeling

REPTILIAN BRAIN
instincts

Figure 2.1 Brain Evolution
Credit: iStock.com / ttsz

Reptilian or Primitive Brain

The most primitive part of the brain is the brainstem, also known as the *reptilian brain*. It is called the primitive brain because it ensures that our basic body functions are working even without our conscious awareness, thereby ensuring our survival. These body systems include, but are not limited to, the heart rate, breathing, and organ functioning. The brainstem sits above the spinal cord and is responsible for receiving information from the body, processing it *up* through various neural connections in the brain, and then *down* again to regulate the body systems. These processes are often referred to as *bottom-up* and *top-down* processes. The brainstem essentially functions as the main *relay station* for information going to and from the brain to create a response that may or may not require conscious awareness. It is at the heart of the *mind–body connection.* The brainstem also plays a role in the body's *motivational systems* that drive us to find ways to get our basic needs met for such things as food, shelter, sexual desire, and safety (Badenoch, 2008; Siegel, 2011). It is also involved in the rapid mobilization required when threat is perceived—to assist in the activation of the fight-flight-freeze response in collaboration with the limbic and frontal cortex areas of the brain (Siegel, 2011).

Neural pathways in the brainstem begin development and come *online* before we are even born. The brain stem begins development *in utero* and is fully operational by the time of birth in full-term infants (Badenoch, 2008), which makes sense when you think about the survival of the species. These functions are needed to ensure our chances of survival beginning in infancy. Therefore, even our earliest experiences *in utero* and within the first year of life begin to shape our perceptions and behavior, which are stored in our implicit memory (discussed later in the chapter).

Limbic System

The limbic system of our brain sits atop the brainstem area in the middle region of our brain (see Figure 2.2). This area of the brain is composed of several parts that function to process emotions, memories, and act as the body's *alarm system.* When information received from the environment is assessed as dangerous, then the limbic system will set in motion a response to the registration of danger with the purpose of survival. It will enact survival behaviors such as fight, flight, or freeze through emotional stimuli that interact with autonomic nervous system and endocrine functions. This area of the brain also facilitates our processing of emotions and is involved in affect regulation development. According to Schore (2000), the limbic system plays a major role in reading facial expressions without conscious awareness due to its location in the brain. The limbic region of the brain is predominantly made up of the *amygdala,* the *hippocampus,* and the *hypothalamus.* Of these, the amygdala in the right brain region plays a key role in the processing of emotions and reading facial cues for recognizing safety within relationships. This is important to understand when working with families because children will be highly attuned to reading the nonverbal facial and voice tone *cues* from

Limbic system

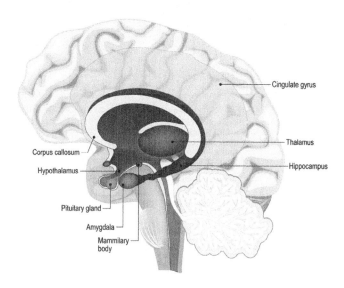

Figure 2.2 Limbic System
Credit: iStock.com/ttsz

their parents/caregivers and will respond in ways indicating their perception of those cues. Memories of these interactions will lay the foundation for our social interaction skills and the quality of our social interactions and relationships throughout our lives.

The amygdala interacts with various brain structures to coordinate a response to danger. It is functional at birth and well developed early in a young child's life (Fishbane, 2007; Weber & Reynolds, 2004). Again, from a survival standpoint this makes sense because infants need to have processes in place that help them to survive. In addition, the amygdala processes the emotional importance of stimuli received (Heide & Solomon, 2006). Coordinated survival responses are set in motion when emotions of fear and anxiety are registered. Whenever sensory information, such as sound, smell, sight, taste, and touch is received, the amygdala filters the information and processes whether or not a threat is present—actual as well as perceived. The amygdala will then trigger the release of neurochemicals into the bloodstream to activate behavioral survival responses via the autonomic nervous system—fight, flight, or freeze (Heide & Solomon, 2006; Hostinar, Sullivan, & Gunnar, 2014). It will also activate the processes in the hypothalamic–pituitary–adrenocortical (HPA) axis to release these stress hormones into the bloodstream until the threatening event has stopped. The HPA axis is involved in the body's response to threat by activating the increase of cortisol production which is required for the body to respond to stress and threat (Badenoch, 2008; Hostinar et al., 2014; Solomon & Heide, 2005).

The *endocrine system* and *autonomic nervous system* work closely together to respond to threat signals. The autonomic nervous system (ANS) includes the *sympathetic nervous system* (SNS) and the *parasympathetic nervous system* (PNS). Using the analogy of a car, our body is the car and the SNS is the *gas* to get the body mobilized to respond to threats of danger. It activates increased heart and breathing rate, allows for easier breathing and for the increased movement of blood from internal organs to arms and legs in order to mobilize one's ability to run and/or fight. The PNS is essentially the *brakes* (Porges, 2011). It slows down the body by slowing heart rate, lowering blood pressure, slowing breathing, and activating pain-numbing opiates to feign death if necessary (Porges, 2011; Schore, 2009). When the presence of a threat requires immobilization, then the PNS is activated in order to elicit the *freeze* response. Dissociation is essentially a *freeze* response to danger.

Generally, after the threatening situation has passed, the HPA axis will *turn off* the production of these stress hormones via the amygdala. People who experience chronic stress continue to produce stress hormones which keep them more prone to being hyper alert to a potential threat. This produces toxic levels of these neurochemicals in the body.

> As soon as the threat is over, the hormones dissipate and the body returns to normal. The stress hormones of traumatized people, in contrast, take much longer to return to baseline and spike quickly and disproportionately in response to mildly stressful stimuli.
>
> (Van Der Kolk, 2014, p. 46)

Several studies of children who have experienced early exposure to maltreatment found that they have increased amygdala volume compared to children who have not experienced maltreatment. (Heide & Solomon, 2006; McCrory, De Brito, & Viding, 2011; Solomon & Heide, 2005).

While studies have shown that childhood abuse can result in increased amygdala volume, other studies have shown that children who have experienced trauma have lower hippocampal volume (Heide & Solomon, 2006; McCrory et al., 2011; Woon, Sood, & Hedges, 2010). McCrory et al. reviewed the research regarding the impact of traumatic stress on children (as well as adults who reported a history of abuse), and found mixed results regarding hippocampal volume for traumatized children with Post-Traumatic Stress Disorder (no reduction in volume) versus adults who reported childhood histories of abuse (decreased volume). However, Woon et al. conducted a meta-analysis of the research regarding the impact of traumatic stress on hippocampal volume. The results of their meta-analysis found that trauma did tend to result in reduced hippocampal volume. Both studies included suggestions that environmental and genetic factors may play a role in the extent of damage to the hippocampus that occurs due to traumatic stress and may vary from person to person (McCrory et al., 2011; Woon et al., 2010).

Smaller hippocampal volume results in difficulty retrieving and recalling details of memories, as well as the ability to sustain attention and concentration. Children who have experienced traumatic events will have much difficulty recognizing and articulating when their traumatic memories have been triggered, or even what is distressing them. Impaired hippocampal functioning can interfere with the ability to accurately interpret information and understand it. Traumatized children may misinterpret social cues from others and then respond in ways that are not appropriate to the situation. Lenore Terr (1990) states that "seeing apparently dominates all other senses following trauma because it is the sense by which most horrible episodes are recorded and reviewed in the mind" (p. 133).

If a traumatized child observes another child's behavior and perceives that behavior as threatening, then the traumatized child will respond in ways to protect himself which may include physical and/or verbal aggression. However, because their brain is not processing the information properly, traumatized children will have difficulty understanding why their response was inappropriate. I have worked with several traumatized teens who develop the reputation of the "bad" kid at school because of their defiant behavior toward others, especially toward adults. Because the memories of the traumatized youth are frequently activated by various sensory triggers in their environment, their brain is registering danger and they respond as though threatened. Their response can be misunderstood as oppositional behavior or even conduct disorder behavior in some cases by adults.

Janet, a 14-year-old female, was sexually abused by an older male peer. At the time of the sexual assault, her attacker was wearing a fragrance that was commonly worn by boys that age. After the event, whenever Janet walked through the school hallways during class change and she passed a boy wearing this particular fragrance, she would become angry and verbally defiant. Her hypervigilance for danger was activated by the memory of the scent associated with her sexual assault. She had no idea why she would become so angry and agitated until we were able to process the sexual assault. Another teenage girl, Mackenzie, was sexually assaulted in a specific place in her home. For months, Mackenzie was unable to go into that part of the home without having a panic attack due to the visual memories of her trauma that occurred there. The neurobiology of these two adolescents was forever changed when the trauma occurred resulting in a heightened state of alert that contributed to the problem they had accurately reading social situations and responding with prosocial behaviors.

Cortex: The Master Mapmaker

The most advanced and complex areas of our brain are contained in the cortex and it provides highly integrative functions for our brain and body. The cortex is also referred to as the *mammalian brain* or *neocortex* since this area of the brain appears in mammals, especially primates and humans. It is categorized into four areas, or lobes (see Figure 2.3), which make up the outside layer of our brain. Of the four cortical lobes, the most advanced is the *prefrontal cortex* and is only present in humans. The *posterior cortex* contains the cortical areas starting at the back and sides of the brain. It is made up of the *occipital cortex, parietal cortex,* and the *temporal cortex.* Siegel (2011) refers to these regions of the brain as "the *master mapmaker* of our physical experiences, generating our perceptions of the outer world—through the five senses—and also keeping track of the location and movement of our physical body through touch and motor perception" (p. 20). The occipital lobe is located at the back of the head and integrates visual information into whole images. Next in order from the back of the brain to the front of the brain is the parietal lobe, which predominantly processes sensory information, such as touch, pressure, pain, and temperature. The temporal lobes are located on the sides of the head. These areas of the cortex have a significant role in integrating memories with sensory information.

HUMAN BRAIN

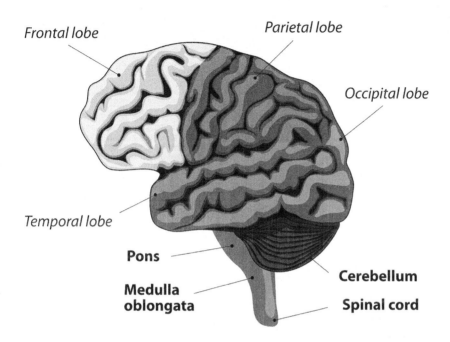

Frontal lobe

Parietal lobe

Occipital lobe

Temporal lobe

Pons

Cerebellum

Medulla oblongata

Spinal cord

Figure 2.3 Human Brain
Credit: iStock.com/ttsz

Frontal Cortex

The most advanced area of the cortex is the frontal cortex located behind the forehead. This area is involved with higher level cognitive functions, emotion regulation, and motor control. The foremost area of the frontal cortex is the prefrontal cortex. The prefrontal cortex is highly integrative and orchestrates complex neural circuitry in the brain and body. My favorite analogy to understand the prefrontal cortex is that of an orchestra conductor who is able to create various sounds in music by directing different sections of the orchestra, and even different instruments within the orchestra sections, when to play, how fast or slow, and when to start and stop. The conductor understands how each of the instruments work and what types of sounds can be produced from instruments. The conductor essentially regulates each of the orchestra sections to produce a coordinated and integrated piece of music. The prefrontal cortex plays a crucial role in behavior inhibition, emotion regulation, and making sense of what is happening to and around us. This part of our brain sets us apart from all other species. Learning to understand the different areas of the prefrontal cortex and the role of the prefrontal cortex in relationships will be discussed in more detail later.

Left/Right Brain

The right and left hemispheres of the brain include processes of the brainstem, limbic system, and cortex. Each of these areas will function differently depending on where they are located—right or left hemisphere. The right brain plays a larger role in nonlinear processes and understanding concepts as a whole. Emotion processing is largely a function of the right hemisphere, which experiences huge growth during the first three years of a child's life (Fishbane, 2007). Schore (2000, 2001) has shown that the right hemisphere plays a critical role in attachment from infancy, since it has a central role in recognizing and processing facial cues and nonverbal information. According to Badenoch (2008), "mental models of the self, the world, and relationships are generated and experienced here, as well as the felt reality of our own story—our wordless autobiography as felt in and by our bodies" (p. 19). The right hemisphere is also thought to play a larger role in processing negative emotions and the left hemisphere is thought to play a larger role in processing positive emotions. The left hemisphere functions to process information in a logical, linear manner and is more focused on facts, cause-and-effect types of processes. The left hemisphere also houses language capabilities and can allow for the use of language to make sense of experiences.

Most of us think in terms of people being more left brain or right brain oriented. The truth is that we all use and need to use processes in both hemispheres of our brain. The corpus callosum is the primary part of the brain that connects the right and left hemispheres and acts as the brain's superhighway of neural connections between the two hemispheres. The neural circuitry in the corpus callosum is fully formed at birth and continues to develop into adulthood, which allows for different regions of the corpus callosum to be susceptible to environmental stressors during the maturation process (McCrory et al., 2011). Bilateral processing aids in the ability to regulate emotions, make sense of events, and manage behavioral responses (Heide & Solomon, 2006; Weber & Reynolds, 2004). The connection between the two hemispheres in young children is not well developed and is influenced by the growing child's experiences in life. Emotion regulation requires the ability to utilize both hemispheres of the brain. The ability to effectively "evaluate, identify, and communicate affect is dependent upon the interaction between both hemispheres of the brain" (Weber & Reynolds, 2004, p. 118). Trauma can negatively impact the corpus callosum region and decrease its volume, which can impair cognitive and emotional processing (McCrory et al., 2011).

The Social Brain

Within the social brain are neural networks that are critical to facilitate understanding of another. According to Daniel Siegel (2011) in his groundbreaking theory of what he calls *Mindsight*, Siegel discusses the concept of internal *mind maps* in which mirror neuron systems help us to experience one another *mind to mind* and understanding one another more fully. These mirror neurons were discovered in 1992 when scientists were conducting research on monkeys to understand neural circuits in the brain (Rodrigues, 2018; Siegel, 2011). What they discovered is that our brain can develop the ability to understand the intentions of others due to specific neural circuits. Based on their research with monkeys, scientists discovered that visual information received by our brain is linked to motor action. Mirror neurons in one person's brain are activated when that person sees another person's intentional, goal-directed action. The sequence of the behavior not only activates neural pathways in the person engaging in the action, it also activates the neural pathway in the brain of the person observing the sequenced, goal-directed behavior. How cool is that? I can watch you perform a predictable behavior and the same neural pathways will *light up* in my mind to give me greater understanding of your behavior.

Siegel (2011) states:

> beginning from the perception of a basic behavioral intention, our more elaborated human prefrontal cortex enables us to map out the minds of others. Our brains use sensory information to create representations of others' minds, just as they use sensory input to create images of the physical world.

(p. 61)

For example, if I raise my hand in a classroom after a teacher asks a question, then the teacher will understand from this sequence of behaviors that she has asked a question and I have raised my hand. She will then read this sequence of events to recognize my intention in raising my hand is that I intend to answer her question. She will then decide whether or not she wants to call on me to answer the question. The behavior of the person must be intentional though. Random or chaotic behavior does not provide a sequence of events to recognize the likely outcome of the other person. This is an important concept to understand when working with traumatized youth. A predictable pattern of behavior can be either positive, neutral, or negative as well as even life threatening.

In addition to providing information about the intentions of others, mirror neurons are critical to empathy and understanding another person from that person's point of view (Siegel, 2011; Siegel & Hartzell, 2003). The same neural pathways that are activated in the person who initiated the action are the same neural pathway activated in the person seeing the intentional action. For example, imagine that you are at a Little League baseball game for your child and you see the first baseman get hit in the arm by a line drive right at him. You see and hear the batter hit the ball, and you see it go in the direction of the first baseman. You see the baseball hit the arm of the first baseman at a fast speed. You see him crouch, his facial expression indicates that he is in pain, and your immediate reflex is to cringe as well. You have felt a baseball and know that it is hard. Since baseball is a popular sport, you might have thrown a baseball with another person and experienced what happens when you are hit by a baseball. You are able to know how painful that was for him because your brain will register the pain to a lesser extent. This predictable sequence of events that you have experienced yourself and now witnessed with the first baseman will activate the same mirror neurons in you as well as the person who was hit by the baseball. Your brain has a map of this predictable sequence of events. According to Siegel (2011):

> the perception of a basic behavioral intention, our more elaborated human prefrontal cortex enables us to map out the minds of others. Our brains use the sensory information to create representations of the others' minds, just as they use sensory input to create images of the physical world.
>
> (p. 60)

Empathy

Mirror neurons play a role in how parents are able to attune to their child, which is critical for secure attachments and affect regulation. Mirror neurons help us to experience empathy with others to understand life experiences from another person's point of view. Essentially, they help us to *see* another person's experience and more fully understand that person. If I have experienced the loss of a loved one then I have experienced the sadness, grief, and emotional pain of that loss. I will also know, in my culture, the rituals that will occur in the mourning process, and the sequence of those rituals such as how we say goodbye to that loved one via viewing ceremonies and funeral services. I will also know the practical tasks of selecting a funeral home, notification to friends and family, costs of the funeral activities, and the need to obtain a death certificate to notify banks, social security, etc. I will know the predictable emotional, cultural, and practical tasks because I would have experienced them and recorded the experience in my brain. Therefore, when I observe or learn of another person losing a loved one, then those mirror neurons in my mind will become activated by my memory, and I will remember all of the aspects of the mourning process which will activate my mirror neurons to experience empathy for that other person who will be going through a predictable process of grieving. My mind will be able to predict how the process may go for the other person experiencing similar grief.

This process of *mapping* the intentions of others is what Siegel (2011) describes as the resonance circuits in physiologically experiencing the emotions and intentions of others. These resonance circuits help to connect us to each other interpersonally. According to Siegel (2011), the resonance circuits include:

> a neural circuit called the insula that seems to be the superhighway between the mirror neurons and the limbic areas, which in turn sends messages to the brainstem and body proper. This is how we come to resonate physiologically with others- how even our respiration, blood pressure, and heart rate can rise and fall in sync with another's internal state. These signals from our body, brainstem, and limbic areas then travel back up the insula to the middle prefrontal cortex.

(p. 61)

These resonance circuits contribute to what is known as *emotion contagion*, which involves syncing up physiologically and emotionally since emotions have a physiological component to them. For example, if I observe a crowd of people huddled together with tears in their eyes and making the sounds of crying, I will likely experience the physiological and emotional manifestation of crying, concern, and/or sadness begin to well up in me before I even learn what has happened. In order to effectively recognize the intention and emotions of another, this requires the ability to recognize our own internal emotional experiences as separate from another person while also sharing the experience because it will be possible to misinterpret what is the reason for the crying.

For therapists, this requires them to be attuned with their own internal emotional process and monitor countertransference material. Therapists need to have empathy and understanding when working with clients to therapeutically *hold* the sacred space of healing during the session and to learn to tap into the resonance circuits to help facilitate change. This ability to tap into the emotional resonance circuits can help therapists to *see* their clients and recognize the nuances of what is taking place interpersonally in the session in order to identify potentially unhealthy relationship patterns and to identify interpersonal strengths in their clients. Therapists need to help parents understand their own internal emotional experiences to recognize their emotions and understand that their emotions are separate from their child's emotional experience during a shared experience so that parents can identify possible misperceptions.

For example, consider an infant who was born to a severely depressed mother who was unable to care for the basic needs of her baby. Mother's face would be blank and unresponsive to her child's cries to change a dirty diaper or feed her child. The predictable patterns of events for the child would be to cry in order to communicate a need to his mother. The child then observes his mother's flat stare and her mouth forming a frown. He has learned that when his mother has this face then he cannot expect her to meet his need to change his dirty diaper or feed him. The threat system in infants can also be activated by depressed affect as well as angry affect. At some point, that same child is removed from the care of his severely depressed mother due to her inability to care for him and is placed in a foster home with foster parents who are able to care for him. When he needs to be fed or is tired, it triggers him to cry. He then observes his foster mother's blank stare and frown with furrowed brow. His mind has mapped a predictable course of action from his mother and now perceives that his foster mother will engage in the same predictable pattern of behavior as his biological mother. He perceives that his foster mother will not be able to meet his needs so he cries harder as if to try to get his foster mother to be alerted to his needs. In the case of his biological mother, this tactic did not result in getting his needs met and he would become emotionally dysregulated. However, in the case of his foster mother, she heard his cries and became alerted to his needs. She would attempt to assess his needs but now he is inconsolable and his emotions are dysregulated.

Researchers have studied the SNS and PNS systems as they relate to trauma and the body's response to threat—real and perceived. Porges (2011) developed Polyvagal Theory to better understand, from an evolutionary standpoint, how humans are able to recognize and respond to threat to ensure survival. Polyvagal Theory is based on the premise of evolutionary changes over time from the lower vertebrates to the advancements seen in mammals, and ultimately in higher level functioning of humans. The theory moves away from a primary focus of understanding the physiology of behavior and emotions as simply a function of the ANS and moves toward viewing behavior and emotion as a bidirectional process "that interprets the brain regulation of peripheral physiology (e.g., neural regulation of both cardiovascular and endocrine functions) as providing a neural platform for emergent adaptive social and defensive behaviors" (p. 3). For example, behavior and emotion are not simply based on one's physiological response of the ANS giving *gas* to our body or putting on the *brakes*. It involves the interaction of the ANS and the vagus nerve, the Xth cranial nerve starting in the brainstem and moving into various organs in the body, including the heart and digestive system. Porges (2011) focuses on the relationship between heart rate and the vagus, and how they regulate various systems in the body to impact behavior and emotions. According to Porges (2011), "the vagus is not a single neural pathway, but rather a complex bidirectional system with myelinated branches linking the brainstem with target organs" (p. 135). As mentioned in Chapter 1, neuroception circuits are the neural circuitry involved in the assessment of threat to determine if survival circuits need to be activated or deactivated.

Porges (2011) states that social engagement cannot occur unless the neuroception circuits have first assessed the presence of danger/threat. His research explored the questions regarding the ability of infants to distinguish safe, familiar caregivers from others, and to assess for the presence of danger. Social engagement refers to the social interactions between people. The social engagement between parent and child aids in the attachment process. In order for social engagement to occur, threat is unconsciously assessed and the defensive circuits must be inhibited to allow for the relaxed engagement to occur. For example, a mother holding her infant and engaging in playful interactions with her baby requires that the baby's neuroception circuits to have assessed the threat and determined that mother and the interactions are safe. This assessment of safety is based on the tone of voice, facial expressions, and communication process that the adult holding him is safe. Once the interaction is determined to be safe, his defensive SNS can be inhibited which activates the PNS processes. The PNS process will allow lowered heart rate, breathing and calm behaviors to occur that let his mother hold him and play with him in close proximity. The neuroception circuits allow for proximity to one another and ability to positively engage in social interactions. These processes are present at birth and are activated at an unconscious level.

In the case of the child who experiences his mother in a predominantly unsafe and unpredictable manner, his neuroception circuits will have assessed his mother's facial expressions, voice tone, and movements which would result in the presence of conflicting information because his mother is both familiar and unsafe. His neuroception system will be impaired and unable to provide him with the ability to accurately assess for safety. This will create challenges for him to effectively engage in the attachment relationship. He will struggle to accurately assess whether or not his foster mother is safe and he cannot not develop a secure attachment with her unless he is able to do this. Neuroception circuits are designed to ensure the survival of the child. However, when not working effectively, this can impede social engagement and attachment. The foster mother will need to recognize that her foster child is not rejecting her, but rather he is unable to determine if the relationship is safe for him.

The child's foster mother will need to recognize her own emotions and thoughts welling up internally for her to see herself and her foster child as separate so she doesn't become emotionally overwhelmed herself— emotional contagion. She will need to focus on her own breathing, heart rate, etc., and recognize that although her foster child does not seem to be positively responding to her attempts to console him and meet his needs, she is not the cause of his distress and he is not trying to be a defiant child. As she is able to regulate her own emotions, breathing, facial expressions, and voice tone, then her foster child will begin to mirror her breathing, emotions, facial expressions, and voice tone. Porges (2011) states, "once the cortical regulation of the brainstem structures involved in the social engagement are activated, social behavior and communication will spontaneously occur as the natural emergent properties of this biological system" (p. 18). As his foster mother is able to consistently and predictably regulate her own internal emotional processes, then she will be able to establish safety within their relationship. Her foster child's resonance circuits will allow him to use his foster mother to effectively co-regulate his own emotions. In order for the foster mother to be used by her foster child, she will need to be aware of her own emotions and thoughts so she does not misperceive his behavior, and she can accurately assess his needs at that moment.

Resonance and neuroception circuits aid in attachment because when children first experience their parents as safe then they can engage in the relationship to experience their parents as fully understanding them. This creates a sense of well-being within the child and strengthens their relationship. Children need parents to recognize and understand their experience of a situation and respond in a way that validates understanding of their children while also simultaneously providing structure. Imagine that your child comes home from school distraught because his friend told him that he is stupid and doesn't want to be friends anymore. Your child is crying and experiencing the harsh realities of life. As a parent, your ability to *feel* your child's hurt can help you to respond in tender ways to validate his feelings without necessarily solving the problem for him. He experiences the interaction in a way that communicates to him that you understand his hurt which will help him to begin to regulate his own emotions. He can use the support of his parent to feel understood and acceptable which will eventually help him to use his parent's support to solve the problem on his own. If a parent has an unresolved emotional wound from her own childhood of bullying and rejection, then this may stir up those old wounds without the parent's conscious awareness which may result in the parent taking this personally as if they were also being rejected. In this case, the parent may become angry and reinforcing that her child has been victimized rather than helping to empower her child. The ability for parents to provide attunement and structure without becoming enmeshed provides the experiences that lay the neural foundation for affect regulation when distressed. Over time, as children experience their parents in a nurturing and supportive manner and parents are able to regulate their own emotions in the face of their children's emotional distress, the children will learn to regulate their own emotions and self-soothe.

Neurobiology of Emotions and Affect Regulation

Affective neuroscientist, Jaak Panksepp (2010), identified what he called the *motivational circuits* for emotions which he separated into primary and secondary motivational circuits. The *primary-process* emotional affective networks are affective states that are inherited and present from birth (Kestley, 2014). Panksepp uses upper case letters to distinguish the emotion circuitry from the emotions. These four circuits are the SEEKING (desire system), RAGE (anger system), FEAR (anxiety system), and PANIC/GRIEF (separation distress system). SEEKING is central to all the circuits and is motivated by desire as it moves us forward. RAGE is the anger system that is activated when we are thwarted in our attempt to obtain something. Any parent of a toddler will recognize these two systems in action. I remember taking my young toddler with me to the grocery store. We were in the checkout line and right at his eye level was a fabulous toy that he was exploring. When it was time for me to check out I instructed him to put the toy back on the shelf and leave it at the store. His desire was to continue to explore the fabulous new toy that had captured his attention and curiosity. When I put the toy back on the shelf, he erupted into screams and fell into a heap on the floor in protest of my refusal to allow him to take the toy home with him. His desire to have the toy was thwarted which activated his RAGE system. The third emotion circuit is FEAR, which is our anxiety system to alert us to danger. This system activates our heightened sense of alertness to help us recognize danger.

Last of the universal inherited emotion circuits is PANIC/GRIEF. This is the separation distress system that is crucial for attachment and mediates the separation-distress calls (crying). This is best illustrated by the Strange Situation assessment in which a mother and her young child are together in a room. At some point the mother will be signaled to leave the room and the child remains in the room without his mother. The young child will become emotionally distressed at his mother's exit from the room. This is the PANIC/GRIEF system activated because mother has left without him in a strange room. The Strange Situation evaluates the attachment relationship by observing the child's response to the mother when she returns to him. His ability to use his mother to help him regulate his emotions and feel safe again helps to identify the child's attachment style. This illustrates how the PANIC/GRIEF system plays a role in attachment. The child will become distressed because his mother is his source of safety and caregiving that helps him to navigate and survive in the world. The PANIC/GRIEF system parallels the CARE system which is one of the Special Circuits that are not universal to all humans.

The *secondary-process* emotional affective networks are networks that occur in special conditions and are not generally active at all times during one's life. These are the CARE (nurturance system), LUST (desire system), and PLAY. These systems tend to come online under special circumstances or during specific developmental stages. LUST is linked with the SEEKING system and not activated until puberty. The CARE system typically comes online when parents have a child. This system acts in collaboration with the SEEKING system to move parents toward taking care of their child's needs. The CARE system is the maternal love and caring that motivates us to move toward our distressed child to take care of his needs.

PLAY systems tend to be online during childhood when a child engages in play to explore and learn about the world and relationships. This system tends to be less prominent during adulthood. PLAY circuits produce feelings of joy, which are also important for the attachment process since children will experience playful interactions with parents as positive. These positive interactions will increase their sense of well-being within that parent–child relationship. The SEEKING system becomes activated in a toddler when he desires to explore his environment in which he is feeling safe. He has experienced his parent in a safe manner and will approach his parent to obtain nurturance and reassurance when his PANIC system has alerted him to potential danger.

Interestingly, Porges (2011) has identified that the PLAY circuits cannot be activated simultaneously with FEAR circuits. The neuroception circuits will assess the presence threat. If threat is determined to be present, these circuits cannot be disengaged to allow social engagement circuits to be active which are the circuits needed for play. Play can quickly turn into the activation of the threat circuits as any parent can tell you. Children can be playing and instantly something happens in which one child perceives that the other child is intentionally causing harm and the interactions quickly change from fun and laughter to yelling and physical aggression.

Stephen Porges (2011) argues that emotion and emotion regulation have their roots in the bidirectional communication between the brain and heart by way of the vagus, which is predominantly a function of the PNS. Vagal tone refers to the control of the rhythm of heart rate, which synchronizes with rate of breathing. He argues that affective neuroscientists (e.g., Panksepp) need to recognize the importance of the neural circuits involved in communication between body and brain. Porges (2011) asserts that to understand the biobehavioral processes of social interactions and emotions, it

> requires an understanding of the neural circuits both between higher brain structures and the brainstem and between the brainstem and the visceral organs (e.g., the heart) mediated through the autonomic nervous system. All affective or emotional states are dependent on lower brain regulation of the visceral state and the important visceral, tactile, and nociceptive visceral regulatory states that foster different domains of behavior.
>
> (p. 258)

Neural circuits involved in facial expressions, tone of voice, and movement are connected with emotion and emotion regulation. Facial expression and striated muscles in the face are linked to emotions (Porges, 2011). To make this point, try this Dialectical Behavior Therapy (DBT) skill developed by Marsha Linehan (Linehan, 2015) to assist in regulating emotion including changing negative emotions. It's called Half Smile. Sit comfortably in your chair and relax your face. Allow your facial muscles to form a half smile and notice the physiological changes in your face and your mood. The connection between body and brain influences our emotions. This is an important point that Porges (2011) makes in order to help therapists understand the need to recognize the role of physiological underpinnings of emotions connecting our lower brain circuits with our higher brain circuits.

The Attachment and Affect Regulation Connection

Affect regulation is a key outcome of secure attachment. Understanding emotions and emotion regulation is an important matter for therapists to understand. The ability to effectively regulate emotions has a tremendous impact on our daily functioning and the quality of our relationships. Allan Schore (Schore, 2000, 2001; Schore & Schore, 2008) has extensively researched the role of the right brain and attachment to understand attachment behaviors and neurobiology. Schore (Schore, 2000, 2001; Schore & Schore, 2008) conceptualizes Attachment Theory as a regulatory theory because of its neurobiological roots and co-regulation function. According to Schore (2000), "Attachment theory is essentially a regulatory theory, and attachment can be defined as the

interactive regulation of biological synchronicity between organisms"
(p. 23). The orbitofrontal cortex regions of the brain play a significant
role in attachment and affect regulation. It is also centrally connected
with the autonomic nervous system and the ability to regulate autonomic responses to social stimuli. The right hemisphere also plays
a role in the expression and interpretation of emotions as well as the
regulation of attention (Porges, 2011). The limbic areas of the cortex
and subcortex are in critical growth for the first two years of life.
These neural networks mediate the stress coping mechanisms throughout one's life. Understanding the relationship between brain–body connection of emotions and ability to access the social engagement system
for attachment repair is critical for therapists to help families impacted
by trauma to engage in the change process. This will be explored in
more depth in Chapter 3.

References

Badenoch, B. A. (2008). *Being a brain-wise therapist: A practical guide to interpersonal neuro-biology.* New York, NY: W.W. Norton & Company, Inc.

Fishbane, M. D. (2007). Wired to connect: Neuroscience, relationships, and therapy. *Family Process, 46*(3), 395–412.

Heide, K. M., & Solomon, E. P. (2006). Biology, childhood trauma, and murder: Rethinking justice. *International Journal of Law and Psychiatry, 29*, 220–233. doi:10.1016/j.ijlp.2005.10.001

Hostinar, C. E., Sullivan, R. M., & Gunnar, M. R. (2014). Psychobiological mechanisms underlying the social buffering of the hypothalamic–pituitary–adrenocortical axis: A review of animal models and human studies across development. *Psychological Bulletin, 140*(1), 256–282. doi:10.1037/a0032671

Kestley, T. (2014). *The interpersonal neurobiology of play: Brain-building interventions for emotional well-being.* New York, NY: W.W. Norton & Company, Inc.

Linehan, M. M. (2015). *DBT skills training manual* (2nd ed.). New York, NY: The Guilford Press.

McCrory, E., De Brito, S. A., & Viding, E. (2011). The impact of childhood maltreatment: A review of neurobiological and genetic factors. *Frontiers in Psychiatry, 2*, 1–14. doi:10.3389/fpsyt.2011.00048

Panksepp, J. (2010). Affective neuroscience of the emotional BrainMind: Evolutionary perspectives and implications for understanding depression. *Dialogues in Clinical Neuroscience, 12*(4), 533–545.

Porges, S. W. (2011). *The polyvagal theory: Neurophysiological foundations of emotions, attachment, communication, self-regulation.* New York, NY: W.W Norton & Company, Inc.

Rodrigues, P. R. G. (2018). The visual neuropsychology of the other. *Psychology & Neuroscience, 11*(3), 231–237. doi:10.1037/pne0000131

Schore, A. N. (2000). Attachment and the regulation of the right brain. *Attachment and Human Development, 2*(1), 23–47.

Schore, A. N. (2001). Effects of a secure attachment relationship on right brain development, affect regulation, and infant mental health. *Infant Mental Health Journal, 22*(1–2), 7–66.

Schore, A. N. (2009). Relational trauma and the developing right brain: An interface of psychoanalytic self psychology and neuroscience. *Self and Systems: Annals of the New York Academy of Sciences, 1159,* 189–203. doi:10.1111/j.1749-6632.2009.04474.x

Schore, J. R., & Schore, A. N. (2008). Modern attachment theory: The central role of affect regulation in development and treatment. *Clinical Social Work Journal, 36,* 9–20. doi:10.1007/s10615-007-7

Siegel, D. J. (2011). *Mindsight: The new science of personal transformation.* New York, NY: Bantam Books.

Siegel, D. J., & Hartzell, M. (2003). *Parenting from the inside out: How a deeper understanding can help you raise children who thrive.* New York, NY: Penguin Books.

Solomon, E. P., & Heide, K. M. (2005). The biology of trauma: Implications for treatment. *Journal of Interpersonal Violence, 20*(1), 51–60. doi:10.1177/0886260504268119

Terr, L. (1990). *Too scared to cry: How trauma affects children … and ultimately us all.* New York, NY: Basic Books.

Van Der Kolk, B. (2014). *The body keeps score: Brain, mind, and body in the healing of trauma.* New York, NY: Penguin Books.

Weber, D. A., & Reynolds, C. R. (2004). Clinical perspectives on neurobiological effects of psychological trauma. *Neuropsychology Review, 14*(2), 115–129.

Woon, F. L., Sood, S., & Hedges, D. W. (2010). Hippocampal volume deficits associated with exposure to psychological trauma and posttraumatic stress disorder in adults: A meta-analysis. *Progress in Neuro-psychopharmacology & Biological Psychiatry, 34,* 1181–1188. doi:10.1016/j.pnpbp.2010.06.016

Trauma and Relationships **3**

Chapter 3 expands on the information discussed in Chapter 2 with a specific focus on how trauma impacts our neurobiology within relationships. Understanding the *why* of trauma behavior helps us identify the emotional triggers that may sabotage healthy relationship building capabilities, as well as help parents learn to read their child's emotional *cues* more effectively, thereby improving parenting responses. In trauma and attachment, adults and children often *miscue* each other when communicating what they need. Memories of traumatic events are often stored in our mind and can be the catalyst for ineffective behavior when triggered. It's important for therapists and parents to understand how trauma memories work to better understand the behavior of traumatized youth. *Dissociation* is an important adaptive survival process for us to understand since trauma can elicit dissociation in an attempt to deal with an overwhelming threatening event during which terror is experienced. Not everyone who experiences trauma will manifest dissociation, but it is important to recognize when dissociation is in play when working with traumatized families. Parents may not spot the signs of dissociation in their child, especially if they have a history of their own trauma which may manifest dissociation to help them tolerate their own trauma triggers. It is important for therapists to recognize dissociation so they can make clinical decisions about the needs of the traumatized child and know how to effectively help parents support their child in the healing process.

Relationships and Memory

For children who have experienced trauma, each trauma memory is wired into their brain with all of these bits of information about the traumatic experience. Age of impact of trauma, and the stage of brain development, all play a role in our wiring. The relationship with parents and the interactions between parents and their children are wired into those memories. The importance of understanding this neurobiology cannot be underestimated because it is related to our ability to understand behavior, and how best to help repair relationship capacity. Our brain and the neural processes activated when threat is perceived will dictate our inter-personal behavioral responses. Our brain directs our behavior. As dis-cussed in the previous chapter, information from our environment is taken in through our senses and is continually processed to identify potential threats. These neural systems in the primitive regions of our brain process a potential threat on an automatic, unconscious level and activate our threat systems—if needed for the purpose of keeping us alive. As discussed in the previous chapters and in more depth later in this chapter, neuroception (Porges, 2011) describes how threat is identified via these neural circuits and how they operate. For people who have experienced trauma, their neural circuitry is forever changed because they have experienced a traumatic event. Their brain circuitry has experienced the threatening situation and set in motion physiological responses to help us to survive.

At the time of the trauma, we may not be fully cognitively aware of what was taking place within our bodies, and yet a response was acti-vated to address the threat. Perception of the event or situation, whether real or imagined, will activate our survival system. People who have experienced a traumatic event will now have an altered understanding of people, situations, and/or events. For a child who has witnessed his father taken away in handcuffs by the police, the child's perception of police has been forever influenced by that experience. When the child observes a police officer after that event, memories of the event will auto-matically be activated, physiological changes will occur in his body and will influence his emotions because the threat circuitry has been acti-vated. At the time of witnessing his father being arrested by the police (especially if the arrest was loud, chaotic, and scary), the child may have experienced increased heart rate, shallow breathing, and fear and/or anger welling up inside of him. Afterwards, every time this memory of the event is retrieved, his body will activate these physiological responses. When he observes a police officer in the future, unconsciously and auto-matically these physiological responses will arise within him and can con-tinue into adulthood. The association between police and traumatic experiences will be made automatically, unless there is a targeted effort to change those associations in the child's mind. The good news is that these trauma responses can be addressed in order to decrease their nega-tive impact. Parents and therapists who do not understand the neurobiology behind their child's distressing behavior may misunderstand the behavior and may respond in ways that do not help the child to effectively establish a sense of safety.

Implicit and Explicit Memory

Our memories are the result of several complex interactions among different areas of our brain. Memories of traumatic events are first processed and stored within the limbic system circuitry, since all incoming information is first processed in the amygdala to assess for threat. Ordinary memories are stored temporarily as *episodic memories* and include one's personal experience of the events, along with a sense of time and a sense of self, so they are more autobiographical in nature (Heide & Solomon, 2006). Aspects of the event that are stored in implicit memory are stored via *sensing* information which does not include language (Weber & Reynolds, 2004). Over time, as the memory is processed, it is then transferred to the frontal lobes of the brain for long-term storage (Solomon & Heide, 2005). The hippocampus plays a major role in memory storage. According to Heide and Solomon (2006), "the hippocampus places our experiences in categories and stores it along with similar memories" (p. 225). Cognitive aspects of the event are stored in the hippocampus and the emotion aspects of the memory are stored in the amygdala (Heide & Solomon, 2006; Solomon & Heide, 2005; Weber & Reynolds, 2004).

When new experiences occur, our brain will access these previous memories to help us know how to understand and respond to the new situation. Remember, our brain is designed to keep us alive, so if we experience novel situations then the ability to access previous, similar experiences will provide us with information to figure out how to respond in the current situation. This can be helpful in navigating new situations. However, if a novel situation activates my traumatic memory then my alarm system will be activated and I will respond as though the traumatic experience was occurring in the moment. This can create significant difficulties for the traumatized person to effectively navigate through the situation at that moment.

Our memories are heavily influenced by our perceptions and our biases associated with our past experiences, which, in turn, impact our behavior (Peres, Mercante, & Nasello, 2005). Since our amygdala is primarily involved with our earliest memories (implicit memories), these memories are accessed via sensory information, such as smell, touch, tone of voice, sight, etc. Therefore, sensory triggers will play a key role in the activation of traumatic memories. According to Solomon and Heide (2005), "we process disturbing memories by thinking, talking, and sometimes dreaming about the experience" (p. 54). Memory is actually a process involving different areas of the brain that take aspects of information about that event and later integrate the information to "create memories, which do not always factually represent what was experienced in the past" (Peres et al., p. 433). In the case of traumatic memories, the brain cannot effectively process the information to store it properly. This is often confusing to adults who are working with traumatized children because these children may recollect bits and pieces of a traumatic event and then fill in the gaps with inaccurate information due to the fragmentation of their memories. Traumatized children often have difficulty processing their memory of the traumatic event because the facts of the event do not match their perception (Terr, 1990).

Activation of these traumatic memories will set in motion the body's stress response and survival behavior. Since memories of traumatic events are not necessarily accurate and these memories contain disturbing content, it can be challenging for traumatized children and adolescents to make sense of the traumatic experience. They are often emotionally distressed by these memories and may act out in an angry or fearful manner—in ways that don't make sense to the adults in their lives. Their SNS processes have been activated and fight or flight behaviors are initiated. For instance, consider a child who was sexually abused at night around the age of 6 over a period of several months. That child may later experience nighttime as unsafe, may have difficulty sleeping through the night, may have traumatic nightmares, or even have tantrums about going to sleep. If the child's parent is unaware of the abuse, these behaviors may seem like manipulation to the adult and treated as such without any knowledge of the fear behind the behaviors. The child may experience these nightmares and become fearful of sleeping or avoid going to sleep as a way of managing their fear.

Dissociation can also be triggered as a way of managing the memories of these distressing events by disconnecting from the overwhelming emotional pain associated with the traumatic memories. Their PNS is activated to manage their feeling of helplessness and become emotionally numb. Dissociation can look like daydreaming or even rage. In infants, dissociation can even look as if the infant is "staring into space." If caregivers are unaware of the trauma, these behaviors will be confusing to the adults who interact with these traumatized children and teenagers. Dissociation during school can significantly interfere with learning. Taylor, a 10-year-old girl, would often dissociate in class if it was a subject that she did not like. Since she did not like the subject matter, her thoughts would wander and eventually intrusive memories of her sexual trauma would come up, triggering her to dissociate. Because Taylor frequently dissociated during that class, she was several months behind in her learning and her grades were poor. Her parents thought she was just not trying hard enough—until she finally disclosed her traumatic experiences. Since such memories can be extremely emotionally distressful, it is important for adults to recognize the underlying cause of the behavior to ensure that when the trauma memories are activated, the outward behaviors are addressed with tact and caution. Dissociation will be discussed in more depth later in this chapter.

Right Brain Processing, Affect Regulation, and Trauma

The interactions between children and their parents lay the foundation for the neural circuitry associated with interpersonal experiences. The tone of a parent's voice, the expression on the parent's face, and the parent's ability to attend to the child's needs will all be received and processed through the neuroception circuits as Porges (2011) identified. These interactions will be stored in the child's memory and will influence behavior, attitudes, and perceptions of the world and people (Shapiro, 2012). Within relationship interactions, the threat systems must be deactivated to allow engagement behavior to occur. We cannot form healthy social bonds if we feel threatened. According to Porges (2011), "to create relationships, humans must subdue these defensive reactions to engage, attach, and form lasting social bonds. Humans have adaptive *neurobehavioral* systems for both prosocial and defensive behaviors" (p. 12). When we engage in interactions with others, our neuroception circuits will help us know how to interact in part due to past memories about interactions, and whether or not we detect potential threat in those interactions. If the majority of our interpersonal experiences have been nonthreatening, then our brain will more effectively assess threat and determine if an alarm for potential harm or discomfort is needed. However, any event that was experienced as harmful will be stored in our memory and influence future behavior. For instance, suppose you grew up in a home in which at least one parent was constantly criticizing you and pointing out what you had done wrong with very little positive feedback given to you. Your experience growing up in a critical home would be hard-wired into your memory. Any possibility of re-experiencing a distressing event such as criticism would result in your brain activating its alarm system to manage the perception of threat. You would most likely be extremely sensitive to any type of corrective feedback and your ability to engage in healthy conflict resolution with loved ones would be significantly impaired. According to Francine Shapiro (2012), "how you respond to people in your life, and how they respond to you, is based as much on past experiences as it is on whatever either of you does or says in the present" (p. 20).

Right brain circuitry has been studied extensively in order to understand the role of these circuits in attachment and in the developing child's social and emotional well-being. The right brain encompasses the dominant neural circuitry that develops during the first three years of life for survival, attachment, and regulation of emotion (Schore, 2001). According to Schore (2001), the *social brain* develops within the context of social–emotional neural networks that interact with the environment and parents. The interactions between infant and parent influence the *use-dependent* networks within the brain. These neural circuits are either strengthened or pruned depending on their use or lack of use. For instance, neural pathways that are not stimulated via interactions and experiences will not be strengthened and will therefore be pruned. Neural pathways that are stimulated will be strengthened and retained. Keep in mind repetitive negative experiences and interactions will be strengthened if those are the predominant patterns. The pruning and strengthening process occurs with both positive and negative experiences. Recall the depressed mother and her young child who was removed from mother's care in the previous chapter? The neural pathways in the child's brain that were strengthened were those that registered his parent as unsafe and unable to help him survive. After moving to a new home with new caregivers who are unfamiliar to him, he and his foster mother will need to disrupt those old neural processes activating his internal alarm system in order to help him rewire his social brain to accept care and support from his foster mother.

Beginning in infancy, children learn to register every nuance of the interpersonal interactions with their parents from tone of voice, facial expressions, and touch. According to Porges (2011), "specific areas of the brain detect and evaluate features, such as body and face movements and vocalizations that contribute to the impression of safety or trustworthiness" (p. 13). In order to create healthy attachment bonds with parents, safety is a critical component within the relationship. Building a positive attachment foundation in children facilitates healthy social emotional development. When parents are able to provide consistent experiences of safety, and of meeting the physical and emotional needs of their children, then those social emotional neural pathways will be activated and strengthened to build on future experiences throughout life. Failure to consistently provide these experiences to infants means that those neural circuits necessary for recognizing facial expressions and voice tones in a parent, indicating physical and emotional needs can be counted on to be met, will be compromised. Those circuits needed to assess threat will not be working properly and the child will have difficulty ascertaining if someone is safe or unsafe. He may perceive everyone as a threat and respond in a defensive manner, or he may think everyone is safe and seek out relationships which make him vulnerable to harm. Neglect can have a significant impact on a child's developing neurobiology in the same way that other types of trauma negatively impact a child's development. It's important to remember here that parental perfection is not the goal since that is an unrealistic expectation. The goal is that these positive attachment experiences happen frequently enough to create and strengthen these neural pathways rather than allowing them to be pruned.

Schore's (2000, 2001, 2009) research on the right brain and the orbito-frontal areas of the brain found that an infant begins to receive information through right brain limbic regions as the foundation for their developing social brain. The right brain limbic circuitry encompasses emotion processing to receive and interpret facial expressions and voice tone without conscious awareness and verbal capabilities. This disputes the common myth that negative experiences, such as trauma and/or neglect during infancy, do not negatively impact children. This is important for therapists to understand because it has been my experience that there is a false belief within the mental health community that early neglect is not as detrimental as physical and/or sexual abuse. These early neglect experiences can influence the ability for a child to develop healthy relationship bonds which may be misinterpreted as the child being uncaring or oppositional. From infancy, children are learning to use their parents for healthy development and survival which is influenced by what they *read* from their interactions with parents.

For me, the *Face-to-Face Still-Face* (FFSF) experiment is a great example of how the nuances of interaction between parent and child influence the relationship, and the infant's ability to regulate himself during stressful interactions with his parent. This experimental framework has been used by researchers to explore the nuances of the interactions between caregivers and infants (facial expressions, tone of voice, behavioral interactions) and the role of these interactions in the infant's ability to regulate his stress response. Recent research using the FFSF model has also explored patterns of infant response across three dimensions:

> (a) engagement (the degree of dyadic reciprocity, shared pleasure and ability to prolong positive mutual interactions, (b) reengagement or return to interaction (infant's ability to self-soothe and signal their desire to return to interactions with the caregiver), and (c) reparation (capacity to restore the disrupted interaction to baseline levels.
>
> (Barbosa, Beeghly, Moreira, Tronick, & Fuertes, 2018, p. 2033)

The FFSF framework has three parts. First, the parent engages playfully and attentively with their infant, the infant registers his parent's tone of voice, facial expressions, and other nonverbal behavior. The second part involved the parent withdrawing socially and displaying a blank, expressionless face with no physical contact with their infant. This in turn impacts the infant's ability to regulate his emotions. The infant typically becomes emotionally distressed at the lack of positive response from the parent to engage his parent in pleasant interactions. The third part of the experiment design is for the parent to re-engage with infant through positive attempts to soothe their infant and repair their disruption. Initially, during the parent–child interactions, the infant responds positively and engages with his parent by smiling, maintaining eye contact, etc. When his parent withdraws her nonverbal positive interactions, the infant immediately notices the change and initiates behavior to regain his parent's positive interaction. When his parent continues her expressionless, blank response, the infant becomes emotionally distressed until his parent resumes her positive engagement with him. Children are wired to read their parents to become attuned with them and learn to depend on their parent/caregiver for physical, social, emotional, and cognitive development.

Attachment and emotion regulation are significantly related and influenced by experiences beginning in infancy (Schore, 2001). Affect regulation neural networks are dependent upon environmental influences via parent–child interaction. Consistent positive experiences within the parent–child interactions strengthen networks for secure attachment and healthy affect regulation. These co-creations between parent and child experienced consistently over time lay the foundation for later resiliency to manage the stressors encountered later in life. Parents provide the stabilizing framework for managing emotional distress when they are able to remain calm and attentive to the needs of the child which in turn results in the child becoming calm and returning to peaceful functioning. Early brain development includes strengthening and fine-tuning active neural pathways. Remember the mirror neurons from Chapter 2? The neural circuits in children will learn to use their parents to co-regulate their emotions and behavior by *mirroring* the predictable behavior observed and experienced by their parents. As children are able to experience this effective co-regulation of emotions over and over, these neural pathways are stimulated for growth and strengthened to provide the ability for the child to learn to self-regulate as they mature.

Imagine a toddler becoming emotionally distraught when told "no" by his parent. Using Panksepp's (2010) theory about affective neurocircuitry, we can say that the toddler's neural circuits for SEEKING to obtain something he wants is now thwarted, which activates his RAGE circuits and he begins to scream, cry, and possibly dissolve into a flailing heap of anger-outburst on the floor. When his parent is able to remain calm and respond to him in ways that effectively help him to decrease the emotional intensity of his outburst, he will eventually regain his happy and cooperative behavior and their relationship will be repaired. The toddler will store that memory of his parent and managing conflict in his nonverbal memory. He will also have stored the memory of his parent's facial expressions and voice tone. His experience of his parent over time will be based on these types of memories stored in his developing brain over and over, probably several times a day, so that he will become adept at reading the cues of his parent. If these experiences have been largely positive, then his threat system will not be activated and he can remain calm. If these experiences are perceived as threatening by the toddler on a consistent basis, then his threat system will be activated based on his perception that he is not safe. For infants and young children, they will not have the verbal capacity to make sense of these threatening experiences, but the memories will be stored nonverbally and can activate a threat response in the child.

As the child enters into adolescence, these early experiences will be built upon over time and become hard-wired into his circuitry. When a secure, positive attachment style between caregivers and an adolescent has developed through largely positive interactions in childhood, this developmental period can result in providing a secure base for the adolescent to accomplish the developmental tasks of this stage of life in a healthy manner. Significant difficulties in adolescence can be attributed to an insecure attachment style with their parents. Family conflict can have its roots in problems that have been unresolved from the child's early years. Some of you may remember the game of Tetherball on the playground in elementary school. There was a metal pole about six feet high with a rope about four feet long attached to a ball. The ball was attached to the pole so the ball didn't go far away when you hit it. It was nice not having to chase after the ball when you missed it. I like to use Tetherball as an analogy for the attachment relationship. In my analogy, parents are the pole, kids are the ball, and the quality of the attachment relationship is the rope. The effectiveness of the rope is dependent on the stability of the pole. If you have a wobbly pole that's not well-grounded, then that affects the quality of the Tetherball experience—because it was hard to hit the ball and feel safe when you never knew if the pole was going to fall over. How far the ball is able to move away from the pole is dependent upon the quality of the rope. If the rope was worn and showing signs of unraveling or detaching from the pole, then again the quality of the Tetherball game was compromised.

When parents are able to be steady during times of stress, then they can remain *upright* regardless of the force to pull away. The quality of the relationship is the rope that *anchors* to the pole (parents). Rope is strong and yet also flexible. When the attachment relationship is flexible yet consistent and stable, then parents are able to adjust to the challenges that occur in life and in their relationship with their child. Parents need to regulate their own emotions and be attuned to the needs of their child. When this occurs, then teenagers do not stray too far away from the *grounding* that their relationship with their parents provides. By the time children hit their adolescence, they are experts at reading the cues of their parents. They may not fully comprehend the extent to which their neural circuits are activated by their interpretations of their parent's behavior. They will be scanning and responding to the cues of their parents. They will know at least on an implicit level that the *Tetherball pole* is anchored or not anchored, as well as whether or not the *rope* is strong. Traumatized teens need their parents to help *ground* them to provide a sense of safety and stability while remaining attuned to their needs. This is true among sibling relationships as well. Siblings will learn to read the behavior of their siblings and the interaction observed between their siblings and parents. The nuances of these experiences will become wired into memory and lay the foundation for the relationship patterns within the family system. In the next chapter, we'll examine more about the nuances of relationship interactions and patterns because therapists need to recognize these nuances in order to identify target points for change.

The *middle prefrontal cortex* (MPFC) region of the brain is made up of the medial, ventral, and orbitofrontal areas of the prefrontal cortex and anterior cingulate. The middle prefrontal cortex processes emotional and cognitive information coming in through the body, which is then understood via the prefrontal areas. This MPFC is key in understanding the social world, and ourselves in the social world. Early experiences between parents and infants begin to lay the foundation for establishing meaning within relationships (Badenoch, 2008; Siegel, 2011). The orbitofrontal prefrontal cortex plays a significant role in processing interpersonal cues during social interactions based on the facial expressions and voice tone of the individuals involved in the exchange. These circuits are also involved in the development of an unconscious sense of self (Schore, 2001; Van Der Kolk, 2014). Schore (2001) describes the role of the orbitofrontal cortex as evaluating the intentions of the social interactions of others to report to the rest of the brain as to what actions may be needed in order to respond.

Van Der Kolk (2014) describes the impact of trauma on the middle prefrontal regions of our brain and our sense of self in relation to others based on researchers who studied traumatized and non-traumatized individuals. He reports that researchers found that traumatized individuals were not able to effectively utilize all the integrative functions of the middle prefrontal cortex regions of the brain. Van Der Kolk (2014) theorized that:

> in coping with trauma itself, and in coping with the dread that persists long afterward, these patients had learned to shut down the brain areas that transmit the visceral feelings and emotions that accompany and define terror … What we witnessed here was a tragic adaptation: In an effort to shut off terrifying sensations, they also deadened their capacity to feel fully alive.
>
> (p. 94)

For people who have become overwhelmed by their traumatic life experiences, they may try to shut out all memories that would activate their threatening emotions and bodily sensations connected with those memories. They try to shut out the "dark" (traumatic memories, physiological responses, and emotions). But you can't shut out the dark unless you also shut out the "light" (joy, contentment, integrated sense of self, emotional connection with others). Meaning, if we try to block out certain emotions and experiences then we cannot fully experience all of life and enjoy an integrated and balanced life.

Dissociation

What exactly is dissociation? For children and adolescents who have experienced ongoing interpersonal trauma, dissociation can be one of the learned *survival responses*. If you remember from Chapter 2, neurologically dissociation is a process that occurs in response to perceived threat. It is a survival response to ensure safety when threat is perceived, whether or not actual danger is present (Schore, 2009). It is essentially shutting out both light and dark. Dissociation occurs when threat within the social interaction is perceived as dangerous and one is helpless, which activates the hypothalamic–pituitary–adrenal (HPA) stress axis circuitry and PNS. As discussed in the previous chapter, the PNS acts as the brakes for our autonomic nervous system activating the freeze or dissociative state. It responds to perceived threat by decreasing heart rate, blood pressure, and breathing as though feigning death as a protective measure to ensure our survival. Imagine seeing a bear ahead of you on a path with teeth bared, ready to attack if you get any closer. If your PNS is engaged, then you will freeze in response to the bear and not allow the bear to sense any threat from you—as opposed to your SNS engaging the accelerator to increase your heart rate, sending blood to your extremities in order to help you fight, or run really fast, and decrease your ability to experience pain. This state of dissociation is a withdrawn state in which one disconnects from the external world as if numb.

Dissociation can occur under non-traumatic experiences as well as traumatic experiences. For example, you may have driven your car home from work using the same route day after day, your thoughts may have drifted back to the events of the day and you completely lost track of sustaining your focus on the actual task of driving. Arriving home, you may have realized you had no memory of your trip. Your thoughts had been on other things and not on your driving. Whenever this happens to me, it usually freaks me out because I wonder, "How did I know what to do, when to turn, when to stop, if I was not paying attention? I could have been hurt or hurt others." At such times our minds are essentially preoccupied with other things to the point that we are acting without conscious focus on the present moment. We are in a dissociative state, in a state of mindlessness—unfocused and unaware.

Dissociation is often considered a symptom of one's response to a traumatic event that is too overwhelming to process in the moment. For some people, dissociation is a coping skill that is needed in order to tolerate severe emotional distress. I like to say to people that our brain is designed to keep us alive first and foremost. When people have experienced a traumatic event, our brain processes will "kick into gear" to help us function and keep safe. Trauma experiences challenge our mind to process terrifying information effectively and make sense of and help us function and survive after a traumatic experience. On a short-term basis, it can provide the ability to tolerate the *intolerable*. Trauma overwhelms our ability to make sense of what has happened.

Many of us in the United States experienced this when terrorists attacked our country in the fall of 2001. My husband was supposed to be in the World Trade Center Towers in New York City on the morning of September 11, 2001. In fact, he was on a train bound for Manhattan about 30 minutes from Penn Station when the first plane flew into one of the towers. He was born in New York City and considers himself a New Yorker, so he was used to the bustling sights and sounds of the city. After arriving at Penn Station, he described the surreal experience of walking to his hotel because there were no available taxis and the subway wasn't operating. Aside from police and fire vehicles, there was no traffic on the streets. The typically bustling streets were empty. He said there was an eerie silence and he described people walking around, as if in a daze, emotionally disconnected. The city was shut down and so were its people. Those of us watching by television, saw people walking with glazed looks on their faces and struggling to articulate what they had experienced. To me, this is an example of people in a dissociative state who experienced something so terrifying and so overwhelming that they needed to emotionally and cognitively disconnect in order to function.

Remember Taylor whose sexual trauma memories activated a dissociative response during class? Her dissociative responses resulted in losing several months of learning. This is not uncommon for traumatized youth. They can have difficulty learning and retaining new information in school because their threat system is activated. Fortunately for Jane, once she was able to engage in healing from the trauma, she was able to catch up academically and was successful in school.

Dissociation can occur on a continuum from mild to severe and can vary in frequency from occurring often, or just occasionally, to perhaps just once or twice in total. Weiland (2011) describes mild dissociation in children as *spacing out* with or without conscious intent, and abrupt changes in emotional state. These abrupt changes are typically extreme with very little "ramping up" or "ramping down." In more moderate states of dissociation, derealization, or depersonalization occurs in addition to the abrupt shifts in emotional state. Numbing of emotions occur to avoid the painful affect that has been triggered. And finally, severe dissociation includes the previous symptoms experienced in mild and moderate dissociation as well as a disconnection with the core self, and compartmentalizing one's experiences into separate parts on self. This is more typical in a disorganized attachment style which may speak to the child's difficulty regulating internal states of *being* due to ongoing perceptions of threat. Trauma dissociation is thought of as a way to adapt to ongoing threatening events that leave one feeling helpless. If one can disconnect internally, then the ability to tolerate the intolerable becomes possible.

I like Joyanna Silberg's (2013) view of dissociation as an adaptive function to a traumatic experience. When conceptualizing dissociation in this way, therapists are likely to be more successful at helping traumatized children experiencing dissociation feel safer and thereby better able to engage in the healing process.

Dissociation as Adaptation

From a psychological perspective, dissociation is generally viewed as a disruption in usually integrated functions of consciousness, emotions, memory, identity, and perceptions (Berry, Varese, & Bucci, 2017; Silberg, 2013). Developmentally, children are in the process of identity formation, learning to regulate their emotions, and developing relationships skills. They do not yet have fully formed personality structures. They are also more dependent on adults to help them regulate their emotions and navigate life's stressors. Silberg (2013) makes the argument that the definition of dissociation as a disruption in usually integrated states is insufficient for children who have experienced ongoing interpersonal trauma. That's because this definition focuses on the usually integrated functions. She states, "a comprehensive theory of dissociation will have to account both for any apparent 'disintegration' as well as the developmental roots of these processes" (Silberg, 2013, p. 15).

Using an *adaptive view* of dissociation requires therapists to explore and identify the purpose and trigger of the dissociative behavior, so that therapists and parents can help traumatized children feel safe and find more effective ways to address situations. Remember, trauma memories will trigger the threat response to activate survival behaviors. In the case of trauma dissociation, threat is perceived and dissociation is activated. Helping the child to identify the threat will allow parents and therapists to help the child identify what he needs in order to feel safe in the moment, and engage in more effective behavior for the situation at hand. During my career, I have worked at adolescent residential treatment facilities, and there were several clients with histories of trauma. Some of the teens I worked with had experienced significant trauma. They would often dissociate and become physically and verbally aggressive when they felt threatened and their trauma memories were activated. They would have very little memory of what they said and how they behaved during these episodes. Afterwards, when they were calm and able to talk with staff, they would explore what triggered their threat system and identify what they needed in order to feel safe when those memories were activated, or they experienced a situation as threatening. Helping them to develop more effective skills reduced their dissociation and increased their ability to function effectively.

It is not uncommon that children with a history of interpersonal trauma have been raised by parents who also had a history of childhood trauma. In these families, parents can become emotionally triggered by the trauma behavior in their children. In some instances, these parents may dissociate in response to their child's behavior and will be unable to respond to their child with a healthy parenting response. For instance, in the case of children raised in homes with domestic violence, it is likely that the child's misbehavior may trigger traumatic childhood memories in the parent resulting in dissociation. The parent will be unable to respond to the child effectively because the parent's dissociative state will essentially paralyze their ability to respond in ways that will help reduce the child's emotional outburst. It is important for therapists to recognize signs of dissociation in parents and help parents recognize their own dissociative behavior in order to receive the help they need to resolve their own trauma. Parents will need help learning to stay emotionally and cognitively *present* with their children in order to be an effective Tetherball pole and maintain a strong Tetherball rope with their children. Parents provide the security and structure to help their children heal from trauma, and to do this, they must be aware of their own trauma histories that may sabotage their parenting. In Chapter 4, we'll examine specific attachment behaviors and processes necessary to help heal trauma in families.

References

Badenoch, B. A. (2008). *Being a brain-wise therapist: A practical guide to interpersonal neuro-biology.* New York, NY: W.W. Norton & Company, Inc.

Barbosa, M., Beeghly, M., Moreira, J., Tronick, E., & Fuertes, M. (2018). Robust stability and physiological correlates of infants' patterns of regulatory behavior in the Still-Face paradigm at 3 and 9 months. *Developmental Psychology, 54*(11), 2032–2042. doi:10.1037/dev0000616

Berry, K., Varese, F., & Bucci, S. (2017). Cognitive attachment model of voices: Evidence base and future implications. *Frontiers in Psychiatry, 8*(111), 1–13. doi:10.3389/fpsyt.2017.00111

Heide, K. M., & Solomon, E. P. (2006). Biology, childhood trauma, and murder: Rethinking justice. *International Journal of Law and Psychiatry, 29*, 220–233. doi:10.1016/j.ijlp.2005.10.001

Panksepp, J. (2010). Affective neuroscience of the emotional BrainMind: Evolutionary perspectives and implications for understanding depression. *Dialogues in Clinical Neuroscience, 12*(4), 533–545.

Peres, J., Mercante, J., & Nasello, A. G. (2005). Psychological dynamics affecting traumatic memories: Implications for psychotherapy. *The British Psychological Society, 78*, 431–447. doi:10.1348/147608305X26693

Porges, S. W. (2011). *The polyvagal theory: Neurophysiological foundations of emotions, attachment, communication, self-regulation.* New York, NY: W.W Norton & Company, Inc.

Schore, A. N. (2000). Attachment and the regulation of the right brain. *Attachment and Human Development, 2*(1), 23–47.

Schore, A. N. (2001). Effects of a secure attachment relationship on right brain development, affect regulation, and infant mental health. *Infant Mental Health Journal, 22*(1–2), 7–66.

Schore, A. N. (2009). Relational trauma and the developing right brain: An interface of psychoanalytic self psychology and neuroscience. *Self and Systems: Annals of the New York Academy of Sciences, 1159*, 189–203. doi:10.1111/j.1749-6632.2009.04474x

Shapiro, F. (2012). *Getting past your past.* New York, NY: Rodale.

Siegel, D. J. (2011). *Mindsight: The new science of personal transformation.* New York, NY: Bantam Books.

Silberg, J. L. (2013). *The child survivor: Healing developmental trauma and dissociation.* New York, NY: Routledge.

Solomon, E. P., & Heide, K. M. (2005). The biology of trauma: Implications for treatment. *Journal of Interpersonal Violence, 20*(1), 51–60. doi:10.1177/0886260504268119

Terr, L. (1990). *Too scared to cry: How trauma affects children…and ultimately us all.* Basic Books: New York, NY.

Van Der Kolk, B. (2014). *The body keeps score: Brain, mind, and body in the healing of trauma.* New York, NY: Penguin Books.

Weber, D. A., & Reynolds, C. R. (2004). Clinical perspectives on neurobiological effects of psychological trauma. *Neuropsychology Review, 14*(2), 115–129.

Weiland, S. (2011). Dissociation in children and adolescents: What it is, how it presents, and how we can understand it. In S. Wieland (Ed.), *Dissociation in traumatized children and adolescents* (pp. 1–27). New York, NY: Routledge.

The Nuts and Bolts of   **4**
Relationships

The first three chapters provided an overview of neurobiology, trauma, and attachment. In this chapter, we'll look at what I call the *nuts and bolts* of relationships. We'll do this by examining attachment styles and the nuances of interaction patterns within relationships. It's critical to recognize the attachment patterns and emotional *cues* within parent–child relationships since they either enhance the attachment relationship or contribute to unhealthy relationship patterns within families. The "devil" really is in the details, by which I mean that, as therapists, we need to be aware of the subtle verbal and nonverbal behaviors underlying family interactions. Recognizing *attachment styles* helps therapists identify the unhealthy patterns in order to target areas for change, as well as identify strengths within the relationship. Concepts of *mentalization, intersubjectivity,* and *attunement* are discussed to provide therapists with frameworks to understand and assess patterns within family relationships and help parents learn more effective ways of parenting their traumatized child.

Attachment Styles in Children

Historically, attachment relationships have been placed into four categories or styles: *secure attachment, anxious avoidant attachment, anxious ambivalent attachment,* and *disorganized attachment.* These attachment styles help to identify interaction patterns within the attachment relationship, as well as identify the child's ability to use his parent as his primary attachment figure. Biringen (1994) describes attachment behavior as "any form of conduct that results in attaining or maintaining proximity to an attachment figure" (p. 405). When examining the attachment relationships, therapists observe the child's response to closeness and distance (proximity) to his attachment figure (parent) and the child's ability to tolerate closeness and distance. For example, when a young child's parent leaves the room and the child can no longer see his parent, does he cry and seek to be reunited with his parent or does he seem oblivious to her absence? How does he respond when his parent returns? Does he seem to be comforted and able to go back out to explore the world? Does he seem unable to be comforted and use his parent for comfort upon her return to him? Does he seem aloof when his parent attempts to comfort him? Keep in mind that it's not unusual for children to have a variety of responses to reunification with their parents, so a single observation of a single interaction is not sufficient for an assessment. Relationship interactions between children and parents need to be observed numerous times over many weeks to make an accurate assessment of the attachment styles. Children and parents will have difficult days, so therapists need to be mindful of making snap judgements which may only hinder the healing process.

Powell, Cooper, Hoffman, and Marvin (2014) developed an adjusted version of the *Strange Situation Protocol* to include feedback from parents about their perceptions of the interactions with their child, and therapists' interactions with parents, in order to gain an assessment of the attachment styles of the child and the parent. In my experience, obtaining information from parents, observing interactions between parents and their children, and using clinical awareness of therapist interactions with parents has been invaluable to help parents and children in the healing process. I think this invitation to parents to provide their feedback and concerns also allows for the parents to feel supported and better able to develop trust in the therapeutic relationship. A strong therapeutic relationship is critical to achieving the ultimate goal of helping family members make necessary changes and improve the quality of their relationships.

Secure attachments have been shown to contribute to healthy development in children across all developmental tasks. Generally speaking, children who have a secure attachment relationship with their parents are comfortable in the presence of their parents, are able to seek parental comfort when distressed, and respond positively to parental comfort. Securely attached children are able to explore their environment and feel confident that their parents will provide support for them in their explorations within safe parameters. Using the framework of Panksepp's (2010) motivation circuits discussed in Chapter 2, in a securely attached child we will observe his SEEKING system activated as he explores his environment. At some point the child's FEAR circuits become activated when he perceives some kind of threat (a stranger approaches, a dog approaches, etc.). This activates the mother's CARE system as she becomes alerted to his distress and his SEEKING system is activated to find his mother to provide safety and comfort to him. Once he becomes comforted and feels safe again, his SEEKING system will propel him to explore his environment once again.

There are two types of insecure attachment styles, ambivalent and avoidant. Generally, both of these attachment styles are seen in children who are not able to effectively use their attachment figure for creating a sense of safety and well-being. Children with ambivalent attachment styles seek to be comforted by their parent, but have difficulty using their parent for support since their parent has demonstrated a pattern of inconsistency in their ability to provide this support. The children aren't confident that they will receive the comfort needed in order to alleviate their emotional distress. They tend to be anxious and often have difficulty learning to effectively regulate their emotions because their parent has not been successful in co-regulating their own emotions. As discussed previously, children need parents to be able to manage their own emotions in order to help their child regulate his own. The co-regulation process is a key component for developing secure attachments.

Insecure-avoidant attachment patterns are seen in children who generally have difficulty accepting support and seem to be more aloof. Children with an avoidant style of attachment seem to be more withdrawn and avoid emotional closeness. They have difficulty tolerating proximity with parents and seem to regulate their emotions by withdrawing from support. As with insecure ambivalent attachment behavior, children with an avoidant style of attachment have experienced their parent's inability to comfort them to be inconsistent and ineffective.

The fourth style of attachment is the disorganized attachment style, typically seen in children with reactive attachment disorder due to a significant history of trauma and neglect. Children with a disorganized style of attachment generally display a pattern of significant emotional distress around interactions with the parent. These children may intensely seek their parent and then intensely try to avoid their parent as if their FEAR circuits cannot be calmed and are also activated by proximity to the parent. Children with disorganized attachment may appear to be frozen as if emotionally disconnected in a dissociative state. A disorganized attachment style "indicates that the infant adopts no organized strategy toward the attachment figure" (Biringen, 1994, p. 406).

An important concept in attachment theory is that of *internal working models* of the attachment figure and the attachment relationship. These are the *representations* of attachment figures based on perceptions of experiences with parents and stored in memory. These representations of attachment figures are activated during relationship interactions. Marrone (2014) describes internal working models as "cognitive maps, representations, scheme, or scripts that an individual has about himself (as a unique bodily and psychic entity) and his environment" (p. 79). Internal working models are complex representations created via our individual experiences and our perceptions of those experiences. These representations or mentalizations are stored in our memories and are activated throughout our life. They may be unconscious or conscious. They are the "stories" we hold in our minds about ourselves, about relationships, and about ourselves in relationships. The concept of internal working models requires therapists to understand two important constructs developed by researchers and theorists to help us understand the nuances of relationship interactions. However, first we'll discuss adult attachment styles since therapists need to recognize attachment patterns within parents if they want to successfully help parents and their traumatized children heal.

Attachment Styles in Adults

Assessing adult attachment styles has been of interest to researchers in order to gain an understanding about the correlation between a parent's style of attachment and their child's style of attachment. One of the most commonly cited is the Adult Attachment Interview (AAI), which is a very structured interview process completed by trained interviewers. This instrument focuses on understanding how adults perceived their relationship with their parents and how they made sense of their lives within the context of the impact of their primary relationships. The AAI seeks to classify adult attachment styles into one of four categories that closely resemble those identified for children. These adult attachment categories are the *secure type*, the *dismissing type*, the *preoccupied type*, and the *unresolved type*.

The secure type of adult attachment style is seen in adults who are able to recollect experiences in their life without becoming overly distressed by these memories and the remembered details about their experiences. They are able to recognize both positive and negative aspects of their childhood experiences and demonstrate a balanced integration of those experiences. They are able to seek out and receive support as well as engage in problem solving to creatively resolve current problems. Adults with this type of attachment style recognize that supportive and mutually positive relationships contribute to overall emotional well-being in life. Marrone (2014) states there are two subgroups of secure type adults:

> (1) individuals who grew up in a stable and supportive family group; and (2) individuals who had difficult experiences during childhood but show resilience and are presently exceptionally thoughtful and developed (these are often referred to as the "earned secure" to distinguish them from the basically secure group).
>
> (p. 100)

The secure type of adult attachment is similar to a secure attachment style seen in children.

The dismissing type of adult attachment refers to adults who tend to avoid connection with their emotions as a way of dealing with distress. They tend to minimize the negative impact of experiences and may report an idealized version of their childhood experiences to avoid the emotional distress of their memories. Since they tend to avoid or minimize their emotions, these adults will have difficulty recognizing their own emotions. They will be more emotionally disconnected in their relationships. They will be more comfortable discussing things on an intellectual level rather than an integration of intellect and emotion. This type of adult attachment style correlates with the avoidant attachment style in children.

The preoccupied type of adult attachment identified by the AAI is demonstrated in adults who tend to become overly emotionally involved with others quickly rather than allowing the relationship to evolve over time. Once they are in a relationship, they tend to struggle with requiring the relationship to be the stabilizing force to help them regulate their intense emotions which puts a high demand on their partner. They are likely to focus on their own emotional needs within the relationship and have poor coping skills for regulating their intense emotions. This unstable attachment pattern contributes to significant anxiety and ambivalence within the adult. Siegel (2011) states that in adults with this type of attachment pattern "issues stemming from the past continue to intrude on experiences in the present" (p. 179). Whereas the dismissing style of adult attachment disconnects from the past and attempts to block it out, the preoccupied style of adult attachment is regularly re-experiencing relationship difficulties within their present relationships. This type of adult attachment style corresponds to the ambivalent attachment style seen in children.

The fourth style of adult attachment categorized by the AAI is the unresolved type. This type of adult attachment is similar to the disorganized attachment style seen in children. Adults with an unresolved type of attachment report childhood experiences of significant loss and abuse. They are unable to develop a coherent understanding of their traumatic childhood experiences and often have difficulty effectively describing and discussing their childhood. They tend to have difficulty maintaining a coherent sense of self and often have a fragmented and disorganized internal working model of themselves and their ability to maintain relationships. They have both a dismissing and preoccupied working model of relationships. This often negatively affects their ability to effectively regulate their emotions and tolerate emotional distress.

These descriptions of attachment styles in children and adults are meant to provide a framework for recognizing the range of attachment behaviors that will manifest within the therapy sessions. Recognizing that attachment relationships contribute to internal working models in children which continue into adulthood provides therapists with the ability to help parents identify the *roots* of their behavior when those working models, or what Ginot (2007) called *enactments*, are activated. In the following paragraphs, the constructs of intersubjectivity and mentalization will be discussed to help therapists better understand the nuances of relationship interactions and the underlying internal working models activating those relationship nuances. Therapists can help parents recognize cues from their children to better understand the *why* of their child's behavior, and not respond only to the *what* of their child's behavior. Viewing behaviors as a child's attempt to communicate their needs to their parents is paramount for parents to help their children heal. As discussed in the previous chapters, traumatized children often miscue their parents and struggle with effectively communicating their needs. Therapists need to tune into the details in the interactions between parents and their children to help parents develop more effective skills for parenting their traumatized child and helping siblings to feel secure in the family.

Nitty Gritty of Attachment Relationships

Liljenfors and Lundh (2015) extensively reviewed the constructs of inter-subjectivity and mentalization. The two separate yet connected constructs have historically been viewed to be mutually exclusive. However, Liljen-fors and Lundh (2015) argue that

> mentalization originally develops within the context of primary inter-subjectivity, and that primary intersubjectivity is a basic prerequisite for the development of mentalization; but also that there is consider-able overlap between the concepts of primary intersubjectivity and those of the implicit and externally focused mentalization.
>
> (p. 36)

Intersubjectivity, Affect Attunement, Shared Attention and Shared Intention

Attachment is a broad concept which helps us understand the importance of the parent–child relationship, and its impact on child development. Bal-bernie (2007) bridges the psychoanalytic concepts of attachment, such as *containment* and *holding*, with intersubjectivity by asserting that intersub-jectivity is essentially the "glue" in the attachment relationship because it allows that ability to provide physical closeness for mutually shared experiences to occur between parent and child. According to Balbernie (2007), "the hard-worked hypotheses may be seen as fine-tuned descrip-tions of aspects of mutually influencing intersubjective contact based on emotional attunement; and they are key constructs that inform infant mental health" (p. 310). Balbernie (2007) further argues that the concepts of holding and containment relate to several "facets of intersubjectivity such as attunement, affect regulation, reflective function, and the sensitive caregiving that promotes security in attachment" (p. 310). It's important to understand the components that help to establish and maintain the attachment relationship.

Remember the resonance circuits discussed in Chapter 2? Resonance circuits help us to physiologically become attuned and connected with another person. Researchers have explored the interactions between par-ents and children to identify key ways of interacting that are essential for healthy attachment in children. These are the building blocks that play a role in the development of the attachment relationship. Attachment is focused on the establishment of safety within the parent–child relationship and its ability to aid in a child's healthy development. When working with families whose relationships are impacted by trauma it will be important to address its relational impact in order to help our young clients overcome all aspects of the trauma. Trauma impacts our ability to trust others and our world and will negatively impact our abilities to form safe and healthy relationships. Therapists need to learn to recognize these components within the interactions between parents and their children in order to help their traumatized clients learn to use their parents as a safe resource to help them navigate through the ups and downs of life.

Intersubjectivity provides a construct to understand the complexity of human interaction and the subjective experiences of these interactions within the individuals. Mirror neurons play a key role in the construct of intersubjectivity since these neural circuits aid in the understanding of the intentions and behaviors of others. "In developmental psychology intersubjectivity has come often to refer to a quality of relating, where sharing, mutuality, and attunement are experienced between infant and caretaker" (Diamond, 2014, p. 280). It is the overlap of the experience between the individuals in which the individuals involved have their own unique experience of the interaction as well as an overlap of their mutual experiences. For example, David and his 6-year-old daughter, Sarah, are having ice cream together at an ice cream store. Sarah experiences the ice cream as delicious, the ice cream store is loud and full of people which she enjoys, and she is enjoying the full attention of her father. David is also enjoying the outing with his daughter, their uninterrupted time together, and the taste of the ice cream. He experiences the outing from a father's perspective and not from his 6-year-old daughter's perspective. He must focus on making sure they are able to get home in time for her bedtime, pay for the ice cream, and drive them home. Sarah has a different focus since she neither has to pay for the ice cream nor drive them home. She will enjoy the sights and sounds of the ice cream experience with less responsibility. Both David and Sarah enjoy the same experience of having ice cream together, yet each of them simultaneously has a different experience. This intersubjective experience occurs in that precise moment when David and Sarah are enjoying the ice cream together—the quality of their relating.

According to Cortina and Liotti (2010), "the main function of attachment is to seek protection, whereas the main function of intersubjectivity is to communicate, at intuitive and automatic levels, with members of the same species and to facilitate social understanding" (p. 410). Ginot (2007) examined intersubjectivity and the notion of enactments within interpersonal interactions to better understand the nuances of these inter-actions. By recognizing these enactments, Ginot (2007) proposed that we could recognize early implicit memories with the emotions, perceptions, and adaptive behaviors in response to these wired-in memories for which we may not have the conscious ability to articulate and understand. Remember, implicit memories are memories stored in our brain without language attached to them. Intersubjectivity, then, will be experienced through our senses and emotions connected with the interaction and are connected to previous implicit memories. Sarah and David will have the ability to fully enjoy their time together because they will have wired-in previous experiences in which they shared other mutually positive experi-ences or enactments. Their intersubjective experience will be influenced by their past positive experiences and will therefore, influence their social communication exchanges.

In cases where there have not been previously wired-in positive experi-ences, then it can result in a less positive intersubjective experience. Let's say that Sarah has often seen her father angry and irritable, short-tempered, and she is often unsure what mood he will be in when he is with her. Her experience of her father will be that he is unpredictable and often angry. She will subdue her behavior when he is with her and she may be focused on reading his cues to know how to respond rather than relaxing to fully enjoy her outing with him to the ice cream shop. Past implicit memories influence her current interactions with him which is demonstrated in the quality of their intersubjective experience. Therap-ists will need to be attuned to the subtle exchanges between parents and their children, as well as the subtle exchanges between siblings. Intersub-jectivity between siblings is also an important aspect of relationships to recognize in order to facilitate relationship repair between siblings.

Affective attunement, shared intention, and *shared attention* form the basis of intersubjectivity between parent and child. Within an attachment framework, these components are focused on experiences that both parent and child experience within an interaction in any given moment. Positive shared attention and shared intention mean that both parent and child experience the interaction in a positive manner. For example, tod-dler and mother playing a game of peekaboo. Mother is laughing through enjoyment of the experience with her child and child is enjoying the experience of the game with mother. Both are fully present emotionally at that moment in time and the attention of both mother and child is focused on that moment of mutually enjoying the game of peekaboo. The opposite would be true if the mother were not fully emotionally present in that moment with her child. Perhaps the mother is thinking about financial stressors or feeling tired from lack of sleep the previous night and she is just going through the motions while emotionally feeling distant, her thoughts focused on other things. The mother's attention is not shared with the child at that moment and they do not share the same intention of enjoying the game of peekaboo together. There are times when parents may be distracted while interacting with their children since no one can be perfect all the time. The goal would be to have regular and consistent positive shared experiences over time to maintain the positive connection when there may be a disruption in the relationship.

Mentalizing: Our Internal Stories of Self and Others

The parent's own attachment history will be activated within the parent–child relationship. Parent and child mutually experience their interactions and respond according to their perceptions of that experience. This intersubjectivity will create experiences within the child that are the foundation for later experiences of relationships. These experiences become the mental and emotional framework underneath much of our behaviors. Dr. Brené Brown (2015) has studied shame and its impact extensively. In her book, *Daring Greatly*, she refers to the stories we tell ourselves when discussing the role shame plays in our behavior. When I think about mentalization, I think about it in terms of the internal stories and images we have stored away in our mind about ourselves, our world, and our place in the world. These stories form the basis of my core beliefs. My core beliefs will influence the way in which I will experience myself and interact in my relationships. Anyone who has ever experienced trauma, especially interpersonal trauma, has shame. Shame and trauma go hand in hand. Therefore, understanding mentalization and its role in the healing process is critical for creating the ability to repair the damage of trauma.

Mentalization is a construct that seeks to explain how we understand ourselves and others. I like to think about mentalizations as the stories we tell ourselves about the meaning of interactions with others and our beliefs about ourselves. These mentalizations influence our core beliefs and play a significant role in emotional wellness and ability to establish and maintain healthy relationships. Other interchangeable construct terms identified in the literature for describing how we understand ourselves and others are social cognition, theory of mind, mind reading, mindfulness, and social intelligence (Ballespi, Perez-Domingo, Vives, Sharp, & Barrantes-Vidal, 2018; Kim, 2015). There are differences among these constructs and all of them seek to explain social interaction phenomenon. Given their relevance to understanding the nuances of relationships, mentalization is an important construct for therapists to recognize within the context of understanding the nuances of attachment. Luyten and Fonagy (2015) concluded that the growth of research on mentalizing from the 1990s to 2014 was evidence of the growing recognition that mentalizing plays a critical role in social emotional development that contributes to either healthy psychological functioning or psychopathology. Several studies have explored the role of mentalizing in the development of borderline personality disorder, anxiety, and other mental health issues, as well as ways in which a high capacity for mentalizing is a protective factor in healthy social and emotional development and attachment (Ballespi et al., 2018; Bo, Sharp, Fonagy, & Kongerslev, 2017; Borelli, Compare, Snavely, & Decio, 2015; Herrmann et al., 2018).

According to Luyten and Fonagy (2015), mentalizing is based on biological aspects of one's self as well as interactions with others. Mentalizing

> focuses on both self and other, and on both cognition and affect. Furthermore, mentalizing also encompasses processes involved in interpreting one's own mind and that of others based on external features (such as facial expressions, posture, and prosody) and balancing this sensitivity with knowledge about the mental interiors of both the self and others.
>
> (p. 368)

Mentalizing plays a role in inferring meaning and intention behind behavior within the context of social interactions. Kim (2015) describes mentalizing as "the fundamental human capacity to make sense of what unfolds in one's own mind and the mind of others" (p. 356). Remember mirror neurons and resonance circuits discussed in Chapter 2? Mirror neurons are neural circuits that play a significant role in *reading* the intentions of others based on predictable patterns of behavior. The construct of mentalizing incorporates the capabilities of mirror neuron circuits in the development of understanding ourselves and others via the resonance circuits.

Resonance circuits identified by Siegel (2011) include the circuitry involved with mirror neurons, limbic regions of the brain and the body via brainstem. These resonance circuits are central to understanding self, and self in relation to others, and influence mentalizing processes.

Mentalizing occurs within a developmental framework which begins in infancy (Borelli et al., 2015; Falkenstrom et al., 2014; Luyten & Fonagy, 2015). Attachment experiences play a crucial role in mentalizations formed and play a critical role in creating the foundation for our core beliefs about ourselves and the world. Our early attachment experiences are based on our interactions with our early caregivers. If our caregivers are able to provide overall positive experiences of love and acceptance and meet our basic needs for food, shelter, and safety then our early concepts of *self* begin forming that we are loveable and acceptable. If our early caregivers are frequently irritated, impatient, and inconsistent, then our early concepts of self will begin to form with a negative foundation about who we are, as well as resulting in negative interactions with others. We are likely to be anxious and insecure in our beliefs about ourselves and others. These experiences become wired into our memory system. Since we have no language in our early development, these experiences are stored in our implicit memory. These early memories influence our later experiences in life and how we make sense of these experiences. Here's where mentalizing helps to explain how these early experiences influence our later understanding of interactions with others, and our beliefs about ourselves, which create our internal working models. If my interactions with my early parent are ones in which I am fed, warm (or cool if the temperature is hot), and the voice tone and facial expressions of my parent are caring and kind, then I learn to trust that my needs will be provided for by this person and that I am loved. Over time, with consistent positive experiences, I begin to trust that my early caregivers are safe and reliable. This pattern of predictable behavior forms the foundation of security and emotional well-being for the infant.

This implicit mentalizing as identified by Luyten and Fonagy (2015) becomes automatic and activated to read experiences and respond without requiring conscious focus thought and intention. For example, if I observe behavior in another person, then I will automatically assign meaning and intention to the action instinctually. I may or may not be accurate in my assessment of that person's intention based upon my early wiring experiences. According to Silberg (2013), affect will activate the memory retrieval system. Silberg (2013) states, "affects are the road signs to the self's navigational system—go closer, go farther, fight, retreat, yield" (p. 21). These implicit mentalizations that are formed early in life will activate behavior throughout life.

Furthermore, when parents are able to mirror affective states to their child, the child develops the ability to recognize their own affective states and learn to regulate independently of their parent. For example, little 2-year-old Sammy is angry that his mother will not allow him to have a toy at the grocery store. When she says no to Sammy, he falls onto the floor and begins to wail loudly in protest of his thwarted desire to have the toy. Mother says to Sammy in a calm and soothing tone, "You are so angry that you cannot have the toy. You really wanted that toy and you are angry that you cannot have it." Mother is mirroring to Sammy that she identified his emotions and the reason for his emotions while she is able to remain calm. Sammy will eventually learn to recognize his own emotions and follow the pattern mirrored to him by his mother of remaining calm when distressed. This becomes an implicit mentalization for Sammy about himself, his emotions, and interactions with his mother.

These implicit mentalizations are not necessarily reliable in all situations, especially since social interactions are complex. Memories that are formed after we have developed the capacity for language are memories that incorporate language—explicit memories. The language areas of our brain help us to use language to make sense of situations using our cognitive thought processes. Therefore, explicit mentalizations as identified by Luyten and Fonagy (2015) can be helpful to correct unreliable perceptions of events and experiences. According to Luyten and Fonagy (2015):

> mentalizing in real time under realistic contextual demands requires the capacity to reflect consciously and deliberately on, and make accurate attributions about, the emotions, thoughts, and intentions of others, and to display an accurate, balanced appreciation of a social situation which relies heavily on the capacity for effortful control and the subtle distinctions language allows us to make.
>
> (p. 369)

Explicit mentalizations utilize higher level mental processing to fully understand the complexities of social situations. If my ability to utilize explicit mentalization is impaired then I will begin to create explicit memories that contribute to my distorted beliefs about myself as well as others. I believe these explicit/controlled and implicit/automatic mentalizations form the underpinnings of core beliefs about ourselves as well as our beliefs about how the world works.

Figure 4.1 shows how my beliefs about myself and the world influence how my mentalizations are encoded in my mind. My core beliefs will influence what emotions are activated, and which will influence my behavior, and this will influence the way in which I engage in the relationship at that moment. If I was raised in an environment in which I was safe and cared about, then my beliefs about myself will be that I am loved, acceptable, and will have seen emotions managed effectively. I will view the world and relationships as safe which will influence my behavior when I am interacting with others. In this scenario, I will view myself as someone who is lovable even when I get irritated and feel sad or disappointed. I will likely view the world and others as safe and I will engage in open, receptive relationship behaviors and be able to navigate conflict effectively. I will be able to regulate my emotions so that I can tolerate distressing emotions within my relationships and find healthy solutions. However, if I was raised in an environment in which my caregiver responded to me in ways that made me feel unloved and unacceptable, and the caregiver did not demonstrate how to regulate my emotions, then I will believe that I am unacceptable which will likely activate feelings of sadness, insecurity, and/or anger. If the emotions activated are intense then I will struggle to regulate my emotions.

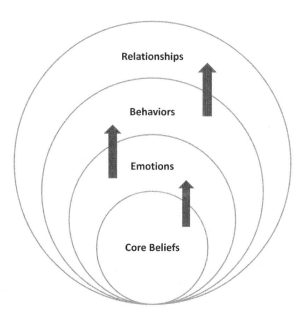

Figure 4.1 The Influence of Core Beliefs

These emotions will likely activate either yelling and blaming behaviors, or maybe withdrawn and isolating behaviors. I will likely engage in relationships that are unhealthy and have difficulty effectively resolving conflict. My core beliefs will influence my emotions which will influence my behaviors and the ways in which I engage in relationships.

These complex neural networks forming the basis of our mentalizations involve experiences over time beginning in early development prior to the acquisition of language coming *online* in our brain and continuing throughout our life. Our life experiences and the meaning we assign to those experiences create our mentalizations and impact the way in which we view ourselves as well as others. Judith Herman (1997) states that traumatic events impact our ability to maintain healthy connection with family, friends, and community because trauma erodes our basic sense of safety in relation to ourselves, others, and our faith in the human experience itself. "Traumatic events have primary effects not only on the psychological structures of the self, but also on the system of attachment and meaning that link individual and community" (Herman, 1997, p. 51).

To illustrate this point, consider the story of Mrs. Jones and her family in which several siblings had been sexually abused by an older sibling. Mrs. Jones brought her sexually traumatized children for treatment. The older sibling who had sexually abused his younger siblings was removed from the home and received specialized treatment for sexual offenders. In the course of gathering information, Mrs. Jones reported she had been sexually abused as a child and found it helpful to go to therapy to resolve her own trauma. However, she reported that her parents were not involved in treatment and she did not address the sexual abuse within the context of how the trauma impacted relationships within her family. She reported a significant family history of addiction and abuse. Mrs. Jones reported that she was divorced from the children's father and her current husband was an active alcoholic. She reported that she did not have close relationships with anyone in her family-of-origin. The cycle of addiction, trauma, and unhealthy relationships continued and was not addressed in her treatment of her sexual abuse as a child.

For children who have experienced developmental trauma that involved parents and/or close family members, attachment and trauma are intricately linked within a child's mentalizations of relationships. Herrmann et al. (2018) state:

attachment relationships characterized by traumatic experiences such as emotional, physical or sexual abuse are assumed to have particularly far-reaching consequences concerning development of emotional self-awareness and affect regulation: in such cases, the caregiver, needed as a psychological safe haven, is a source of danger at the same time, creating a so-called "fright without solution" situation for the child.

(p. 2)

When possible, it's important to address the impact of trauma within the family since trauma negatively impacts relationships, including sibling relationships. Adopted children who experienced early childhood trauma will need their adopted parents to help them work through their early childhood traumas. Repairing the impact of trauma within relationships will help to provide an environment to create safe, secure attachment relationships in the healing process for the child which will also help to repair the child's faulty self-perceptions.

Repairing relationship ruptures that occur within family systems will require parents to recognize their own mentalizations since their beliefs about the world, relationships, and safety will become activated and influence their behavior when parenting. Research by Burkhart, Borelli, Rasmussen, Brody, and Sbarra (2017) examined the link between attachment anxiety and parenting satisfaction. The need for self-reflection is an important part of parenting and helping our children to develop healthy attachments with us. Siegel (2011) underscores the importance for parents to recognize themselves as separate from their children while allowing engagement of the resonance circuits to help them remain attuned to the needs of their child. Chapter 5 focuses on identifying skills needed to effectively repair relationships after ruptures in the relationship occur as they do in all relationships.

References

Balbernie, R. (2007). The move toward intersubjectivity: A clinical and conceptual shift of perspective. *Journal of Child Psychotherapy, 33*(3), 308–324. doi:10.1080/00754170701667213

Ballespi, S., Perez-Domingo, A., Vives, J., Sharp, C., & Barrantes-Vidal, N. (2018). Childhood behavioral inhibition is associated with impaired mentalizing in adolescence. *PLoS ONE, 13*(3), 1–16. doi:10.1371/journal.pone.0195303

Biringen, Z. (1994). Attachment theory and research: Application to clinical practice. *American Journal of Orthopsychiatry, 64*(3), 404–420.

80 Neurobiology of Trauma and Attachment

Bo, S., Sharp, C., Fonagy, P., & Kongerslev, M. (2017). Hypermentalizing, attachment, and epistemic trust in adolescent BPD: Clinical illustrations. *Personality Disorders: Theory, Research and Treatment, 8*(2), 172–182. doi:10.1037/per0000161

Borelli, J. L., Compare, A., Snavely, J. E., & Decio, V. (2015). Reflective functioning moderates the association between perceptions of parental neglect and attachment in adolescence. *Psychoanalytic Psychology, 32*(1), 23–35. doi:10.3389/fpsyg.2019.01062

Brown, B. (2015). *Daring greatly: How the courage to be vulnerable transforms the way we live, love, parent, and lead.* New York, NY: Avery.

Burkhart, M. L., Borelli, J. L., Rasmussen, H. F., Broday, R., & Sbarra, D. A. (2017). Parental mentalizatizing as an indirect link between attachment anxiety and parenting satisfaction. *Journal of Family Psychology, 31*(2), 203–213. doi:10.1037/fam0000270

Cortina, M., & Liotti, G. (2010). Attachment is about safety and protection, intersubjectivity is about sharing and social understanding: The relationships between attachment and intersubjectivity. *Psychoanalytic Psychology, 27*(4), 410–441. doi:10.1037/a0019510

Diamond, N. (2014). On Bowlby's legacy: Further explorations. In M. Marrone (Ed.), *Attachment and interaction: From Bowlby to current clinical theory and practice* (pp. 266–292, 2nd ed.). New York, NY: The Guilford Press.

Falkenstrom, F., Solbakken, O. A., Moller, C., Lech, B., Sandell, R., & Holmquist, R. (2014). Reflective functioning, affect consciousness and mindfulness: Are these different functions? *Psychoanalytic Psychology, 31*(1), 26–40. doi:10.1037/a0034049

Ginot, E. (2007). Intersubjectivity and neuroscience: Understanding enactments and their therapeutic significance within emerging paradigms. *Psychoanalytic Psychology, 24*(2), 317–332. doi:10.1037/073609735.24.2.317

Herman, J. (1997). *Trauma and recovery: The aftermath of violence—from domestic abuse to political terror.* New York, NY: Basic Books.

Herrmann, A. S., Beutel, M. E., Gerzymisch, K., Lane, R. D., Pastroe-Molitor, J., Wiltink, J., Zwerenz, R., Banerjess, M. & Subic-Wrana, C. (2018). The impact of attachment distress on affect-centered mentalization: An experimental study in psychosomatic patients and healthy adults. *PLoS ONE, 13*(4). doi:10.1371/journal.pone.0195430

Kim, S. (2015). The mind in the making: Developmental and neurobiological origins of mentalizing. *Personality Disorders: Theory, Research and Treatment, 6*(4), 356–365. doi:10.1037/per0000102

Liljenfors, R., & Lundh, L.-G. (2015). Mentalization and intersubjectivity towards a theoretical integration. *Psychoanalytic Psychology, 32*(1), 36–60. doi:10.1037/a0037129

Luyten, P., & Fonagy, P. (2015). The neurobiology of mentalizing. *Personality Disorders: Theory, Research and Treatment, 6*(4), 366–379. doi:10.1037/per0000117

Marrone, M. (2014). *Attachment and interaction: From Bowlby to current clinical theory and practice* (2nd ed.). London, UK: Jessica Kingsley Publishing.

Panksepp, J. (2010). Affective neuroscience of the emotional BrainMind: Evolutionary perspectives and implications for understanding depression. *Dialogues in Clinical Neuroscience, 12*(4), 533–545.

Powell, B., Cooper, G., Hoffman, K., & Marvin, B. (2014). *The circle of security intervention: Enhancing attachment in early parent-child relationships.* New York, NY: The Guilford Press.

Siegel, D. J. (2011). *Mindsight: The new science of personal transformation.* New York, NY: Bantam Books.

Silberg, J. L. (2013). *The child survivor: Healing developmental trauma and dissociation.* New York, NY: Routledge.

Repairing Ruptures in the Attachment Relationship 5

This chapter reviews behaviors and processes that are necessary for the repair of attachment injuries and trauma within families. It's important for therapists to have a framework for helping parents learn new patterns of relationship interactions with their traumatized child. Repairing relationship *ruptures* is critical. Even in the most healthy relationships, all of us get frustrated with those closest to us—our family members. You cannot be part of a family and not know each other's "warts," so to speak. We all have our strengths and warts and those are most evident to people who are around us the most. Effectively repairing and maintaining healthy family relationships is essential to helping traumatized children heal in all areas of their lives.

The ability to form healthy attachments between parents and their children is a fluid process, both constant yet ever-changing over time. The day-to-day interactions between parents and children are impacted by numerous factors, such as emotional states, sleep habits, stressors, illnesses, hunger, etc. Parents who are well-rested, experiencing low stress, and in good physical shape will be more likely to respond positively to their child, even if their child is not yet emotionally regulated or able to receive parental support at the moment. Parents who are ill, stressed, and/or tired will have a decreased capacity for patience, thinking clearly, or being emotionally responsive. These are simply the realities of life. All families experience varying amounts of stressors over time and sometimes families go through difficult periods in their lives. Children and parents who are able to experience one another in predominantly positive ways will be better able to navigate the ups and downs of life while maintaining a healthy, supportive relationship. The building blocks, so to speak, of attachment relationships are built upon the day-to-day experiencers between parents and their children. Thankfully, it is not necessary to be a perfect parent because that's an unrealistic expectation. This is an important point for parents to keep in mind when raising their children so they don't become entrenched in guilt and shame over not being perfect because guilt and shame can become debilitating.

Good Enough

As a parent myself as well as a mental health professional, I tend to think about all the mistakes I have made with my own children. One of my many theories about parenting is that when you give birth (actual birth—or "birth" through adoption) to a child, you give birth to guilt. Parents worry about being a "good" parent. This seems to be universal to all parents. Whenever I start to feel guilty about times when I have "blown it" with my own children, I have to remind myself of this truth: I can either practice self-compassion during those times when I blow it, regain my balance and respond in ways that will help my child to navigate life successfully, or I can give in to guilt which will reduce my effectiveness to parent, which will not help my child to be successful in life. That usually helps me get back in balance and focus on how to be a more effective parent. Parents need to be *good enough* more often than not so that they can maintain a healthy attachment with their child (Powell, Cooper, Hoffman, & Marvin, 2014). The ability of parents to repair their relationship with their child is also an important part of the attachment relationship process.

Parenting involves working to provide healthy boundaries and to ensure that our children are safe from harm—to the extent that we are able to do this. From a realistic standpoint, the goal is not to remove all negative experiences from the lives of our children because that's an unrealistic expectation. Parents must realize that while they need to shelter their child, they also need to allow their child to grow and learn from life experiences in order to be resilient. Sometimes, despite our best efforts to protect our children, traumatic experiences happen. When this occurs, the parent's goal is to help their child overcome the negative impact of the traumatic event and thrive. Life is stressful so parents need to help their children learn to tolerate their emotional distress while using their parent's support in navigating through their difficulties. When parents are able to effectively support their children during times of emotional distress, this helps the children develop resilience. Resiliency will allow them to navigate the "ups and downs" of life in order to gain internal strength and mental toughness while maintaining their integrity and a healthy moral compass.

As therapists, our job is to provide support and care for parents so that they, in turn, can do this for their child. When therapists mirror support and guidance for parents it helps them engage in the change process. Parenting is a difficult, often overwhelming, task. Many enter therapy feeling like failures, which is accompanied by a tremendous amount of guilt and shame, especially if their own childhood histories include trauma and/or neglect. So therapists need to provide a therapeutic environment where parents feel supported in order to do the difficult work of repair with their children, help facilitate their healing, and help them engage in relationship repair with each other. This mirroring process will help parents to develop the necessary skills for supporting their traumatized child and strengthen the relationships within the family.

All families experience relationship disruptions through conflict, differences of opinions, and just having a "bad day." Consider a father who is experiencing stress at work because he's afraid of getting laid off due to company budget cuts. His main focus is on financially supporting his family, so he's feeling impatient and irritable, and he's having trouble sleeping. Because of his negative mood, he may respond to his child's demanding behavior with irritability, which might not have been the case had he been less stressed. This influences the emotional environment in the home, and relationships are impacted. To help stabilize the family, parents and children will need to adjust within the home. If parents are able to tolerate their own stress levels while focusing on helping to ensure consistency in the home, then they will interact in effective ways with their children and the family will most likely navigate through this difficult period effectively with healthy attachments intact. The important thing for parents to remember is that they need to find ways to maintain positive connection in their relationships within the family despite the challenges they face. The overwhelmed father will need to go back to talk with his child when he is calm and repair their relationship that may have been shaken by the father's irritability. Perhaps he will apologize and reassure his child that he is loved and they are able to talk about the child's behavior and address the misbehavior in more effective ways.

It's been my experience that when children feel loved and valued by their parents, they tend to be willing to engage in the repair process. Traumatized children who have unstable attachment patterns with their parents and are unable to use their parents for support will likely struggle to trust until their relationship is repaired and visa-versa. Traumatized children who have acted in unsafe and aggressive ways over an extended period of time will struggle to gain the trust of their parents. This can be a difficult process to work through without the assistance of a therapist. Trust lost is difficult to regain. This is also true with sibling relationships. If a child's sibling has regularly acted in an aggressive and hurtful manner, then the child will not experience the sibling as a safe person and will most likely act in ways to protect himself, even retaliate. Therapists will need to help family members work through these complex family relationship patterns in order to repair their relationships.

In families in which children have experienced trauma, typical developmental parent–child interactions may be more difficult to establish and maintain because traumatic memories will be activated which will influence the child's behavior. Traumatized children will struggle with tolerating their emotional distress and will require parents to learn to understand what is underneath the child's dysregulated emotions and behavior. Traumatized children can respond in ways that don't fit the current situation or may be easily emotionally triggered by a parent's bad day. A child who has experienced trauma will learn to read the cues of parents to better know how to respond and maintain safety, and can misperceive their parents' intentions. Earlier we discussed the neural processes involved from infancy that are focused on reading their parents to ensure their survival. Those neural pathways become more hard-wired the longer those neural connections are maintained.

If a child was raised for the first two years in a home in which the parent was loud, angry, and aggressive toward others, and/or toward the child, that most likely resulted in the child feeling unsafe. After that, the child will read the angry face of the parent as dangerous and will adjust his behavior to maintain safety. Think about all the brain development that occurs in the first two years of life. These neural connections have been well-used even by the age of 2 years old. This implicit memory of caregivers and anger, now linked, will be activated in future interactions with the parents and negatively impact the child's ability to effectively regulate his emotions and behaviors. For example, if 2-year-old Hailey was raised in a home in which her mother was frequently irritable, displayed an angry face and voice tone with Hailey, in an inconsistent manner, then Hailey will quickly learn to recognize that facial expression and that voice tone to mean she will be treated in a harsh, unpleasant manner by a caregiver. This activates feelings of anxiety in Hailey because she is not experiencing safety within the relationship with her mother, especially if the mother's behavior is inconsistent and unpredictable.

Now it's hard for Hailey to know if she can effectively use her mother's support to help her when she is distressed and needs help.

In Chapter 2 we discussed mirror neurons and their role in perceiving *intention* in the behavior of another person. The key to recognizing intention is the goal-directed sequence of behaviors that are predictable. In this case, Hailey recognizes the facial expressions and voice tone of her mother which is associated with negative experiences that activate emotional distress. Hailey's mother's behavior is inconsistent and unpredictable—sometimes the mother is able to regulate her behavior and sometimes she's not. Hailey will have difficulty recognizing the intent of her mother's behavior, making it difficult for Hailey to use her mother as a secure attachment figure, someone she can trust in this caregiver relationship. Now, a year later, little Hailey is living with adoptive parents who are working hard to help Hailey feel safe. However, they are confused by Hailey's excessive response to being corrected by them. What Hailey's adoptive parents may not understand is that Hailey is interpreting their facial expressions and voice tone as harsh because she's basing it on her past caregiver experiences. For Hailey, those caregiver behaviors made her feel unsafe and fearful that perhaps her new parents do not like her. Hailey is not able to accurately perceive the intention of her new adoptive parent's behavior because of her early experiences of a caregiver who was unpredictable and inconsistent. Of course, she is not able to verbally communicate this to her parents because she is only 3 years old.

Hailey's parents will need to recognize her behavior cues and help her learn that when they are irritated, Hailey is still safe and loved. It will probably take some time for Hailey to learn how to be in a relationship with her parents, and for her parents to learn how to read Hailey's cues more effectively. Again, this doesn't mean that parents of traumatized children are expected to be perfect all the time; that's impossible. It does mean that parents of traumatized children will need to be aware of their own emotions, body language, and voice tone, and be aware of the responses of their child in order to help the child learn to trust them and use them for support to regulate their emotions and behaviors. Therapists working with parents of traumatized children will need to provide them with support and reassurance since this process can be emotionally exhausting for them. It takes a lot of patience. Therapists will also need to help parents use *self-care* to make sure they are refilling their "emotional tank" back up.

This supportive stance by parents provides the opportunity for traumatized children to begin using their parents for support as they learn to effectively regulate their emotions and behaviors. According to Powell et al. (2014), for a healthy attachment connection to be successful, parents need to be *bigger, stronger, wiser, and kind*. I love this mantra because it gets right to the heart of the framework needed to parent children effectively. Essentially, this means parents can reconnect with their child after a rupture in the relationship and help their child learn to experience the benefits of this process. Parents who are able to remain calm and think through the difficulty will be able to respond in more effective ways to their child. It means parents are able to regulate their emotions well enough to provide structure and security for their child. This structure and security creates a sense of safety and well-being allowing their child to explore and navigate the world around them, using their parents for support when needed, and helping them recover effectively when life is distressing. This is especially true during the teenage years when teens are out exploring the world and learning to become independent adults. Remember my Tetherball analogy in Chapter 3? Parents are the pole, the relationship is the rope, and the child is the ball. At some point, teens will encounter difficulties and will need parents to provide support to help them figure out how to effectively navigate difficult situations. The strength of the pole and the quality of the rope are what influence a teenager's ability to effectively use his parents to help him navigate those difficult situations.

A rupture is any conflict or negative interaction that decreases the positive feelings between the parent and child. Ruptures in relationships are typical occurrences; therefore, the repair process is an integral part of healthy attachment. For example, suppose a child has become angry when a parent says "no" to buying a new toy when shopping at a department store. The child will experience angry feelings toward his parents at that moment and may lash out by throwing something or shouting. The parent will likely remove the child from the store and go home. The child may spend some time in his room to help him calm down, if he has not already calmed down during the car ride home. The repair work will facilitate addressing the impact within the relationship and the importance of tolerating limits imposed by the parent while positively reconnecting on an emotional level. It's important to understand that children need to experience parental limits and structure. Setting those limits will create emotional distress in the child in the moment but will result in helping children learn to tolerate their emotional distress, inhibit non-prosocial behavior, and develop emotion regulation. It's the glue to help parents maintain a secure attachment with their children. Interactions between parent and child will fluctuate from day to day, and over time these interactions need to involve consistency regarding appropriate expectations and emotional connection. For traumatized children, parents need to be aware of their own emotions and triggers in order to successfully navigate through relationship disruptions, and help their child to engage in the relationship repair process with them. Understanding the essential components of attachment relationships in the parent–child relationship will be important to help traumatized children establish a sense of safety within their relationship with their parents.

Relationship Skills Needed for Attachment Repair

Relationship disruption is a normal part of life and a parent's capacity to use skills to effectively repair their relationship with their children is crucial for the healing process and health attachment. This section discusses several types of parenting abilities needed for effective relationship repair and healthy social emotional development in children. Therapists need to assess parents' ability to use attachment skills and identify their strengths and weaknesses in these areas. Therapists also need to maintain an ongoing mindset of assessment to evaluate treatment progress and treatment targets for the change process. They need to observe relationship patterns within the context of the sessions and obtain feedback from parents about the effectiveness of the skills when implemented at home, which is where the real change occurs. Our goal is to help parents feel confident and effective to implement the changes in *real time* at home. That's where the "rubber meets the road" so to speak. Are parents able to implement the changes and effectively navigate challenges as they occur at home when the therapist is not present? Our goal as therapists is to ask ourselves this question as we are working to help families successfully complete treatment. We need to know what it "looks like" when families are ready to discharge successfully.

Empathic Attunement

Attachment theorists have identified the importance of *maternal warmth* and *maternal sensitivity*. Maternal warmth is not the same as maternal sensitivity. According to Van Rosmalen, van der Horst, and van der Veer (2016), Ainsworth described maternal sensitivity as the mother's "appropriate response to the baby's initiative. In Ainsworth's view, attachment was indeed being formed by the (continuous) presence of the attachment figure, but the security of this attachment was being formed by the sensitivity of the attachment figure" (p. 17). It's not just about parents' ability to be kind and caring. It's about their ability to be tuned in to their child's personality wiring and emotional needs. This is *empathic attunement*.

First and foremost, parents need to help their child feel safe. Stephen Porges (2011) states that the neural pathways for fear and safety cannot be activated at the same time. Therefore, the ability to help a child feel safe will increase his ability to engage in relationship building and adapt to the world around him. Feeling safe is a critical need in order for a child to want to use support from his parents. Children feel safe with their parents when they know the parents understand them. A parent's ability to provide empathic attunement to their child will rely heavily on resonance circuits. Empathic attunement is the ability for parents to recognize the emotions of their child and see their child as a separate self and not a reflection of the parent. As discussed in the previous sections, resonance circuits aid in a parent's ability to be empathically tuned in to their children. Parents need to have the ability to be self-aware in order to recognize their own emotions separately from their child's emotions so they can respond effectively to the needs of their children.

This ability to be empathically attuned to our children while recognizing our separateness as parents provides the ability to understand and recognize our child's needs and respond in ways that will address the situation effectively. Parents need to be able to recognize what a child is trying to communicate through their behaviors, even when the behaviors are anger and irritability. For example, think about that child who had a tantrum in the middle of the store because his mother would not buy him a desired toy. Empathic attunement would allow the mother to recognize that a 3-year-old child seeks gratification in the moment and when that gratification is thwarted, he will likely show his displeasure by crying and yelling in the store. An empathically attuned mother will recognize that her child did not sleep well the night before because he has been recovering from a cold which contributed to his increased irritability, so she understands that his behavior is due to his cold and lack of sleep and not due to her being a bad parent or her child being a "spoiled child."

As discussed in Chapter 4, the intersubjectivity between parent and child will greatly influence their attachment patterns. The nuances within the parent–child relationship help or hinder a child's ability to use his parents to establish a sense of safety and security. Children need their parents to be able to recognize and understand their behavior in order to help them manage life's ups and downs. Children communicate their emotional distress to parents through their behavior. While their cognitive functioning is developing during childhood, children lack the ability to effectively recognize and understand their emotions and what triggers their emotional response via behaviors. Therefore, it is important for parents to understand their children's personality and to *see* their children. Empathic attunement requires parents to be fully present in the moment from a mindfulness standpoint. This *mindfulness presence* engages the resonance circuits to allow parents to recognize and understand their child's behavior in order to respond more effectively. For example, in his book, *Peace is Every Step*, Thich Nhat Hanh (1992) provides the following example of a parent's ability to be mindfully present with a child:

> if we are not fully ourselves, truly present in the moment, we miss everything. When a child presents himself to you with his smile, if you are not really there—thinking about the future or the past, or preoccupied with other problems—then the child is not really there for you. The technique of being alive is to go back to yourself in order for the child to appear like a marvelous reality. Then you see him smile and you can embrace him in your arms.
>
> (p. 43)

Brown (2015) has researched the impact of shame on compassion and empathy and identified the importance of shame resilience within healthy relationships. Compassion and empathy are key factors for healthy attachment. In her book, *Daring Greatly*, Brown (2015) discussed the ways in which shame negatively impacts our ability to establish healthy connection with our children to provide a secure emotional base within our family systems. Recognizing our own emotional defensiveness and factors contributing to our emotional triggers is essential for establishing empathic connections with our children because these emotional triggers can contribute to disconnection and interfere with healthy emotional repair work needed to maintain the connection between parent and child. Therefore, it's essential for therapists to provide a safe place for parents to examine their own emotional triggers so they can more effectively read their child's cues and respond accordingly.

Reading Cues Effectively and *Seeing* the Child

Parental warmth and the ability to respond to the *cues* given by the child are essential to building healthy attachment patterns with children.

Parents need to look for the *root* of the behavior to better understand it and respond effectively. This does not mean that parents do not maintain appropriate boundaries and set realistic limits or that parents do not set limits because the child will be distressed. It means that parents will focus on the *why* of the behavior and respond to the *why* (emotional need) rather than the *what* (behavior). Parents are better able to read the cues of their child when they are self-aware and recognize their own emotions and beliefs, as stated above, that are separate from their child's behavior and emotions.

Mentalizing plays an important role in parenting and in understanding children's behavior. Parents' ability to understand that there is an underlying reason that has resulted in the child's behavior will increase their effectiveness in addressing the issue with their child. This is especially true with traumatized children who can become emotionally overwhelmed and dysregulated when their unresolved trauma is triggered, resulting in an unhealthy behavioral response. Parents with strong mentalizing abilities will be able to navigate through the process with their child. However, parents with their own trauma and attachment difficulties can struggle with accurately recognizing the underlying need in their child's behavior. Parents with low mentalizing abilities will likely misinterpret their child's behavior as negative or even hostile. For example, a parent with low mentalizing abilities may view their child's crying as negative attention seeking and ignore the behavior rather than assess what is the underlying cause of the crying behavior. Researchers have examined the relationship between parental attachment style and attachment security in their children. Parents with low mentalizing abilities tend to have higher attachment insecurity themselves which tends to decrease their ability to effectively read the behavior cues of their child (Borelli et al., 2019; Burkhart, Borelli, Rasmussen, Brody, & Sbarra, 2017; Fonagy, Steele, Steele, Moran, & Higgitt, 1991). Burkhart et al. (2017) state that "it is possible that anxious parents' hypervigilance toward attachment threats, and thereby their hyperactivation of negative emotion, prevents them from making accurate attributions about their child's thoughts and feelings" (p. 205).

For example, your 5-year-old having a tantrum may just be upset because he is tired or hungry, not "trying to make me mad and ruin my day because he just wants to be selfish." It will be more effective to recognize that the root of the child's behavior is hunger or fatigue and respond by feeding him or having him take a nap instead of responding to the behavior by getting angry at the child. In the case of traumatized children with attachment difficulties, it's important to remember that traumatized children will let parents know their trauma has been triggered by their behavior, and that trauma triggered behavior will not likely match the *triggering event* of the behavior. For example, a traumatized child's response to being told that he cannot have his favorite treat before dinner because it will "ruin his appetite" may then sneak into the kitchen to obtain the coveted snack and then lie to the parent. When disciplined for the "sneaky" behavior and lying, the parent may give a consequence of no snacks for the next two days only to experience the child erupting into screaming and calling the parent unkind names.

Trauma memories are activated predominantly via implicit memories, which means their brain's alarm system will be activated and their ability to communicate will be impaired until they feel safe again. These implicit memories are stored in the body, without language, and can be triggered when sensory information is received which activates the memories and results in behavior that does not fit the situation. If a child has been raised for the first five years of his life without basic needs being met, then he may feel compelled to sneak food and lie about it even though foster or adoptive parents have plenty of food in the home and the child is now well cared for by his caregivers. His brain has initially been wired to make sure he has food, and food then becomes a trauma trigger for him because his early experiences have influenced his present life. For this child, he may see the removal of food as a threat to his safety and well-being which will negatively impact his ability to trust his current caregivers if food becomes a source of conflict. Parents will need to understand their child's emotions, personality, and behaviors to learn how to effectively read their child's cues which will require strong mentalizing skills.

Therefore, it will be critical for therapists to assess the parent's ability to accurately read the behavioral cues of their traumatized child by gathering a thorough history of the parent's childhood attachments to include trauma experiences. Therapists need to work with parents to recognize the parent's own emotional triggers and increase their mentalization capacities to better understand their child's behavior. The root of empathy and understanding are the mirror neurons. The difficulty here for parents of traumatized children is that when their child's traumatic memories have been triggered, then their child's behavior will not seem to follow predictable, intentional behavior until the parents have learned to recognize that the intention behind their child's behavior is to protect against perceived threat. The task for parents then becomes learning to recognize the intention of the behavior and responding to the intention of the behavior to help the traumatized child learn to recognize perceived versus actual threat so that they can effectively regulate their emotions. Parents will need to first make sure that they are able to recognize their own internal response to their child's emotionally dysregulated behavior and remember that their child is separate from them during their shared experience. The resonance circuits within the parent will become activated which will result in the parent experiencing an internal response to their child's emotion dysregulation. According to Siegel (2011), "when we sense our own internal state, the fundamental pathway for resonating with others is open as well" (p. 62). Parents with a higher capacity for mentalization will be more successful in reading the cues of their child, and have more ability to attend to their child's needs effectively. The therapist's goal here will be to help parents increase awareness of their internal responses when their child becomes emotionally dysregulated and learn to regulate themselves to effectively mirror to their child how to regulate their own emotions.

Empathic Responding and Recognizing Parent Triggers

Parents need to have the ability to regulate their own emotions if they are to be successful in helping their children regulate their emotions in order to effectively engage in healthy relationships with others. Empathic responding involves the parent's ability to regulate their own emotions, accurately understand their child's behavior, and respond to misbehavior with empathy rather than with irritability and anger. As stated earlier, this does not mean that parents do not set limits. Limit setting is an important part of parenting as will be discussed further in the next section. However, *how* parents set limits is the key to effectively helping traumatized children learn to regulate their emotions and engage in healthy relationship behaviors. Empathic responding can help parents learn to help their traumatized child regulate their emotions by helping their child to feel understood and supported.

When children are emotionally dysregulated and engaging in disruptive behavior, it is important for parents to learn to emotionally "hold" the behavior in the moment because in that moment of emotion dysregulation, their child's brain has been hijacked by the limbic system to help them respond to threat. Parents will need to help their traumatized child learn to use their support in order to feel safe, which will in turn help their child's brain turn off the threat response system. When a traumatized child has been emotionally triggered and experiences an event as unsafe, as discussed earlier, the limbic system in the brain will activate the threat response system in order to respond to the threat that has been perceived. However, if there is no actual danger then the child's behavior will be excessive and will further confuse the situation. Parents need to recognize that their child's trauma system has been activated and work toward helping their child's threat system to deactivate before trying to engage their child in a discussion about their behavior. *Empathic responding* will help the child to feel understood and able to receive support from his parent, which will establish a sense of safety to help the child reduce his threat response.

Jane, a 14-year-old female, had been sexually assaulted in her home by an older peer in her basement. It was difficult for her to go into the basement because her trauma memories were activated which then triggered her threat system. She would become hostile and defiant toward her parents when they asked her to go to the basement to clean or retrieve something for them, which they in turn interpreted as disrespectful. By using empathic responding, her parents could respond in a much different manner and help her to use their support rather than to emotionally push her parents away. Empathic responding would look something like this:

Father: Jane, it's your turn to clean the basement. I noticed that you have not cleaned it yet.

Jane: Yeah, I'm not cleaning it! You always make me clean the basement.

Father: It sounds like you're really upset about cleaning the basement. What's going on?

Jane: Nothing! I hate cleaning the basement and I'm not going to clean it because you never make Sam clean the basement.

Father: Sounds like cleaning the basement is really frustrating for you. I'm just wondering what's going on because I noticed that you have not gone down to the basement in a few weeks now. That seems unusual because you used to go down there a lot. I noticed over the last couple of months that when it's your turn to clean the basement that you get really upset. I love you and want to make sure that you are okay.

Jane: Well, I hate cleaning the basement now and why do you keep nagging me about it!

Father: Jane, I'm sorry it feels like I'm nagging you. I'm actually worried about you because I've noticed a big change in you about the basement since you told us about what happened down there. I'm wondering if the basement reminds you about what happened and upsets you. I'm asking because I love you and really want to help you.

Jane: Yes! So why are you asking me to go down there! You know what happened and why are you yelling at me to go down there?!

Father: I can definitely see how it would be hard to go down there and be reminded of something terrible that happened. That would definitely be really scary and hard to do. I want to help you feel safe in your own home. I'm wondering if it would help if I go down there with you and we just start with small steps to help you feel safe. We can go down together and you can let me know how you are doing. It will be important for you to not let what happened to you keep you from doing things and I know that will be really hard. Let's just go down together and we can leave when you need to leave. You are strong and I am here to help you.

Jane: Okay, but I'm not staying down there long and I'm not going to clean anything down there!

Father: I'm so proud of you for doing this hard thing and we don't have to stay down there any longer than you are able to stay. Sam can help to clean the basement until you are ready to help with the cleaning. In the meantime, you and I can work on helping you to feel safe and we can figure that out together. You can go as slow as you need it to go.

Jane: Fine. Let's go and get this over with.

In this scenario, Jane's father did not take Jane's negative attitude as disrespectful because he had noticed that Jane seemed to be avoiding the basement and he knew that his daughter had experienced a traumatic event there. He was able to read her behavior cues as emotional distress rather than disrespect which also helped him not to get emotionally reactive to her negative behavior. He was able to regulate his own emotions and hold her emotions while they explored the reason for her avoidance of her chore of cleaning the basement. Since he was able to regulate his own behaviors, Jane was eventually able to decrease her defensiveness and use his support to begin finding a way to overcome her avoidance of the basement. In this mirroring process, Jane's father was helping Jane to regulate her emotions and stay in the conversation with him. If Jane's father had gotten angry and irritated with Jane for disrespect then she would not be able to trust him to tolerate her strong emotions of fear and help her to use him as a safety support. Jane's emotions would likely escalate which would have resulted in both of them becoming angry at one another. Jane would have lost the opportunity for her father to help her learn to effectively regulate her emotions as she worked through the difficult task of overcoming her traumatic experience in the basement and learning to become resilient.

It's important for parents to understand that empathic responding does not mean that they are reinforcing disrespectful behavior in their child or letting their child think that their behavior is acceptable. This is often a concern for parents when learning about empathic responding. Empathic responding focuses on the underlying reason for the misbehavior and then helping their child to make healthy behavior choices and help parents emotionally connect with their child before addressing the behavior. This emotional connection with parents will help children to feel emotionally safe with them. When children feel understood and accepted, despite their behavior, then they are more likely to use the support of their parents when they are struggling.

Empathic responding can be exhausting at times and takes a lot of patience. Parents and therapists need to practice their own self-care, as mentioned earlier in this chapter. Therapists need to use empathic responding to help parents feel safe in the therapeutic relationship and accept caring feedback. If parents have unresolved trauma and insecure attachment patterns then therapists will need to provide that same empathic responding to parents to help them feel supported while they work to identify when they are emotionally triggered and learn to get their own emotions regulated before they respond to their child. Adopted or foster parents will need to recognize that their traumatized child will need them to respond in ways that help them feel safe and that may take time to develop. Traumatized children will need to feel safe before they can learn to use support from them.

Structuring

Children thrive when there is consistency and structure in their lives. Children vary in their requirements for structure and they all need some measure of structure. Some children require high levels of structure and predictability in order to feel comfortable and calm throughout the day. Some children need less structure and predictability. A parent's ability to recognize and provide the level of structure that their child responds to best will help to create a sense of safety. Often, children within the same family will require varying amounts of structure, and the type of structure required will change with their child's developmental needs. In our household, we have two sons. When we went on family vacations, my husband and our youngest son would develop a schedule for the week based on our family discussion of what we wanted to accomplish during our vacation. My husband and our youngest son would review and adjust the schedule each evening or the following morning. This seemed to provide a sense of stability for our youngest son and he thoroughly enjoyed this planning process with his father. Our oldest son is much more laid back and basically followed what the schedule stated for the day. Once he gave his input into the activities for the week, he did not seem to be as interested in the structuring process for our week. He was just happy to hang out as long as he had access to video games or television when we were not enjoying our planned activities. As children get older, the type of structure they need changes. When parents are consistent with their behavior, then children learn to trust their parents and others. Children learn that their parents will take care of their basic needs, such as providing food, clothing, and shelter. Additionally, when parents consistently and appropriately respond to a child's emotional needs, the child learns that he can emotionally trust others. Routine helps children trust in predictability and predictability contributes to a foundation for trust and reduces anxiety.

In the interaction between Jane and her father about cleaning the basement, Jane's father provided structure in the relationship by identifying the problem and helping to find creative solutions to ensure the basement is cleaned. He helped Jane to connect her reluctance to go into the basement and then offered to help her in the moment to challenge herself with his empathic support. He also offered to talk with Sam (her brother) to help out with the basement chores until Jane could overcome that traumatic memory. In this scenario, Jane can probably take over one of Sam's chores so that Sam does not become resentful of Jane, which would cause a rupture in Sam and Jane's relationship. Here, Jane's father was demonstrating his ability to provide structure by being bigger, stronger, wiser, and kind. I sometimes like to think of parenting in terms of leadership. Leaders need to find effective ways to get people to work together to accomplish a common task. Wise leaders will know how to get their team to accomplish a task using a respectful approach and providing the structure needed to accomplish the task.

Structuring also includes establishing and maintaining boundaries through limit setting, which is essentially where we challenge our children to learn to develop healthy boundaries and behaviors. I like to think of boundaries as a protection for relationships. Think about it. If I don't like that my child is constantly leaving the door open and letting our dogs out of the house, then I need to have a conversation with my child to discuss my need for him to close the door after him when he leaves the house so the dogs won't escape and get hurt. If I don't have this discussion with him, and it's a big concern for me, then I will likely let this fester and build up resentment, which will cause a rupture in our relationship.

This is where the discussion of discipline generally comes in. It is important to hold age-appropriate and realistic boundaries with children so that they learn to inhibit behavior that is not effective within their relationships and experience success in life. This is part of life. If I speed and a police officer pulls me over for speeding, then I'll likely get a traffic ticket and be expected to pay the fine or risk going to jail. Structure through appropriate implementation of laws and regulations provide the foundation for safety and security in society. There is a difference between punishment and discipline. Parents need to be able to recognize that the goal of discipline and holding boundaries is actually teaching a child to develop healthy life and relationship skills. Punishment is generally more focused on inflicting painful consequences in an attempt to prevent further violations. Our jails are an example of punishment on a more macro scale. Punishment does not help to protect the relationship and can actually harm the relationship. How many times do we see videos of police officers attempting to build positive relationships with people in the community? Police officers who want to be a positive influence in their community know that when people in the community know, like, and trust them, then the community is safer and relationships with police are based on trust. Punishment is based on the threat of harm. Discipline is generally based on a parent's values and a desire to instill those values in their children. It is important for parents to identify their family values and age appropriate expectations because they will teach values to their children through their communication and boundaries they hold with their children.

Flexibility

While children need structure, they also need parents to be flexible with them so they can adjust to the day-to-day experiences of life. I like to think of the goal as creating a sense of balance and teaching this to our children. We need both structure and flexibility to create a sense of balance. Flexibility allows children to feel loved and valued by their parents. Rigid and rules focused relationships with parents can actually interfere with the goal of teaching children because the focus of the parent's interactions with her child is not on the relationship, but on compliance and behavior. Rigid parenting tends to be more punishment oriented than discipline oriented. Flexibility and emotional attunement go hand-in-hand because parents need to be able to recognize their child's cues and adjust their response to behavior based on the needs of the child and the family. Parents who are able to be attuned to their child's needs in the moment, and aware of their own internal working attachment models operating in the moment, will be able to use wisdom to know when to maintain the structure and when to be flexible. Of course, parents cannot be expected to be perfect all of the time and the ability to be flexible when flexibility is needed will help to maintain a strong attachment with their children.

Traumatized children need parents to be flexible because their traumatic memories may become activated and their behavior may seem inconsistent or defiant. These trauma triggers will activate their threat systems and parents will need to help their child feel safe in that moment first before even being able to address the behavior. After their child feels safe, then parents can explore what happened in that moment and find more effective ways for their child to handle difficult situations. In this way, parents can be flexible in the moment to help their child feel safe and address the crisis. Then, once their child is calm and receptive, then they can explore what happened, discuss the outcome of the behavior (for example, yelling and hitting a sibling and the impact of that behavior on the sibling relationship), and then provide structure by identifying how the situation can be handled differently in the future.

Playfulness

Play is natural to all children regardless of culture. All children play. The key to authentic play is the ability to be mindfully present in the moment. Have you ever watched children fully immersed in their play? Their attention, thoughts, emotions, and behaviors are engaged in that moment. They are not thinking about what happened the day before or what will happen tomorrow. To be playing, children are fully present at that moment—emotionally, socially, cognitively, and physically. Children learn about the world around them by playing. It is how they explore the world. According to Porges (2011), the PLAY system can only be engaged when children feel safe. If a child experiences fear then they are unable to engage in play because the fear and safety neural systems cannot both be activated at the same time. This is true for parents as well. Parents cannot fully embrace authentic playfulness unless they are feeling safe to play with their child.

Playfulness helps to engage children in the relationship. If you want to have a relationship with adults, you first need to talk to them because most grown-ups have long ago lost the ability to enjoy the moment in playfulness, so you have to meet them where they are—by talking to them to establish safety. Children, on the other hand, play in order to establish relationships. This is evident to anyone who watches children on a playground. Children approach one another through play and the enjoyment of the play experience creates the relationship bond. Adults who are serious all the time with their children lose valuable opportunities for relationship building and trust building. It is important for parents to learn to play with their children and to be playful with them. If you think about relationships using the analogy of a bank account, parents can make emotional "deposits" in their relationship with their children through playful experiences. There will be times that parents need to make relationship "withdrawals," such as enforcing boundaries and setting limits, which means parents need to have enough relationship deposits to maintain the attachment bond with their child.

In addition to building relationships with children through playfulness, it can also help to reduce defensiveness in children. Children cannot be guarded (FEAR circuits) and yet receptive to exploring new ways of doing things if they aren't able to have positive intersubjectivity experiences via playful exchange with their parents. The treatment model proposed in this book integrates the therapeutic powers of play, identified by Schaefer (1993) that were briefly discussed earlier in the book, to help facilitate the change process for traumatized children and their parents. In my experience, it's one of the most effective ways to help the whole family be engaged during therapy sessions. Play and expressive arts can help reduce defensiveness in the sessions, which helps therapists to gauge the level of safety within the session experienced by each family member. Play-based interventions can be developmentally appropriate to teach children new skills and how to engage in healthy relationship behaviors, often much more effectively than strictly talk-based therapy. Adding playfulness into the session, and teaching parents to be playful, will provide traumatized children an avenue to communicate, learn, and experience relationships in a new, safer way.

References

Borelli, J. L., Cohen, C., Pettit, C., Normandin, L., Target, M., Fonagy, P., & Ensink, K. (2019). Maternal and child sexual abuse history: An intergenerational exploration of children's adjustment and maternal trauma-reflective functioning. *Frontiers in Psychology, 10*. doi:10.3389/fpsyg.2019.01062

Brown, B. (2015). *Daring greatly: How the courage to be vulnerable transforms the way we live, love, parent, and lead.* New York, NY: Avery.

Burkhart, M. L., Borelli, J. L., Rasmussen, H. F., Broday, R., & Sbarra, D. A. (2017). Parental mentalizatizing as an indirect link between attachment anxiety and parenting satisfaction. *Journal of Family Psychology, 31*(2), 203–213. doi:10.1037/fam0000270

Fonagy, P., Steele, M., Steele, H., Moran, G. S., & Higgitt, A. C. (1991). The capacity for understanding mental states: The reflective self in parent and child and its significance for security of attachment. *Infant Mental Health Journal, 12*(3), 201–218.

Hanh, T. N. (1992). *Peace is every step: The path of mindfulness in everyday life.* New York, NY: Bantam Books.

Porges, S. W. (2011). *The polyvagal theory: Neurophysiological foundations of emotions, attachment, communication, self-regulation.* New York, NY: W.W Norton & Company.

Powell, B., Cooper, G., Hoffman, K., & Marvin, B. (2014). *The circle of security intervention: Enhancing attachment in early parent-child relationships.* New York, NY: The Guilford Press.

Schaefer, C. (Ed.). (1993). *The therapeutic power of play.* Northvale, NJ: Jason Aronson, Inc.

Siegel, D. J. (2011). *Mindsight: The new science of personal transformation.* New York, NY: Bantam Books.

Van Rosmalen, L., van der Horst, F. C. P., & van der Veer, R. (2016). From secure dependency to attachment: Mary Ainsworth's integration of Blatz's security theory into Bowlby's attachment theory. *History of Psychology, 19*(1), 22–39. doi:10.1037/hop0000015

Part II

Attachment-based Family Play Therapy

The Model

Framework of Attachment-based Family Play Therapy

6

This chapter provides an overview of the unique neurobiologically informed, attachment-based treatment model proposed in this book. While traumatized young people need individual psychotherapy in order to have a safe and protected emotional space to address the impact of their traumatic experience, they also need to heal within a relational context. This model is not intended to replace individual therapy for the traumatized child, but is designed to aid in recovery for traumatized children by including family members to repair the relational impact of trauma. Integrating play and expressive arts into therapy sessions is one of the foundational aspects of this treatment model. Traumatized children will require a developmental approach that can meet their needs in the healing process to help promote post-traumatic growth and establish healthy relationships within their family. Play allows children of all ages to express themselves and feel safe in the sessions. From a developmental perspective, children build relationships using play primarily because it is fun and helps to reduce defensiveness.

Attachment-based Parenting Skills

The framework proposed for implementing a neurobiologically informed attachment-based family play therapy approach is intended to provide therapists with a structured process to help traumatized clients navigate through treatment from start to finish. Family SPACE is an acronym that stands for the five main attachment skills that will be taught to parents to help them learn how to establish healthy relationships within their family. SPACE stands for *Structure and Flexibility, Playfulness, Aware and Present,*

Curiosity, and *Empathy and Acceptance.* These specific attachment-based skills will be taught to parents during feedback sessions and practiced during the family sessions. Providing specific skills to parents will teach them how to be a therapeutic agent of change for their traumatized child and their family.

The *Three Rs of Relationship* are essentially the mechanics of what to do to implement the Family SPACE skills which will be taught to parents during parent coaching sessions and practiced during the family sessions. To achieve this, parents of traumatized children will learn skills necessary to help their child overcome the negative impact of trauma and help family members heal. Since it is not uncommon for parents of traumatized children to have also experienced trauma, this treatment framework will help parents learn healthy parenting practices to parent their child with more confidence.

Where to Begin

Therapists will begin with an initial session with the parents to obtain a family history and gather information about the trauma. During this session, therapists will also orient parents to the skills that will be taught and the rationale for the framework. After gathering all this important information, the family therapy sessions will begin. Family members will meet with the therapist for four sessions, then the fifth session will be a parent coaching session. This structure will repeat for the duration of treatment—four family sessions, a parent coaching session, then four family sessions, and another parent coaching session, and so on.

During the parent coaching sessions, therapists will elicit information from parents about the effectiveness of the skills at home and to provide feedback and suggestions to parents. Therapists will obtain feedback from parents regarding the family play therapy sessions, such as the pacing of the change process, feedback about situations that occurred after the sessions, concerns that arose during the sessions, etc. The purpose of the parent coaching sessions will be to create a parent–therapist coaching partnership that will provide the foundation for parents to become the *therapeutic agent of change* within the family. As the therapeutic agent of change, parents will play a crucial role in the healing process for their children. Therapists will also prepare parents for what to expect from the next four family therapy sessions. This gives parents a chance to ask questions and partner with the therapist in the change process. Therapists will show video clips of targeted interactions from the family therapy sessions. This will be discussed in more depth later in the chapter. Videotaping can be an invaluable tool to help parents recognize relationship interaction patterns, so they need to be willing to give consent for videotaping the sessions.

The therapist's clinical judgement can be used when necessary to adjust the format of the sessions. For example, if a parent is struggling to use some of the Family SPACE skills, then perhaps scheduling an additional parent coaching session makes sense. The main idea is that the family needs to have enough sessions to practice and engage in the change process, plus they need dedicated time with the therapist for feedback and review. In my experience, four consecutive family sessions provide ample opportunity for learning and practicing new relationship skills before meeting with parents again.

"How" Skills for Creating Family SPACE

This treatment model teaches parents to create Family SPACE. The Family SPACE framework uses specific attachment-based skills parents need to use with their children that will teach parents how to effectively engage with their children. Therapists will model, or mirror, these skills with parents and other family members. These Family SPACE "how" skills, as stated earlier, include: Structure and Flexibility, Playfulness, Aware and Present, Curiosity, and Empathy and Acceptance. Therapists will help parents to incorporate these skills which enables them to increase their ability to help their traumatized children manage their emotions effectively and engage in healthy relationship behaviors. These skills will help parents to be present in the interactions with their child to establish and maintain a caring and safe relationship. See Figure 6.1.

Let's look at the Family SPACE skills one by one:

Structure and Flexibility skills focus on helping parents to create a balance between providing structure for a sense of security, and also flexibility to maintain a family culture that can adjust to the needs of the child and the stressors of the day. As discussed in Chapter 5, creating a structured and flexible family culture is important for establishing and maintaining strong family relationships.

Playfulness helps parents make emotional deposits into the relationship *bank* with their child. It's important for parents to make sure there is genuine caring in their playful interactions, and not a way to mask

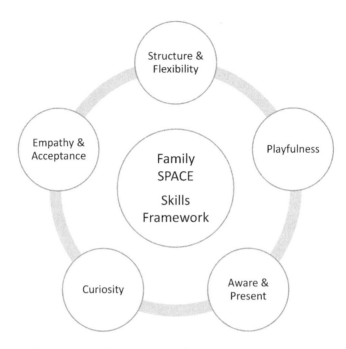

Figure 6.1 Skills Framework for Creating Family SPACE

sarcasm or unresolved anger. Children do not always understand sarcasm so parents need to recognize how to engage in playful interactions with their children in a way that is received positively, not negatively. Parents also need to recognize how and when to be playful with their child. This will require parents to learn to effectively engage their resonance circuits with their child, which brings us to the next skill, Aware and Present.

To be *Aware and Present*, parents will need to understand how resonance circuits and mentalization play a key role in their ability to be attuned to the needs of their child. As discussed in Chapters 2 and 4 (respectively), parents use their resonance circuits to tune in to their child's emotions and needs, and mentalizations play a key role in the meaning that parents make of their child's behaviors. Learning to use mindfulness skills allows parents to learn to settle themselves into the present moment and be aware of what is taking place in that moment. A parent's ability to be aware of their own internal emotions and thoughts, as well as what has triggered their own emotional reactivity, is essential to their ability to recognize themselves as separate from their children so they can more proficient in *tuning in* to their child. It's critical to create and maintain a strong parent–child attachment and to help siblings navigate their relationships well. Kids need their parents to help them learn how to be in relationships, which requires parents to be aware of their own internal working models and emotions.

To provide an example out of my own parenting experiences, I'll share an interaction I had with my youngest son when he was about 10 years old. We were in the kitchen, and I was stressed about something, probably something at work. I was in a cranky mood, and when my son asked me to do something for him, I had a snarky response to his request. You guessed it, at 10 years old, he had a snarky response back to me and now the argument was on. I now shot back to him that he was being disrespectful and I was tired of his disrespect. Being the highly intelligent and intuitive child that he was (and still is as a young adult), he called me out on my crankiness. He challenged me using sound logic that it was I who was disrespectful to him when he was simply making a request, and why was it okay for me to be disrespectful but not him? Busted. At that moment, I had to make a decision: I could take ownership of my behavior and apologize, or I could continue to blame him for the cranky interaction between us. At this point, I needed to be present enough in the moment to be aware of what was going on with me. I realized that at the moment I was actually stressed out and looking for a way to "offload" my cranky mood on to him. He was simply making a request, asking me for what he wanted and needed. My job as his parent was to consider his request and determine what course of action to take. I realized that I was simply tired of people making requests of me because I had allowed myself to be overstretched and hadn't been doing a proper amount of self-care. So, I told him that he was right and that it was I that was in the wrong. I apologized and we moved on. To be honest, I think he enjoyed calling me out on my cranky attitude a little, and we were able to repair our relationship.

I have found that mindfulness skills are the best way to be "Aware and Present." In Dialectical Behavior Therapy, mindfulness skills are part of the foundation for learning to effectively regulate emotions. How and What skills provide the ability to tune in to our bodies and emotions to identify what is happening in that moment so we can learn to use this wisdom to make decisions about our behavior, rather than allowing our emotions to rule our behavior. We'll discuss this more in Chapter 9 in the Engagement phase. I like to teach my clients how to use mindfulness early in the treatment process to give them skills for managing difficult emotions.

Curiosity provides a gentle way to explore and challenge behavior which minimizes the intensity of defensiveness. For those of you who remember (or have seen reruns) of the TV show back in the 1970s and 1980s, *Columbo*, you'll recall that he was a detective with an unassuming curiosity-based style of relating to people in order to obtain information from them. Using this *curiosity* stance helped him to navigate around defensiveness in people. When I'm trying to understand the intention underlying behavior from others, I use my "Columbo-mode." I will be curious about what's going on with a client, and I am genuinely interested in their response because my goal is to fully understand what happened from their perspective. Therapists need to help parents engage in curiosity with their children, rather than make assumptions about the behavior. Parents need to first seek to understand their children's behavior before making decisions about the consequences that need to be applied to address the problem. Children need to experience their parents in a way that ensures that their parents want to understand them.

I often find that parents worry that embracing a curiosity stance with their children will mean that parents do not hold boundaries. Therapists need to help parents understand that seeking to understand their children first will help parents recognize the cues their children are giving them. Parents will then use the information obtained from their child in their decision-making about what needs to happen to address the situation. Here's an example of a dialogue between 7-year-old James and his foster father:

Foster father: James, I noticed that the cookies are missing from the pantry again and there's an empty cookie package under your bed. I'm wondering how the empty cookie package got under your bed because we talked about the need to eat only in the kitchen to keep the bugs out of your room.

James: I didn't take them! (yelling) You're lying! You just want me to get in trouble!

Foster father: I know you are worried about getting in trouble and I'm sorry you feel like I don't trust you. That must be hard to feel like you are always getting in trouble. I'm just curious why the cookies were in your room?

James: Well, you are always yelling at me for stuff. I can't do anything right! (yelling less loudly).

Foster father: I'm sorry it feels like you are always getting in trouble. I'm guessing that makes it hard to feel like you can trust me. I just want to make sure we don't have ants in your room again. There were a lot of ants in your room last week. I'm wondering what will help you feel like you can eat the cookies in the kitchen so you don't feel like you can only eat them in your room?

James: Well, you told me that I couldn't eat snacks right before dinner last week and I was hungry. You were really mad at me.

Foster father: I'm sure that must have been kind of scary for you to think I was mad at you and maybe I didn't like you anymore. I know you had to leave your last two foster homes. That must be really hard not feeling like adults like you so you need to hide things. I'm sorry that happened to you. I'm sorry you thought I was mad at you. I was kind of frustrated about all the ants in your room. I'm wondering if there is something we can do so you feel comfortable eating in the kitchen and not your room?

James: Well, you can stop yelling at me for stuff.

Foster father: It sounds like you feel like I yell at you a lot and that makes it hard to trust me. Sometimes, I need to have boundaries to make sure you are safe and we have a clean house to live in. There were a lot of ants in your room from the cookies that were under your bed for a long time. I want you to have a clean room to live in to keep you safe. And sometimes, it's important for you to eat healthy food before having dessert so you can grow up strong and healthy. I want you to have snacks, though, because I know you really like to have snacks. Is there a way we can help you to only eat snacks in the kitchen and not right before dinner? Maybe you can decide what kind of dessert you want to eat after dinner? Maybe you can eat snacks right after you get home from school and you can pick the snacks?

James: Okay.

In this scenario, James' traumatic childhood experiences made it hard for him to trust adults. James' foster father recognized James' cues of not trusting adults and trying to find ways to take care of his needs without having to rely on adults. However, this mistrust of adults caused difficulties in his ability to develop a healthy relationship with his caregivers, and often caused significant ruptures in the parent–child relationship. The foster father was able to use curiosity to help him better understand James' behavior and problem solve ways to address the situation in a way that maintained connection with James.

Empathy and Acceptance were also critical in the interaction between James and his foster father in helping them to maintain the connection in their relationship while addressing the issue at hand. In the interaction you will notice the foster father used empathy with James by recognizing how difficult it must be for James to trust adults due to his trauma history that included removal from two previous foster homes. The foster father also demonstrated acceptance with James. This is seen in the foster father's recognition that James' behavior, while not appropriate, makes sense within the context of James' life experiences. Traumatic experiences erode our ability to trust others and also influence our beliefs about ourselves and most often includes shame.

Shame is inherent in traumatic experiences and requires parents to embrace empathy and acceptance toward their traumatized child. Empathy and acceptance are the "antidote" needed for healing. Therapists need to help parents adopt empathy and acceptance with their traumatized child in order to build trust in their relationship, and help to improve their child's self-concept. This does not mean that structure and discipline are not applied within the family. It means parents need to emotionally connect with their child to help their child feel understood and acceptable despite their behavior. *They are not their behavior.* Their behavior is a manifestation of what is happening internally. Empathy and acceptance help parents to help their child make changes internally by changing their core beliefs that were discussed in Chapter 4.

"What" Skills to Use Family SPACE: The Three Rs of Relationship

The mechanics of relationships within the Family SPACE framework are the Three Rs of Relationship. These focus on teaching parents what they need to do in order to appropriately implement the Family SPACE skills. For example, parents will need to use reflexive communication skills when they are using curiosity to explore the underlying reason for a behavior problem. The Three Rs are: *Reflexive communication*, *Regulate emotions*, and *Repair* when a relationship rupture occurs. Therapists will need to orient parents to the Family SPACE and Three Rs skills during the Engagement phase of treatment during a parents only session. See Figure 6.2.

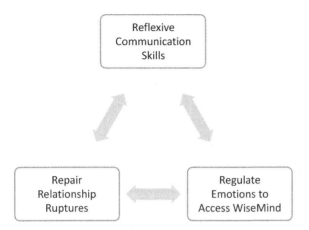

Figure 6.2 The 3 Rs of Relationship Skills

Reflexive communication is a style of communicating that focuses on gathering information during the interaction to ensure an accurate understanding of what is being discussed, using an empathic and attuned presence. Parents of traumatized children need to acquire the ability to engage in communication with their children that will facilitate understanding of the issues from the perspective of their children, since that will give context for the behavior. From an attachment standpoint, I believe the goal of communication within our relationships is to enhance understanding of one another and communicate needs in order to feel felt and understood. This is the healing aspect of relationship, and communication is one of the avenues through which we can achieve this goal.

In a Norwegian study by Sommer, Finlay, Ness, Borg, and Blank (2019), the researchers explored the role of what they called *nourishing communion* in providing healing support to young adults with a history of mental health difficulties. This study was the third in a series of studies exploring support to young adults with mental health issues. Interestingly, researchers in this study were exploring ways in which support from professionals could aid young adults with mental health issues to find healing and existential meaning in their lives. To achieve this goal, the researchers utilized intersubjectivity constructs, reflexive dialogue using curiosity, and resonance circuits to establish a strong therapeutic rapport when gaining the analytical information needed for their research. From this research stance, the authors concluded the following:

by drawing on our own experiences of communion that give a sense of nourishment, mirrored and refracted in the light of the participants' experiences, we came to identify five overarching intertwined themes: (a) trusting the other to hold vulnerability safely; (b) flourishing in mutual participation; (c) acceptance in a felt togetherness; (d) feeling found and received; and (e) feeling an attuned resonance.

(p. 9)

The goal of reflexive communication is to seek information rather than making assumptions about what is communicated, and be curious to better understand the other person. This stance of curiosity will facilitate more effective avenues to understand the intention of the other person and to be clear about what you are communicating with the goal of maintaining a strong attachment with our children. Essentially, we are reflecting back to the other person what we perceive about their intention and need in their communication to us. The conversation between Jane and her father in the previous chapter is an example of reflective communication. Jane's father recognized that Jane was distressed and he reflected back to her that he noticed she did not want to go into the basement. He also reflected back to her that she seemed irritated, and then used curiosity to obtain more information as to the reason she was irritated, which he then also reflected back to her.

When conflict arises in sessions with parents, their children, and siblings, it can be helpful for therapists to be more directive and show families how to use reflexive communication with each other. The problem is, when there's conflict, people often become defensive and focus on their own response rather than actually listen to one another to try to understand their intentions and/or needs. Reflexive communication within a Family SPACE framework can use the conflict to learn how to improve the understanding of one another, rather than allowing conflict to increase tension and mistrust within relationships.

Regulate emotions to access wisdom. Emotion regulation is a critical skill when using Family SPACE within relationships. For example, it will be difficult to maintain Awareness and Presence with their children if parents are emotionally dysregulated. When parents are emotionally regulated then they can use the critical decision-making areas of their brain to help them navigate situations and conflicts effectively using the Family SPACE skills. When parents are emotionally dysregulated, then their access to those areas of their brain are temporarily suspended until they are calm again. I love the Dialectical Behavior Therapy (DBT) skill of *Wise Mind* to help me get to that wise place within myself for decision-making and getting calm. Wise Mind is essentially a synthesis of the beneficial aspects of two other states of mind: *Emotion Mind* and *Logic Mind* (also referred to as *Reasonable Mind* and *Rational Mind*) using mindfulness practice. These two states of mind also correlate with right brain and left brain functions. Logic mind is only focused on facts, cause and effect, and logic. It does not include emotions and is strictly more intellectual focused. Emotion Mind is—you guessed it—focuses on our emotions, both positive and negative emotions. Our emotions give us a lot of information so they are important for Wise Mind. For example, if I am angry, then it will be important for me to identify what is actually triggering my anger. Maybe I have been frustrated because my child continually disregards the family rule to call me when he is going over to a friend's house so for hours I never know where he is or if he's okay. Maybe I'm frustrated that because he doesn't check with me before going to a friend's house, he continually neglects his chores which means the rest of us in the family always need to do his chores. This anger is a signal to me that there is a problem in our relationship that needs to be addressed, and I may need to hold a boundary so he will be considerate of others which is an important relationship behavior.

Wise Mind is using the benefits of identifying what my emotions are communicating to me, as well as the benefits of Logic Mind. If I want to buy a car, then I need to use Logic Mind to determine if I can afford a car at this time, what monthly payments can I afford, how much will car insurance cost, where do I want to shop for the car, and maybe when I can begin my search. Since I want to enjoy my car, then I want to use the benefits of Emotion Mind, such as what color do I like for the exterior and interior, how comfortable are the seats, and what kind of vehicle do I want. Wise Mind will help me to buy a car that I can afford, meets my needs, and a car I enjoy driving.

Regulating emotions helps parents to access Wise Mind, which will help them stay effectively engaged with their child when communicating and resolving conflict by increasing their window of emotional distress tolerance. Parents with a narrow window of tolerance will have high emotional distress levels and low ability to tolerate that distress. Parents with a wider window of tolerance will have a higher threshold for emotional distress and higher ability to regulate their emotions. Effective emotion regulation also helps parents to use effective decision-making with their child which will help to improve trust and understanding within the parent–child relationship.

Repair the relationship rupture when it occurs. Parents need to repair their relationship with their child and teach their children how to repair their own relationships. Relationship repair skills, when done sincerely, can be a powerful way to strengthen and maintain good relationships. It will be difficult for parents to use the Family SPACE skills with their children to establish and maintain a secure attachment with their children if there is an ongoing rupture in their relationship. Parents need to recognize their role in the rupture and identify what triggered their behavior. When both parent and child are calm and ready to talk, then parent and child discuss what happened, and their respective roles in the conflict, with the goal of better understanding one another and identifying solutions as needed. I find that children are receptive to parents who are able to take ownership of their role in the conflict, and will more readily accept discipline from their parents.

Repairing any ruptures within the relationship helps to re-establish trust, which is critical for traumatized children to feel safe. In the interaction between James and his foster father, James' foster father acknowledged the hurt that James experienced in his short seven years of life and helped to maintain James' ability to remain in their dialogue by apologizing for those negative things. Even though James' foster father did not cause those experiences, he could let James know that he was sorry those experiences happened to James. In my interaction with my son in which I was cranky, it was important to re-establish trust with him by acknowledging my cranky behavior.

Getting Started

Gathering Multigenerational Information

Prior to integrating the child and siblings into the therapy sessions, it is critical for the therapist to meet first with parents to obtain a thorough multigenerational family history. This session with parents will identify family history information that has influenced the relationship and attachment patterns within the family system presenting for treatment. Using a multigenerational lens will help therapists to identify any family history of trauma, abuse, and/or neglect, attachment patterns and resiliency factors. It will be important for parents to identify their own trauma and attachment histories since the trauma work with the traumatized child will most certainly activate all those memories for the parents and influence their parenting. First and foremost, therapists need to establish a sense of safety within the sessions which means identifying any history of trauma within the family so that therapists can be more aware during the therapy sessions, especially if parents have a history of dissociation. Parents with a history of their own trauma are likely to have the experience of their own emotional triggers becoming activated within the sessions. Therefore, therapists should assess a parent's tendency for dissociation and their ability to effectively participate in the sessions. Therapists will need to help caregivers manage their own trauma triggers while helping the child resolve their own traumatic experiences. Parents will need support from therapists to navigate this successfully. Because trauma impacts the ability to engage in healthy relationships, it is critical to heal the relational impact of trauma to help traumatized kids fully resolve the impact of trauma and develop posttraumatic growth. Post-traumatic growth is the ability to overcome and thrive after experiencing the devastating impact of trauma. It is the ability to grow and become resilient after trauma. Kids and teens need to move beyond surviving trauma to thriving. And because children and teens live within the context of family relationships, I believe it's important for the family to develop post-traumatic growth as well.

Therapists will also need to gather as much information as possible about the nature of the trauma; the severity, duration, and extent of the traumatic experience, its impact on the child's daily functioning, age of the child when the trauma was experienced, relationship of the child to the abuser (in the case of abuse), as well as what was done to address the impact of the trauma (removal of the child from parental care, counseling, medical care, etc.). All of this information will provide the therapist with the ability to conceptualize the clinical issues to be addressed and formulate an initial plan to begin addressing the trauma with the child and family.

The information about the traumatic experience can be gained from a variety of people to include parents, child, reports by social workers, school personnel, and/or attorneys. Once the initial history information has been obtained, therapists will also need to be aware of how family members and the traumatized child respond to stressors and identify trauma triggers since the treatment process can be an emotionally difficult experience. It will be important to identify possible trauma triggers and how family members manifest their distress in order to develop a safety plan with caregivers to implement and pace the treatment process. The pacing of treatment will be critical so that all family members feel emotionally safe and able to remain engaged in treatment. Remember that when the brain registers danger, it will activate the threat systems and clients will have difficulty staying engaged in the treatment process unless they have the support and structure to "weather those storms" during the healing process. I usually like to use the first session with the child, siblings, and parents present to discuss any concerns about what is said during the therapy process and then identify a plan that all family members can agree upon.

Things to Consider When Getting Started

Therapists will need to assess the ability of parents to engage in the sessions with their child to facilitate change. Parents who cannot be supportive to the traumatized child, who may be mentally unstable and/or actively abusing substances, will not be appropriate to engage in this treatment model because there will not be a way to establish emotional safety within the family sessions. When considering the addition of integrating family members into the treatment process with the traumatized child, it will be important to meet with parents without the child present to discuss the purpose of the family sessions, the role of parents in the family sessions, and the role of the therapist. This orienting process will help to build rapport with parents and help them see the therapist as an ally and not their judge. It can be intimidating for parents to engage in the family sessions with their children because they typically feel they have failed in their job as a parent to protect their child or do a good job of parenting. Therapists will need to determine if there is a history of trauma in the parent's childhood so the therapist can help parents to manage their own emotional triggers while engaging with their children. In this way, the therapist can help to facilitate healing within the parent–child relationship, and the child's relationship with siblings. It can be a difficult task for some parents to manage so many emotional needs within their family with their children. Therefore, it will be important for the therapist to have an idea of what situations may be triggering for the parent in order to help the family navigate effectively through these challenging situations when they occur in the session. Therapists may need to request that parents with an unresolved trauma history participate in their own individual therapy while also participating in their child's treatment.

It has been my experience that children worry about one or more of the following things in joint sessions with parents and family members: 1) that they will get "in trouble" if they say something that activates a parent's reactivity, 2) that they will hurt their parents' feelings, and/or 3) that if they say something in sessions that upsets their parent then the parent will use it against the child in the future, and the child will "never hear the end of it." If these concerns are not addressed at the beginning of treatment then the child will have difficulty being open and honest in therapy. Think about it from a child's perspective—who rules the universe? Adults! Children need adults to understand that they, the children, are in a position of disempowerment and don't want to upset their parents for fear of rejection, and then their life may become worse.

Parents need to recognize that in the therapy sessions it will be important for the *unspoken* to become *spoken* so that misperceptions, hurt, and fear can be replaced with accurate understanding and improved ability for children to utilize the support of their parents. With all of this in mind, I will start the first session with children and parents by stating in the session that kids tend to worry about one or more of the three things previously stated. Then I ask each child to identify which of the three things they are worried about. Each child then identifies one or more of the concerns. Once we have started the session by identifying an important "elephant in the room," we can now identify a plan for managing those concerns.

At this point I will say to parents and children: "It's been my experience that families tend to want to agree to one of these things: 1) What's discussed in the therapy session is not discussed outside of the therapy session until the next session, 2) after the session then you all agree that you can continue to discuss what was discussed in the therapy session as much and as often as you like (kids rarely like this option, and parents usually like this option), or, 3) you can try talking about what was discussed in the therapy session at home and if things don't go well then someone can say they need to stop and wait till therapy to continue addressing it." I present these options to the family for discussion and there needs to be a unanimous decision about which plan the family will adhere to for the duration of the session. I usually use a little humor (adding an element of playfulness) with the kids saying that if their parents don't follow the plan, then the kids can "tell on them" during the next session. This usually helps the kids to engage in the decision-making process and use their voice in the discussion. Once the family members unanimously agree upon the plan, then we proceed with the initial session. I have found that it's helpful to have this discussion at the first session to set the tone for the treatment process.

Overview of the Treatment Framework

This model focuses on working through several phases of treatment to address the impact of trauma within the family relationships to facilitate healing for the traumatized child and the family. First and foremost, therapists need to develop therapeutic rapport to build trust within the family system and then to help families identify behavior patterns that contribute to ongoing problems, and to change those patterns. Creating and maintaining a safe, therapeutic space in the therapy office is the foundational framework needed for effective treatment. Since this model is not meant to replace individual therapy for the traumatized child, it will be important to ensure that the individual therapy needs for the child are addressed in order to help the child heal.

There is one caveat at this point that will need to be addressed and considered when therapists are considering who will be present in the family sessions. If the child experienced abuse by one of the family members who will be participating in the treatment sessions, then the ability of that family member to take accountability and commit to making repairs with the child is critical. Otherwise, it will undermine the ability for the child to feel safe in the sessions. The abusive family member cannot repair the relationship with the child unless he or she recognizes the impact of his or her behavior on the traumatized child and is willing to repair that relationship as well as respect the traumatized child's need to see proof of the abuser's ability to maintain a safe and healthy relationship. Trust will need to be built with the traumatized child.

The therapist may need to slowly integrate the abusive family member into the family sessions and in a way that ensures the traumatized child will feel comfortable. I've worked with several families over the course of my career in which an older sibling sexually abused the younger siblings for extended periods of time. In these cases, the older sibling was required to participate in treatment for adolescent sex offenders while the traumatized child received individual therapy. I coordinated services with the therapist of the adolescent sex offender to ensure that the older sibling was able to engage in his treatment to take accountability, understand why the abuse occurred, and demonstrate the ability to maintain healthy relationship behaviors. Both therapists worked together to ensure the traumatized child was ready for the older sibling to join the family sessions to begin the repair process. In these cases, it is important for the traumatized child to be willing to integrate the older sibling so that the traumatized child can feel safe and empowered.

This is also true if the abusing family member is the parent of the child. Children need parents to keep them safe and help them navigate the ups and downs of life. When a parent is the abusive family member, then it shatters the ability for the child to use the support of that parent in a way that supports their social and emotional growth. Therapists need to ensure that the abusive parent is able to take accountability and acknowledge to the child that their behavior was wrong and that their behavior hurt the child. Children generally tend to want to repair their relationship with their parents and it is the responsibility of the parent to demonstrate the ability to change and learn healthy relationship and parenting skills. Therapists also need to recognize that some parents who have not resolved their own trauma and tend to function more in a dissociative state may not be able to participate in family therapy. If parents are frequently dissociative in the session and unable to engage in the change process, then it will be difficult for the child to develop a secure attachment relationship with that parent without significant intervention with the traumatized parent. Remember, we want parents to be bigger, wiser, kinder and strong for their children. It will be difficult for a dissociative parent to demonstrate the ability to provide the structure and empathic attunement needed for healing their relationship.

Traumatized clients often want to know why they were targeted for the abuse so it will need to be important for the abusing family member to address that with the traumatized child. The abusing family member will also need to be able to tolerate the traumatized child's assertion of anger without becoming defensive or blaming. These are key elements of healing for the traumatized child as well as for the repair to occur in the relationship with the abusing family member.

Overview of the Observational Assessment Phase

Once the therapist gathers all the important information and conducts the initial session to orient the family to the treatment process, then the *Observational Assessment* phase can begin. The focus of the Observational Assessment phase is primarily to get a sense of the family interaction patterns with little to no intervention by the therapist. This will help the therapist know what relationship patterns to prioritize and begin to identify interventions that will help the family to make the necessary changes. The therapist is also working on developing rapport with family members and creating emotional safety within the session. I like to use the analogy of an emotional bank account. Therapists will make a lot of emotional deposits in the bank accounts of the family members through the use of positive feedback, identifying strengths for family members, being playful when appropriate, demonstrating positive regard for each family member, and structuring the sessions. I need to make sure that I have made enough emotional deposits before making any emotional withdrawals such as constructive feedback and challenging unhealthy behaviors.

Therefore, during the Observational Assessment phase, I focus on providing activities that can match the developmental needs of all family members as much as possible and are fun so that the children can engage in the process and feel safe. I take the role of observer in the sessions with minimal interaction so that I can observe the relationship patterns. This phase generally lasts 3–4 sessions.

Overview of the Safety and Engagement Phase

Once the Observational Assessment phase is completed, the *Safety and Engagement* phase begins. This phase focuses on helping family members to develop a sense of safety within the change process, and commit to the process. The therapist works on providing structure and activities that will help all family members recognize the importance of repairing their relationships and developing healthy relationship skills. The therapist begins to take a more directive role in the sessions by identifying specific activities for each meeting. Activities introduced during family sessions in this phase of treatment will focus on developing coping skills, emotionally tolerating the sessions, and feeling safe. This phase lays the foundation for building the necessary trust with family members by making lots of deposits in the family emotional bank so that withdrawals made in the next phase of the treatment process can be tolerated by family members. The Safety and Engagement phase of treatment can take many sessions depending on the needs of each family. Some families will be able to establish a sense of safety in the sessions and engage in the treatment process quickly and others will need more time. The role of the therapist will be to structure the sessions, continue to demonstrate positive regard for all family members, and use activities that will help family members to fully participate in the session activities.

Overview of the Realignment Phase

Once family members have demonstrated that they are engaged in the treatment process and feel comfortable in the sessions, therapists will begin the next phase of treatment—the *Realignment* phase. During the

Realignment phase, therapists will therapeutically challenge unhealthy relationship patterns within the family. It will be important for therapists to monitor the family's ability to tolerate emotional distress. Therapists will need to monitor for signs of emotion dysregulation and dissociation and help family members recognize triggers for these behaviors to aid in the effectiveness of the interventions and pacing of the sessions. Dissociation and/or emotion dysregulation can be a sign that the pace of the treatment process is going too fast, so it will be important to monitor the family's ability to tolerate emotional distress. Therapists might need to return to using Engagement phase type of activities to help families stabilize before moving back to therapeutically challenging family members.

When family members become emotionally distressed in the sessions, it can be a great time to explore and identify what triggered the emotional distress, how those behaviors occur at home, how those situations are generally handled at home, and identify ways to help family members learn new patterns of coping and interacting. One of my previous employers used to say, "Why waste a good crisis?" meaning that for family members, these events can be an opportunity for learning and repairing. Of course, as therapists, we need to be comfortable tolerating the emotional distress of our clients so that we can effectively and therapeutically help our clients navigate through those emotional withdrawals.

The Realignment phase of treatment is primarily focused on helping family members learn and implement healthy changes and improve their relationships. Family members will essentially *realign* their relationships by changing unhealthy relationship behaviors and establishing healthy relationship patterns. This is where the bulk of the change occurs in the treatment process. Time in this phase of treatment will most likely be the longest part of the therapy process, so it will be important for therapists to make sure they have established trust in the Engagement phase of treatment.

The Final Phase of Treatment Is the Attunement Phase

This is essentially the termination phase of treatment. Parents and their children will have successfully identified and replaced unhealthy relationship patterns, creating a safe and nurturing environment in the home. This phase ensures that parents are able to effectively use the skills learned in treatment with their children. Children will be able to use the support of family relationships and demonstrate resilience when challenges occur. Helping parents and children to say goodbye is an important part of the process. It's a wonderful time to reflect on the progress made by family members and affirm their resiliency.

Use of Videotaping

Each session is videotaped to capture relationship patterns in real time. The videotaping is an important part of the framework because it will be impossible to observe all interactions among family members within each session. Therapists can review the sessions to identify interactions among family members and assess these interactions to determine effective and ineffective relationship patterns. These videotaped sessions can be a powerful tool to use when helping parents recognize and explore these relationship patterns during the parent coaching sessions. Once the therapist has established a therapeutic alliance with parents, then parents can tolerate examining their roles that are supporting the unhealthy interactions because they will experience the therapeutic relationship as a safe place to be vulnerable. The therapist will then identify portions of the session to use for the parent coaching sessions that will highlight these patterns.

Furthermore, any seasoned therapist will acknowledge the certainty of becoming pulled into the family system dynamics. Since therapists are human, we need to be aware of our own ability to be drawn into the system in order to know how to get back out of the family dynamics. If we don't know how we get drawn in, then we will find it difficult to get back out of the system in order to have a more neutral position within the family system. The old saying, "You can't see the forest for the trees," is a perfect way to think about the wisdom of making sure to stay out of the "forest" in order to have a better understanding of the interaction patterns and where families get stuck in order to help them create change. Therapists are the change agents and need to have the ability to keep the focus on the bigger picture. Families will get stuck "in the weeds (or lost in the forest!)," so to speak, because their focus will be on external issues rather than the core issues that keep perpetuating the problem. For example, parents and their teenage daughter constantly argue about the rules that their daughter keeps breaking. The daughter is rebellious and skips school, using drugs and alcohol, and hanging out with friends who are also using drugs and failing school. The parents see this as disrespect and worry that their daughter will be unable to successfully maintain a job and independent life. The daughter sees her parents as restricting her independence and trying to control her life. The root of the problem lies in their inability to have a healthy relationship in which trust and boundaries can be managed effectively through communication and problem solving. Children will accept boundaries from their parents when they trust that their parents really do have their best interest in mind, even when they don't like the boundaries set for them. Therapists must be able to see the forest so that they can help parents navigate through it. Videotaping the sessions will also help therapists to recognize when they are getting pulled into the family dynamics and to identify how they need to get back out so they can be effective change agents.

The use of consultation is an accepted practice and, when working with families, it can be important to receive feedback and support. The ability to use the videotape sessions in the consultation process is an invaluable tool to help therapists help their clients navigate the change process.

Therapist Role and Modeling

Therapists need to be fully present in the sessions using play and expressive arts. This requires them to be attuned to their own internal experiences so that they can be attuned with their clients and stay present when clients are working through difficult emotions. Creating the *free and protected space* within the therapy office requires therapists to create an environment in which there is unconditional positive regard for children and parents to feel comfortable to express what is underneath their behaviors. When therapists are fully present in the session, then clients feel *seen*, *heard*, and *understood*. This may take time because being vulnerable will feel unsafe for some clients.

Presence and Acceptance are key aspects of mindfulness practice and essential to creating safety and maintaining therapeutic rapport. Mindfulness requires the ability to be fully emotionally and consciously present in the moment without judgement. It is accepting the moment in the moment without judging the moment or the experience. It requires paying attention to one's thoughts, emotions, and physical body sensations. According to Daniel Siegel (2011), "the presence of a caring, trusted other person, one who is attuned to our internal world, is often the initial key to widening our windows of tolerance" (p. 139). Think about it—have you ever struggled with a difficult situation and been with someone who was fully emotionally present with you and fully able to sit with you in compassion, without judging you or giving you advice? Feeling fully accepted and your pain understood? The healing quality of compassionate presence is an essential part of the therapeutic relationship.

Within the attachment framework, the role of the therapist is to create a safe and secure environment for vulnerability and change to take place. Therapists who are able to establish a therapeutic relationship with their clients will be more successful in giving permission for parents to be self-reflective and to explore vulnerable emotions. It will be important for family members to get to the deeper level of change required to create vulnerability and intimacy within family relationships, so that all family members can experience their relationships as safe and authentic. Therapists need to be able to tolerate the negative emotions of clients, including parents who may feel tremendous shame and guilt—or perhaps their own trauma has gotten triggered in the session. Therapists who practice mindful presence during the sessions will be able to recognize their own internal responses and regulate those in order to therapeutically hold family member interactions during the sessions. Daniel Siegel (2011) states that being mindfully present in sessions with distressed clients provides an opportunity for assisting clients to learn to regulate their emotions due to the benefit of mirror neurons. The mirror neurons of clients who observe and experience a calm and regulated therapist, one who is able to regulate her own emotions, will help her clients learn to engage emotion regulation circuitry within themselves. Therapists will use mirroring with parents in the same way we want parents to mirror for their children.

Therapists need to understand their own potential barriers to intimacy. Clients will never progress further than their therapists are able to take them in the healing process. We can only take our clients as far as we, as therapists, are willing to go on our own healing journey. The human condition is one in which we need to recognize our strengths as well as our weaknesses. Therefore, as therapists, we need to recognize and remain constantly aware of our shortcomings and work to mitigate the impact of those shortcomings on our clients. Our *use of self* in therapeutic relationships by tapping into our resonance circuits can be a powerful tool to help family members change and learn to build authentic relationships. Therapists can model healthy boundaries, effective problem solving, and communication.

As therapists, we need to know when to provide nurturing support to clients and families and when we need to challenge them outside their comfort zone in order to make the necessary internal changes. One of the hallmarks of Dialectical Behavior Therapy (DBT), developed by Dr. Marsha Linehan (1993), in working with difficult clients with Borderline Personality Disorder, is the concept of dialectics. Dialectic essentially means that two different things can be true at the same time. For example, within an attachment framework, we can understand that parents and children can be angry with one another while also loving each other. They may not feel the soft feelings of love when angry, but at the same time those feelings of love do not diminish. Their love still exists. Therapists can be both nurturing and challenging in helping their clients make the necessary changes to overcome barriers within their relationships.

Therapists need to understand the importance of taking a strong yet empathic stand with parents when parents are struggling to make the necessary changes. It is best to establish therapeutic trust via emotional deposits before undertaking benevolent challenging (emotional withdrawals) to increase the likelihood that parents will remain in treatment. If parents believe therapists are challenging them because the therapist cares about them, then they are more likely to work through the repair process with the therapist. Challenging parents will likely cause a rupture that will need to be repaired.

A therapeutic dialectic identified by Dr. Linehan (1993) for mental health professionals is the dialectic of *Nurturing and Benevolent Demanding*. Therapists need to establish a therapeutic non-judgemental alliance in which clients feel accepted. This will allow the safety net to maintain the therapeutic alliance when therapists demand change from their clients in a firm, yet caring manner. In the same way, therapists mirror to parents how to hold firm boundaries to provide healthy structure for their children to grow. This is particularly important when working with difficult family systems in which there are several generations of attachment difficulties because those relationship patterns and behaviors will most likely be entrenched. Consider, also, children in foster care or adopted after the age of 3 who have experienced the world as unreliable and unsafe. These children will struggle with making deeper level changes unless parents are able to hold firm boundaries and challenge them to be emotionally vulnerable and begin to trust their caregivers.

References

Linehan, M. M. (1993). *Cognitive-behavioral treatment of borderline personality disorder*. New York, NY: The Guilford Press.

Siegel, D. J. (2011). *Mindsight: The New Science of Personal Transformation*. New York, NY: Bantam Books.

Sommer, M., Finlay, L., Ness, O., Borg, M., & Blank, A. (2019). "Nourishing communion": A less recognized dimension of support for young persons facing mental health challenges? *The Humanistic Psychologist*. Advanced online publication. doi:10.1037/hum0000122

Guiding Principles of the 7
Model for Implementation

Core Principles of Attachment-based Family Play Therapy

The core principles in this model, which provide the foundation for its implementation, are based on understanding the connection between behavior, and quality of the relationships within the family. Working with families requires the ability to understand the needs of each individual within the family, and how the members work to simultaneously meet the needs of the family. This is a delicate balance in which therapists must be vigilant in recognizing the nuances of interactions among all the family members and understand the possible purpose underlying the observed behaviors. Since many of the families we work with include children from different developmental stages, therapists must also understand typical developmental tasks for each child, then be aware of how family members manage the different needs of each developmental stage. Families provide the "building blocks" for learning about the world and relationships. For instance, our relationship with our parents provides us with opportunities to learn how to engage in healthy interactions with people in authority. Parents provide us with experiences related to taking direction, living within structure with boundaries, and taking correction. Our relationships with our siblings give us the opportunity to learn how to engage in healthy relationships with peers. Our siblings challenge us, frustrate us, and engage with us as peers rather than those in authority. Therapists working with children need to be able to help families navigate through the complexities of dynamic relationships to find healing. This will require therapists to therapeutically hold these complexities while helping families during the change process.

Families Are Generationally Complex

Families are complex systems that are made up of complex individuals, and families can also be generationally complex. Modern families consist of a variety of individuals, but all families have two main things in common—caregivers and children. The reality of what constitutes *family* for the raising of children has changed over the past two decades and children within these families will require their parents to provide them with the amount of safety and security to help them grow and mature. Traditional family systems include mother, father, and children. Within a traditional family system, there can be children who are biological children as well as adoptive children or foster children. Grandparents and other family members are also raising children when children are removed from the care of biological parents. Same gender parents have increased in our society and require family systems to figure out non-traditional models of parenting. Stereotypes of parenting roles will be challenged in non-traditional families and mentalizations of what makes a family a family will need to be challenged in order to allow the opportunity for new types of conceptualizations for family.

There is a rise in the number of single parents raising children over the past two decades as well as blended families. Single parenting reduces the number of parental resources within the nuclear family if the single parent does not have access to supportive resources for raising children, such as childcare, financial resources, emotional support. Blended families require family members to adjust to including additional sets of parent figures into their family system and figure out the roles of the stepparents in the family system. Some of these families can become embroiled in high conflict between parents, often pulling their children into the middle of their conflicts.

High-conflict divorced families create significant instability for their children due to the level of intense conflict between the parents. This instability interferes with a child's ability to establish a sense of safety and security, especially when child protective services becomes involved due to ongoing allegations of abuse by one or both parents. Often, the court is involved in an attempt to facilitate resolution to the legal issues of visitation and custody. These families are often quite frustrating to the court and child protective services staff, mostly due to the inability of these parents to co-parent their children effectively. For many of these children, the parental high conflict can be experienced as traumatizing and the quality of their relationships with parents is impaired, especially in the case of Parental Alienation. Parental Alienation occurs when one parent purposefully attempts to sabotage the relationship of the child with the other parent.

Many of the families experiencing complex trauma and attachment difficulties consist of parents who are either a sibling of the birth parent, such as an aunt or uncle, or the parent of the birth parent, such as a grandparent. These caregivers have taken on the role of parent when the birth parent is unable to care for their child due to mental illness, substance abuse, or incarceration. Children in foster care have experienced some sort of trauma, which resulted in their inability to live with their birth parents. Most cases of foster care are the result of removing a child from the home due to revealed cases of abuse and/or neglect. In some cases, children are removed from the home due to the death of their parent or legal guardian. Multiple disruptions in foster care placements increase a child's difficulties with healthy attachments resulting in more complex social emotional difficulties.

Trauma tends to be experienced across the generations. When working with traumatized children, therapists need to obtain information about trauma across several generations to identify the prevalence and impact of trauma within the family. This information gathering should also include trauma histories of foster parents and adopted parents. Borelli, Comparc, Snavely, and Decio (2015) examined intergenerational child sexual abuse and the role of reflective functioning, also known as mentalizing, and discuss the evidence of intergenerational risks factors of sexual abuse across generations citing research that mothers who were exposed to sexual abuse as children were 3.6 times more likely to have children who were exposed to sexual abuse. Many of the families experiencing trauma and attachment difficulties have long histories of attachment difficulties across the generations, which speaks to the ingrained patterns passed along from one generation to the next. Bowen Family Systems theory explains that across the generations, there may be some well-functioning adults as well as low functioning adults. Understanding the relationship and emotional patterns across the generations provides therapists working with these families a better understanding of the issues involved and the intensity of those issues. Attachment theory helps us to understand the nuances of the caregiver–child relationship and its impact on the child's ability to regulate emotions and engage in healthy behaviors.

Children Innately Desire to Have a Positive Relationship with Their Parents and Feel Connected to Their Siblings to Have a Sense of Belonging

Children are born with an innate drive to connect with their parents. Their survival at its most basic level is dependent upon a child's relationship with his parents. Infants are neurally wired to become attuned to their parents to read the cues. This attunement facilitates the ability for children to get their basic needs for survival met. According to Van Der Kolk (2014):

> children have a biological instinct to attach—they have no choice. Whether their parents or caregivers are loving and caring or distant, insensitive, rejecting, or abusive, children will develop a coping style based on their attempt to get at least *some* of their needs met.
>
> (p. 117)

In early childhood, a child's misbehavior is not due to a desire to detach from parents or hurt parents. Sometimes parents misinterpret a child's misbehavior as "willful" attempts to hurt them, but it is more likely a child's attempt to let the adults in his life know that something is wrong or just simply childish misbehavior. It is important for parents to identify their own mentalizations so they can address the misbehavior effectively and do the necessary repair work to maintain a strong positive relationship between parent and child. For example, if a mother grew up in a family in which a sibling was frequently angry and aggressive toward her and her siblings and her parents were unable to provide the necessary structure to create a sense of safety within the family, then mother's internal working model (mentalization) about a child's anger is that he will become an angry and aggressive adult just like her aggressive sibling, especially if that sibling grew up to be an angry and aggressive adult. If she viewed her sibling as intentionally hurtful toward her, then she may see anger as intentionally harmful and destructive. Mother will need to identify that this mentalization has been activated and learn to recognize that her child is a separate person who has the capacity to develop into an emotionally regulated adult. She will also need to recognize that anger is an emotion, like any other emotion, and is intended to communicate something. Her child's anger may be her child's attempt to communicate displeasure about a limit set and that this is developmentally age-appropriate for her child.

I believe that sibling relationships are important for children and their sense of belonging. Sibling relationships enhance a sense of connectedness within a family system. The ability for siblings to establish healthy relationship patterns with one another is important in the healing process. Trauma tends to isolate and make one feel separated from others in a way that feels ostracizing by the very nature of the traumatic experience itself. Herman (1997) discusses the impact of trauma, including disconnection, which in my opinion, is an overlooked area of the healing process for victims of trauma. She states, "traumatic events call into question basic human relationships. They breach the attachments of family, friendship, love and community. They shatter the construction of the self that is formed and sustained in relation to others" (Herman, 1997, p. 51). Traumatized children need to heal relationally and learn to trust again, which is why their ability to heal within the context of family relationships, including sibling relationships, is an important part of the healing process. Trauma shatters the ability to feel connected to others in a way that feels safe. Trauma impacts many families generationally and impacts the ability to engage in healthy relationship patterns. Traumatized children and their siblings need to learn to navigate relationship ups and downs effectively, especially in families where multiple siblings have experienced trauma.

While several siblings may have experienced trauma, their developmental age and personality structure will determine how they process and resolve the trauma and whether or not it interferes later on with their ability to engage in healthy relationships with adults and peers. Let's go back to some of the basic neurobiology of relationships—social engagement system. We are wired to be social beings. On the most basic level, my ability to understand other human beings and make sense of their behavior will help me to survive. In a family, siblings learn the social nuances of relationships to help them navigate their social world. Attachment and trauma have been widely studied and written about over the last several decades. Family therapists understand the value of examining family relationship patterns among parents and children and between siblings. If we are going to help traumatized children heal, then I believe it is important to explore the impact of trauma within the family system to help traumatized children and their families, including siblings, develop emotional connection within their relationships. It will be important to examine the concept of mentalization within sibling relationships and the impact of emotional connection within sibling relationships.

I have worked with many families impacted by abuse and have found it useful to gather information about what siblings know about the trauma and how they feel about the trauma. If we think back to the concept of resonance circuits and mirror neurons, we need to consider that this process also occurs within siblings. Consider a family in which one child was sexually abused and the other sibling was not abused. The non-abused sibling will likely experience guilt as well as relief that that trauma did not happen to him. He may not know what to say to his sibling about the abuse and the guilt and shame of knowing about the trauma can cause emotional distress as well as interfere with their healthy relationship building, contributing to increased disconnection for the abused child as well as the non-abused child. What will happen to that sibling relationship if the traumatized child consumes much of the family's time and resources due to emotional meltdowns and court involvement? The court process is an intensely stressful process for families as well as being time consuming. Parents may blame each other that the traumatic event happened which increases conflict within the family system.

These relational experiences within the family will form the foundation of interpersonal *maps* regarding relationships for the traumatized child and her siblings. Schermerhorn, Cummings, and Davies (2008) explored the internal representations of children regarding multiple family relationships. The authors examined family relationship processes to understand children's mentalizations of relationships within a family and attachment security with parents. Regarding family relationships, the authors proposed a transactional family process to conceptualize the reciprocal influences of family members on one another. Schermerhorn et al. "define transactional family dynamics as the collection of ways in which family members and family relationships influence one another, that is, mutual influence processes within the families over time" (p. 99).

Children Thrive When They Have a Positive Loving Relationship with Parents That Is Balanced with Structure and Limit Setting by Parents

Children thrive when they have a balance between a positive loving relationship with their parents to feel loved and when parents are able to provide leadership by establishing and maintaining healthy boundaries. Maintaining healthy boundaries helps to protect the relationship. Parents provide a leadership role to their children by helping to guide a child's social emotional development and learn to regulate their emotions.

It's important for children to learn to accept *no* and internalize self-control. When children believe their parents love and care for them, they will accept discipline because they know their parents love them. Van Der Kolk (2014) states, "a secure attachment combined with the cultivation of competency builds an *internal locus of control*, the key factor in healthy coping throughout life" (p. 115). As discussed previously, discipline is about teaching children to behave in ways that will help them to navigate the world by learning to engage in healthy relationships while also learning to live within healthy boundaries. Discipline is different from punishment in that punishment is designed to inflict pain as the primary motivator for changing behavior. Discipline takes the focus of teaching children about themselves and the need to behave in ways that will help them to be successful in life. Too much discipline without a positive relationship with parents will be experienced by children as harsh and uncaring. Too much positive relationship with parents and not enough discipline will not help children learn self-control in order to tolerate emotional distress.

Children learn to inhibit their behavior in order to think through problems and make positive choices. All human beings must learn to live within boundaries. For example, if I drive my car over the legal speed limit and a police officer is monitoring my speed, then I am going to get a speeding ticket (limit setting and boundaries). I must be able to think about my behavior in a calm rational manner to make choices that will enhance my life. During adolescence, our children must be able to come in contact with numerous influences that are outside of our control as parents and still make healthy choices by saying *no* to harmful influences (drugs, sexting, etc.) and *yes* to positive influences (maintaining good grades, choosing positive friends, etc.). A positive, healthy relationship with parents will help to facilitate the ability for their children to have a sense of being loved and belonging that will provide the foundation for making healthy choices.

Parents Provide the Foundation for Developing a Healthy Sense of Self and Developing a Sense of Security

Parents are the key to their children developing a positive sense of who they are as people, their ability to be successful, and feeling a sense of security that will allow them to venture out into the world and engage in life. Children gain a sense of themselves based on what parents mirror back to them. When parents engage with their children in ways that communicate love, acceptance, and value, both verbally and nonverbally, then children internalize those messages. For example, when parents are able to engage playfully with their children, as seen in their facial expressions and voice tone, then this intersubjectivity with their parents allows children to experience their parents as safe and loving. Parents can set limits with their children by remaining firm and loving. This communicates that parents are able to provide structure for children, which in turn creates a sense of security. According to Powell, Cooper, Hoffman, and Marvin (2014), children need parents to support their exploration of their world to gain a healthy independence. This healthy independence helps to develop self-competence, which provides the ability for children to tolerate frustration and accomplish their goals. When children feel safe, they will venture into the world to explore and that in turn will also increase a child's ability to learn about himself and what he is capable of achieving.

An Effective Parent Is a Self-aware Parent

As we have seen in the previous chapters, our experiences as children impact our realities of the present day. As a parent, the importance of recognizing our own emotional reactions and the factors contributing to those reactions are key to positive relationships with our children. Parents who can recognize their own emotional reactions and take responsibility for them are more likely to be able to respond to their children's misbehavior effectively. For example, if I have had a difficult day at work and my frustration level is high, then I am likely to respond in ways that reflect that high frustration level. If I am not able to manage my frustration effectively or even recognize it, then I may take it out on my family over things that otherwise might not have bothered me. Children need their caregivers to be able to help them to manage their own emotions as part of their development. Learning to manage our emotions is part of our growing up so that we can respond to the frustrations of life in ways that are productive. If parents are not able to recognize their own emotional reactivity, then they are likely to respond to their children in ways that do not fit the situation. Reflective functioning, or mentalizing, plays an important role in parenting because it helps parents to recognize the emotions and underlying intent of their child. Siegel (2011) states that "our awareness of another person's state of mind depends on how well we know our own" (p. 62). Parents need self-awareness to recognize when their emotional reactivity has been activated so they can accurately assess and understand their child's needs and intent in the moment.

Another important factor to consider is that parents have their own experiences regarding interactions with parents and family relationships. If a parent has grown up in a family in which parents were able to respond to their children with generally stable, calm interactions with a balance between healthy limit setting and strong positive relationships, then parents have those experiences wired in to their emotional circuitry. Parents will be able to respond to their children in a similar manner because their internal alarm systems are not activated. However, if parents were raised in homes in which one or both parents yelled and/or had rigid or unrealistic expectations, then it will be difficult for these parents to remain calm because "their past is their present." What I mean by this is that our past experiences are encoded into our memory and will influence our present perception of events. Previously discussed in the book, we examined memory and emotional triggers. Our brain will respond to an event and will set in motion a safety response via our neuroception circuits to alert our brain to potential danger. If our memory of an event is encoded with danger signals, then events occurring in our present that activate our memory of traumatic events from the past will elicit a danger alert. We see our present through memory of our past. Our past becomes the *lens* through which we understand what is happening in our present. When parents are able to recognize their danger signals, it will allow an opportunity to *stop, detach, think, and then respond* rather than instantly react in a manner that can trigger their children instead of helping to calm them.

Borelli et al. (2015) examined the role of reflective functioning, or mentalizing, in mitigating the negative impact of mother's history of childhood sexual abuse on their children. The study investigated intergenerational child sexual abuse and the role of mother's sensitivity to their children regarding exposure to child sexual abuse. According to Borelli et al., mentalization is

> the capacity to place oneself in the mind of others, imagining the intentions and reasons underlying others' and being aware of one's own reactions and their impact on others may facilitate the enactment of sensitive responses to others' emotional needs.
>
> (p. 3)

The authors found that mothers with their own histories of childhood sexual abuse who had high understanding of the impact of their abuse tended to be associated with lower risk of their child experiencing sexual abuse. Additionally, these mothers were able to provide more effective support to their child who had experienced sexual abuse. Borelli et al. (2015) stated that the research supports the notion that parents with unresolved trauma tend to be less able to engage in effective parenting behaviors to support secure attachments in their children. Since it is not uncommon for parents of traumatized children to have experienced their own childhood trauma, it is important for parents to develop the capacity for self-awareness that will help them to develop high mentalizing abilities.

Parents Provide the Foundation for Learning to Regulate Emotions

Parents are critical as role models for children to learn how to regulate their emotions. As parents are able to remain calm and attuned to the needs of their children, they provide the structure needed for children to learn to tolerate emotional distress and manage their emotions effectively. We see this early in child development. When infants become distressed, they will cry in order to communicate to their parents that something is wrong such as being hungry, wet diaper, etc. The baby's cry will alert the parent to be attentive to the child to determine what is needed. The parent's alertness triggers the parent's arousal system to move toward the child to determine what their baby is trying to communicate. If the parent is able to respond calmly and address the reason for the baby's distress, then the baby will be able to return to a calm state. Over time, when the parent is able to respond to the baby's needs with consistency and in a calm manner, then the neural circuitry is put in place to manage emotional distress effectively. This process occurs over time and parents just need to be good enough consistently in order to help their child learn to regulate their own emotions effectively. However, if a parent's arousal system is alerted and the parent is not able to regulate their own emotions to attend to the needs of their infant, then the infant will not be able to be soothed and will remain in a state of arousal. If the experience of the child has been that his or her parent is not able to respond consistently in a calm manner, then the child will have difficulties learning how to regulate his or her own emotions. Parents provide the framework for helping their children to manage emotions effectively.

Our Biology Directs Our Behavior and Is Heavily Influenced by Environment

The question of "nature versus nurture" in regard to childrearing has been an ongoing discussion among the experts. With the last three decades of brain research, most experts will agree there is an interactive process between our personality wiring at the biological level and the environmental experiences of the child. Our brain is plastid, which means that experiences will influence our neurobiology. As the brain develops over time, the experiences we have during our childhood will influence our neural circuitry. Our brain circuitry directs our behavior. When working with traumatized children and their families, this is a key point to remember. It is essential for therapists to help parents of traumatized children to fully understand the connection between the neurobiological impact of trauma and their child's behavior. If this connection is not fully understood by parents, then their ability to become therapeutic agents of change for their traumatized child will be impaired because they may not learn to implement the necessary attachment-based parenting skills taught in this treatment model.

References

Borelli, J. L., Compare, A., Snavely, J. E., & Decio, V. (2015). Reflective functioning moderates the association between perceptions of parental neglect and attachment in adolescence. *Psychoanalytic Psychology, 32*(1), 23–35. doi:10.3389/fpsyg.2019.01062

Herman, J. (1997). *Trauma and recovery: The aftermath of violence- from domestic abuse to political terror.* New York, NY: Basic Books.

Powell, B., Cooper, G., Hoffman, K., & Marvin, B. (2014). *The circle of security intervention: Enhancing attachment in early parent-child relationships.* New York, NY: The Guilford Press.

Schermerhorn, A. C., Cummings, E. M., & Davies, P. T. (2008). Children's representations of multiple family relationships: Organizational structure and development in early childhood. *Journal of Family Psychology, 22*(1), 89–101. doi:10.1037/0893-3200.22.1.89

Siegel, D. J. (2011). *Mindsight: The new science of personal transformation.* New York, NY: Bantam Books.

Van Der Kolk, B. (2014). *The body keeps score: Brain, mind, and body in the healing of trauma.* New York, NY: Penguin Books.

Observational Assessment Phase 8

In this chapter you'll meet the fictitious "Johnson" family, a composite based on several years of clinical experience with actual clients. This is just to maintain their privacy, but the situations are real and they represent the dynamics commonly seen when working with families who have experienced sexual abuse.

Throughout the four phases of treatment, you'll get to see how to apply the framework proposed in this book using clinical case information of two families, first the Johnson family and then the fictitious "Smith" family. You'll meet them in the next chapter. The Johnson family is made up of Helen (the mother), John (the stepfather), Helen's two daughters, Makenzi (11 years old), and Samantha (9 years old), and John's son, Thomas (14 years old). Helen's first husband died of cancer when Makenzi was 5 years old and John's first wife died in a car accident (hit by a drunk driver) when Thomas was 3 years old. Makenzi and her family received grief therapy through a hospice program. Thomas and John did not participate in therapy to help them grieve their loss.

Helen and John married when Makenzi was 8 years old and Thomas was 11 years old. The sexual abuse started gradually and had advanced by the time Makenzi finally disclosed to her guidance counselor what was happening to her. Upon disclosure of the sexual abuse, and investigation by child protective services, Thomas was removed from the home at the age of 13 and sent to a specialized residential treatment program for male sex offenders. Makenzi has been participating in individual therapy for about 10 months to address the impact of the sexual abuse.

Thomas had no history of trauma. However, his father had a history of being a victim of childhood sexual abuse multiple times by an extended family member when he was 8 and 9 years old. John had never disclosed the sexual abuse to anyone and had disconnected from his memories of it. Helen had no history of trauma. However, her parents divorced when she was 7 years old and her father moved away from the family. Helen grew up with her single mother and younger brother, and had no contact with her father who had a history of alcoholism when her parents divorced. Helen's parents divorced as a result of her father's extensive alcohol abuse. Helen learned that her father had died of complications from his alcoholism when she was in her early twenties. While Helen's first husband did not have an addiction problem when he died of cancer, there was a significant family history of addiction in her first husband's family.

Purpose of the Observational Assessment Phase

The purpose of the Observational Assessment phase and the role of the therapist during this phase of treatment are examined with the Johnson family. During this phase of treatment, therapists need to begin assessing parents' ability to use Family SPACE skills and their children's responses to them. Therapists will identify behaviors within the relationship interactions between parents and their children that are strengths, as well as any ineffective behaviors that need to change to increase the secure attachment relationships within the family. Therapists will also observe how family members regulate their emotions, and begin to assess each family member's window of tolerance for emotional distress. The ability to effectively regulate emotions is critical to establishing safe relationships and managing life stressors. The therapy process will elicit uncomfortable emotions and experiences, so it will be important to assess windows of tolerance and interaction patterns. Our window of tolerance is essentially the extent to which we are able to tolerate distressing thoughts, emotions, and experiences without becoming emotionally dysregulated (Porges, 2011; Siegel, 2011). People with a low window of tolerance will have difficulty regulating their emotions effectively in the midst of the distressing experience, and their subcortical limbic regions will likely dominate. People with a high window of tolerance will be able to more effectively tolerate emotionally distressing thoughts and experiences by remaining emotionally regulated, which will increase their ability to utilize their higher level prefrontal cortex regions to effectively address issues. Most people fall on a continuum from a high window of tolerance to a low window of tolerance. The goal of the treatment process is to assist family members to widen their windows of tolerance so they can engage in the change process.

Sexual abuse by an older sibling destroys safety within the family and parents need to carefully navigate supporting the needs of the trauma-tized child and re-establishing a sense of safety within the family. There-fore, it will be important to assess Helen and John's windows of tolerance during therapy sessions and observe how they are able to help their chil-dren work through the impact of the trauma. Siblings of traumatized chil-dren experience the secondary effects of the trauma within the family and, in my opinion, are often unseen in the healing process. Creating a safe, therapeutic space for Makenzi and her family members to address the impact of the sexual abuse within the family is a critical first step, while simultaneously allowing the initial observational assessment to take place.

The Observational Assessment phase begins after completing the biop-sychosocial assessment and obtaining information about the child's trauma, and determine if parents have a trauma history. It is critical to obtain information about family history of trauma, addiction, and mental illness, since this provides valuable information about trauma and attach-ment patterns. Observing interaction patterns within the family during this phase of treatment, helps therapists identify a starting point for what relationship interaction patterns to begin targeting during therapy ses-sions. The purpose of this initial phase of treatment is not so much a formal assessment of the attachment relationship patterns as it is to get an understanding about the family relationships and their attachment pat-terns in order to know how to help the family begin the process of change. There are good instruments to use to obtain information, how-ever, discussion of those instruments is outside the scope of this book.

Objectives Achieved during This Phase

Based on the family history gathered, there are several things that we can identify as starting points to examine within the family dynamics. First, there is a history of unresolved sexual trauma within the family since John had never disclosed his childhood sexual abuse—until his son was sent to a residential treatment center for adolescent male sex offenders. One of my favorite clinical frameworks to use for the ongoing assessment process is the concept of *running hypothesis*. As therapists, we gather *data* in the form of getting information from our clients about their presenting symptoms and histories. We use this data to form our *hypothesis* of the family dynamics as well as strengths and weaknesses to address in therapy sessions, based on our clinical training and experience of the information gathered. As we move through the treatment process from session to session, we are constantly gathering new information about what is working, what is not working, issues that arise during the treatment process, and how clients are responding to treatment. This information is adjusted as needed throughout the treatment process to maintain a running hypothesis. Throughout the phases of treatment, we are assessing and evaluating the information and forming a running hypothesis about the issues we need to address to help our clients successfully achieve their goals. This helps therapists provide structure and flexibility with families, since treatment and relationships are dynamic not static.

My initial running hypothesis for John about potential his strengths was that he chose to disclose his childhood abuse in order to help his son confront his own behavior. However, the negative impact of compartmentalizing such a profoundly negative experience would most likely be that he was emotionally cut off and, therefore, most likely had been unable to provide the emotional support Thomas needed to deal with the impact of his mother's death and John's subsequent remarriage. Going forward, he will likely struggle with connecting to his emotions enough to be Aware and Present with his wife and children. This hypothesis was further strengthened based on the fact that John and Thomas did not go to counseling to grieve the loss of Thomas' mother. Unexpected death due to a drunk driver is hard on families and can be traumatic due to the nature of the death. The grieving process is painful and John did not seem to be able to help his son and himself work through that grief. John's window of tolerance for emotional distress is likely to be low, which means he was not likely to effectively mirror that to Thomas. For John, the grief of losing his wife would be exacerbated by unresolved trauma. Additionally, my hypothesis would include the likelihood that Thomas was not able to develop a secure attachment with John due to John's emotional unavailability. John will likely need much coaching to develop Family SPACE skills.

My working hypothesis about dynamics within Makenzi's family would be that the family history of addiction has potentially impacted her parents' ability to form secure attachments with their children, and the death of Makenzi's father due to cancer likely exacerbated coping with difficulties. Cancer has a devastating impact on families due to extensive medical procedures and watching a loved one mentally and physically decline. As a therapist, it will be important to gather information from Helen and observe family interactions to assess her ability to provide emotional connection and structure for her children.

Another working hypothesis as part of my starting point with the Johnson family would be that blended families can take several years to fully re-establish a sense of family since two distinct families with two distinct family relationship patterns are merging into one family system. This is a complicated process and the adults need to figure out how the parenting dynamic will work in the family with the stepchildren. The children of both parents need to establish relationships and adjust to a new adult in a parenting role. The decision to remarry is one that is made by the adults and the children typically do not feel like they had a *voice* in that decision of their parents. Sexual abuse early within that transition period will destroy trust and create high tension in the home since these relationships within the family have not yet had time to be fully and positively established.

It would be important to assess the impact of the sexual abuse disclosure on the marital relationship between John and Helen. There are several questions to keep in mind when assessing family relationship dynamics. Since John is likely emotionally disconnected due to his own history of childhood sexual abuse and the death of his first wife, how will he manage his emotions that will become activated when dealing with the impact of his son's sexual abuse of his stepdaughter? How does Helen manage her own emotions that will be activated when addressing her stepson's sexual abuse of her daughter? What's going to happen to Thomas when he completes his treatment since his mother is deceased? What is the impact on Helen's ability to trust her husband whose son sexually violated her daughter? And, what has Samantha been told is the reason Thomas is no longer living in the home?

Sexual abuse victims often have ambivalent feelings when the perpetrator is removed from the home and child protective services and legal professionals become involved with family. While they are often relieved that the sexual abuse has stopped, they often feel tremendous guilt and worry about the perpetrator if that perpetrator is a member of the family. My running hypothesis was that Makenzi will likely struggle with her relationships in her family and feel tremendous guilt about being the reason Thomas was *made* to leave the family and go to a residential treatment center. Since sexual abuse often causes the victim to feel isolated and defective, Makenzi will probably have a strained relationship with her sister. Makenzi may struggle with feeling resentment toward Samantha for not having the abuse happen to her as well as possible anger that Samantha seemed to have a close relationship with Thomas. Helen and John reported that Makenzi tends to be bossy and rude to Samantha. They reported that Samantha would like to have a better relationship with Makenzi, but Makenzi emotionally pushes Samantha away. Samantha most likely feels confusion about all the changes in her family and unsure how to seek support. It will be important to help family members have an honest, developmentally appropriate discussion about the abuse and how to create safety.

These questions identify important data that needs to be identified and can identify a starting place to know where to start with this family. Clinically, our running hypothesis will adjust as we obtain more information through coaching sessions with parents, observations during sessions, and information reported by family members during the sessions. Using the concept of a running hypothesis helps me to clinically hold a lot of information and make clinical decisions about next steps to accomplish the overall goal of healing for the traumatized child and the family.

During the Observational Assessment sessions, therapists integrate the information obtained during the history gathering session with the observations of interaction patterns and the nuances of those interactions during sessions in this phase of treatment. Therapists need to consider and understand healthy parent–child interaction patterns as well as how siblings interact and the parental oversight of those sibling interactions. For instance, how do parents respond to the differing personality styles of each child and the differing developmental needs of each child? With the knowledge of what secure parent–child attachments look like and how parents manage the day-to-day challenges within family relationships, therapists will observe these relationship interaction patterns and identify strengths and weaknesses using Family SPACE skills.

Therefore, the objectives that need to be achieved during this phase of treatment are gathering information, and observing interaction patterns to assess the parents' ability as a starting point for *target points* for change, while also beginning to create a safe space for the family. These target points are the nuances within the interaction patterns and attachment relationships regarding parents' ability to use Family SPACE skills and their children's response. It will be important to identify strengths in the family to enhance and maintain them so that the focus is not just on the negative aspects of the family dynamics. Families already feel like they have failed when they initiate treatment and it's important to help them identify their strengths while also working on changing unhealthy dynamics.

Role of Therapist during Observational Assessment Phase

Since this is the initial phase of treatment, therapists also need to establish a therapeutic relationship with the family as a whole as well as each family member. Therapeutic relationship building with the family system is critical to helping the family prepare for change. As therapists, when we work with clients and invite them to engage in the therapeutic relationship, we are asking them to risk vulnerability because change requires a willingness to be open, honest, and willing to trust the clinician with their most private information. We are asking parents to trust that we will not pass judgement on them and treat them as bad parents. The ability to create an environment in which parents will begin to be more emotionally vulnerable will help therapists to help parents gain increased self-awareness. One of my many theories about what happens when we become parents and give birth (biological or adoption) to a child is that we give birth to guilt. As parents, we worry about the well-being of our children, are we doing right by them? During this phase of treatment, it's important for therapists to understand that we are asking families to invite us into their most private lives and to risk vulnerability. In order to achieve the therapeutic relationship, family members need to trust us and believe that we will treat them with respect and compassion. Families with long histories of trauma and attachment difficulties will have significant difficulty trusting us and allowing us into their lives because vulnerability may be not safe for them. Rather than write these families off as bad parents, we need to help them to experience the therapeutic relationship at the beginning of the healing process and that will happen when parents feel safe.

Therapeutic presence is a foundational component of effective treatment. It is the ability for a therapist to be attentive and emotionally present in the moment with clients. Siegel (2011) states that "the presence of a caring, trusted other person, who is attuned to our internal world, is often the initial key to widening our windows of tolerance" (p. 138). Therapists use of a mindfulness approach helps to bring a stronger sense of awareness and empathic attunement into the present moment with our client and help to establish a sense of safety. Geller and Porges (2014) explain the relevance of Polyvagal Theory in understanding the neurobiological underpinnings of therapeutic presence to facilitate emotional healing for clients. The authors state:

> according to the polyvagal theory, effective social communication can only occur during states when we experience safety, because only then are the neurobiological defense strategies inhibited. Thus, we suggest that one of the keys to successful therapy is for the therapist to be present and promote client safety so that the client's involuntary defense subsystems are down-regulated and the client's newer social engagement is potentiated. Functionally, during therapy, the repeated present moment encounters provide a "neural" exercise of the social engagement system.
>
> (Geller & Porges, 2014, p. 181)

Therapists also need to keep in mind that all family members need to experience these family sessions as safe. Different children may be more ready to engage in the therapeutic relationship than other siblings. It will be important for therapists to respect the needs of each sibling and parent while also working to engage everyone in the family. During this phase of treatment, therapists observe how parents are able to help their children engage in the treatment process and establish safety within the sessions with their children. Parents and their children will often play out their attachment struggles with the therapist as part of the transference process. Therapists can use this transference and countertransference by tapping into their resonance circuitry to obtain information that can help facilitate change, but first families will need to establish a sense of safety within the therapeutic relationship.

Purpose of the Interventions

The focus of this phase of the treatment process is to gain clinical information about the family's ability to engage in healthy relationship patterns that promote a positive self-concept, effective communication and problem solving, effective conflict negotiation, and enjoyment of interpersonal relationships. Therapists need to choose activities that require limited direction and involvement from the therapist to allow an opportunity for families to engage in the activity with very little oversight. The activities need to provide an opportunity for therapists to observe how family members work to accomplish a task, and how the children respond to parents and one another. The activities will provide an opportunity for therapists to observe how parents facilitate the accomplishment of the activity with their children. Since this phase lasts between three and four family sessions, therapists will have the ability to observe the family over a period of several sessions and use those observations to evaluate the relationship interaction patterns.

The observations of the family interactions will provide a starting point for therapists to assess strengths and weaknesses in the parent's ability to be attuned to their children while also providing structure. Therapists will observe how parents initiate structure and help the children to work toward accomplishing the task using Family SPACE skills. During this phase of treatment, therapists need to recognize the nuances of interactions between family members, but not intervene at this point unless there is a safety concern. Families with children in differing developmental stages require therapists to observe how the family system manages the needs of each child as well as accomplishing the overall family needs.

Choosing Play and Expressive Therapy Interventions

When choosing interventions for this phase of treatment, it's important to choose activities that have a low challenge quality to them while also allowing for the therapist to observe the interactions of family members with very little direction needed. The therapist will need to identify ways to include all family members in the activities. The activities need to be simple in format and general in nature to allow the possibilities of the activity to unfold, but will not be overwhelming for the family to problem solve ways to include all the family members. Activities also need to take into consideration the developmental stages of each of the children participating in the family. For example, a family with school-aged children and adolescents will need activities that can incorporate the developmental needs of school-aged children as well as the developmental needs of teens. Therapists can observe how the family adjusts the activities to include all family members with very little guidance from the therapist. It will be important for therapists to observe how the family adjusts the activity to include all family members. Most of these families are used to having to accommodate the different developmental needs within the family, and it will be important for the therapist to observe how the family achieves this goal.

During this phase of treatment, I like to use interventions described in the *Family Play Therapy* DVD created by Eliana Gil (2006) and its accompanying manual because these play therapy interventions provide ample opportunities to observe family interaction patterns with limited direct involvement from the therapist. Gil (1994) was one of the pioneers in play therapy to develop interventions that included all family members in the play sessions to help families heal. Her family play therapy interventions include the use of art, puppets, and sand tray. There are numerous resources available for therapists to find interventions to use with families, including their own creativity. See Resources at the back of this book for more information about play therapy intervention resources. Essentially, the goal in this phase of treatment is to use play and expressive arts interventions that allow therapists to observe the interactions patterns with minimal involvement that will also be non-challenging enough to help family members feel safe.

Identifying Relationship Patterns

In the first session with the Johnson family, Helen, John, Makenzi, and Samantha were present. The activity for this first session is to create their Ideal World in the sand tray using the sand tray figures (aka figures) supplied in the play therapy room. I like to use this intervention in the beginning stages of treatment because it has a positive focus, which helps to reduce defensiveness and negativity. It also does not require drawing which can create a sense of inadequacy because teens and adults tend to believe they need to be artists, which activates perfectionism in the session. Since I want to focus on creating safety, I try to choose interventions in the first session that will decrease potential negativity because family members come to the first session with heightened sense of anxiety and guardedness. Sand tray figures allow family members to simply choose what they like and what makes them feel good in the moment.

During the first session, I will introduce family members to the sand tray and the figures on the shelves so they understand what they are allowed to use for the intervention. Next, I will provide the following instructions:

Choose the figures to create your Ideal World as a family. It can be any type of world your family chooses and however you want your world to be. Each family member can choose up to ten sand figures maximum, which means if you want more than ten figures, you will need to choose which figure or figures to return to the shelves so you don't use more than ten figures per person. Also, if you did not choose the figure to include in the world, then you cannot remove the figure because we need to respect that each person in the family gets to have a choice in what goes into the Ideal World.

After I give that direction, I allow family members to get started with creating their Ideal World in the sand tray.

It's often hard for parents to know how to get started because they are more used to talking than playing, so therapists must resist the temptation to *rescue* parents as much as possible so you can observe how parents manage their uncertainty and help their children engage in the process. In the first session with the Johnson family, Samantha was the first to begin accumulating figures. Samantha initiated interaction with Helen to invite Helen to enjoy the activity with her and begin creating their Ideal World together in the sand tray. This resulted in Helen becoming more comfortable, though still somewhat cautious, and she invited Makenzi to join them in the activity. Makenzi and Samantha interacted with their mother independently of each other initially. John seemed to hang back as he watched his wife and stepdaughters begin to pick figures and place them in the sand tray. His eyes moved between watching his wife and stepdaughters as they talked and smiled with Helen and placed their figures in the sand tray. Helen eventually encouraged John to join in the activity by inviting him to pick figures as well, though he continued to hang back and observe. Helen began to ask her daughters what they wanted their sand world to be like and how they wanted to use the space in the sand tray. Samantha was smiling, picking figures, and placing her figures in the sand tray. Helen helped Makenzi join in the activity by talking with her about what she might like to pick and showing Makenzi her own figures to get her opinions on the figures and invited discussion about what theme they might have in their Ideal World.

Eventually, John slowly made his way to the shelves and began to methodically explore his options for sand tray figures. Helen noticed John moving toward the shelves and smiled at him as if to help him feel comfortable in the session so that he could join them in the activity. John quietly and slowly picked some figures and methodically placed the figures in the sand as if in his own world. He did not verbally interact with his stepdaughters initially. Helen posed a question to the family to elicit ideas for a theme for their Ideal World. John then also asked his stepdaughters what they would like to be in their sand world. Eventually Samantha and Helen took the lead in the discussion since Makenzi did not offer ideas. Makenzi seemed to pick figures and quietly placed them in the sand tray. John followed the lead of Helen and Samantha, and chose figures that fit the theme of their choosing. Helen and Samantha reminisced about past pleasant vacations to the mountains and hiking, so that was the theme for their Ideal World.

Samantha began picking figures in excess of her allotted ten figures, which caught the eye of Makenzi. The following is the interaction in the session:

Makenzi: Hey! You have 12 figures in there and you're only allowed to
    have 10. You need to put some back!
Samantha: You don't get to tell me what to do!
Helen: Samantha, you do have more than ten figures, so which ones to
    you want to put back?
Samantha to Makenzi: Fine! You're always bossing me.
Makenzi: Well if you followed the rules, then I wouldn't need to be bossy.
    Anyway, you know you're the favorite one anyway.
Helen: Makenzi, you know that's not true. We tell you all the time that
    we love you. I wish you would stop saying that. Samantha, just put
    some back, and Makenzi, why don't you tell us what you want to have
    in our world?
John: Girls, let's just focus on doing what we were asked to do.
Makenzi: Fine!

Samantha spent time thinking about her choice of figures and which figures to switch out in the sand tray. She continued to interact with Helen and observed Makenzi, but did not interact with Makenzi directly. Helen seemed to be the moderator to help Samantha and Makenzi remain engaged in the activity. Helen cautiously initiated playful interactions with John at times. John cautiously interacted with Helen and followed her lead helping the girls to complete the activity. He remained predominantly quiet during most of the session. Samantha initiated asking John if he liked the figures she picked and he affirmed her choice of figures in a quiet manner. John and Makenzi did not interact directly with one another.

During the session, therapists quietly observe and allow parents to take the lead in the session. Therapists only observe interactions, facial expressions, voice tone, body language, and how family members respond to one another. Parents may try to enlist the help of therapists to provide more instructions for the activity and may be unsure what therapists are expecting of them. Therapists can calmly reassure parents and family members that there is no wrong or right way to complete the activity, then remain as peripheral as possible. Maintaining a calm, peripheral presence provides the ability to allow parents to take the lead in the session and therapists to observe interactions.

In this first session with the Johnsons, several observations are made that provide information about relationships in this family. John seems to be less active in providing structuring and engaging in playful interactions with his stepdaughters. He is slower to engage in the activity than wife and stepdaughters, choosing instead to be more peripheral in the session. Samantha is more extroverted in the session and invites Helen to engage in the play activity with her. Helen positively responds to Samantha's invitation to join her, although somewhat cautiously. This intersubjectivity between Helen and Samantha is observed in their mutual enjoyment of their interactions and the activity. Helen is playfully present with Samantha once she was more comfortable with the activity, and both of them seemed pleased with their mutual enjoyment of the activity. Helen also demonstrated the ability to provide structure with flexibility to adjust to both daughters. However, she seemed to struggle to know how to help Makenzi feel like a valuable member of the family.

Helen seemed to be attentive and attuned to Makenzi's reluctance to engage in the activity and gently invited her to join in the activity. Makenzi responded positively to Helen's invitation to join the activity, but was still somewhat guarded and reluctant to fully mutually enjoy the activity with her mother. She did not engage in the activity with her sister. In fact, Makenzi seemed focused on policing Samantha to ensure Samantha did not break any rules during the activity. Based on her statements to Samantha, it appears that Makenzi resents Samantha and perceives Samantha to be more accepted than Makenzi in the family. It might be hypothesized that Makenzi feels unacceptable due to the sexual abuse and possibly judged for "ruining the family" since Thomas was removed from the home after her disclosure about the sexual abuse. Additionally, Makenzi may be experiencing shame about the sexual abuse which makes her feel different and unacceptable in relationships. Makenzi may view Samantha as getting special treatment because Samantha does not appear to be "damaged" like Makenzi. Samantha approached her mother to engage in the activity and not Makenzi, which may indicate that Samantha likely feels rejected by Makenzi and constantly judged by her. This seems to be interfering in the ability of the sisters to have a healthy sibling relationship.

It might also be hypothesized that John has an emotionally distant relationship with his stepdaughters and depends on Helen to take the lead in parenting. Allowing Helen to take the lead in parenting may be due to being the stepfather and not a biological parent. Stepparents often need to establish a positive relationship with their stepchildren before their stepchildren will accept correction for their misbehavior. Parents in blended families also need to identify what role the stepparent will play when it comes to structuring and discipline. This can be a conflictual area for blended families.

Since we know John spent most of his life making sure to disconnect emotionally due to his childhood sexual abuse, we can hypothesize that it is difficult for him to emotionally connect with his stepdaughters. We may also hypothesize that John may be struggling with his own shame due the impact of his sexual abuse which may be exacerbated by his shame that his son sexually abused his stepdaughter and he did not see the signs to be able to protect his stepdaughter and his son. Parents experience significant shame and guilt when their child is sexually abused about not protecting their child. If they have their own history of sexual abuse, those trauma memories will be activated and impact their relationships in the family.

Parent Coaching Session

After the first three to four family sessions, therapists will have obtained data to form their initial running hypotheses. Therapists will review the video of the family sessions and identify several video clips to view with parents in the parent coaching session. Since therapists are focused on building therapeutic rapport to create safety within the session, they need to make emotional deposits into their relationship with parents. It will be important to identify several video clips of positive interactions to show parents. This will serve two purposes: (1) establish safety and trust in the therapeutic relationship and (2) show examples of what parents are doing well and need to continue to do. Therapists also need to help parents understand interaction patterns between siblings and explore ways to help parents encourage healthier relationship behaviors between siblings. I generally like to use the analogy of a *sandwich approach* when working with parents. In the first several parent coaching sessions, therapists want to identify several positive interaction behaviors to one ineffective parenting behavior, and then follow that ineffective behavior example with a few more positive examples. This is especially true in the first parent coaching session because parents will be expecting you to show them all the wrong things they are doing. Therapists can *sandwich* feedback about the ineffective behavior with positive examples, while also observing parental responses to the constructive feedback.

Therapists need to have an idea of what positive and constructive feedback they want to show parents in the video clips and elicit feedback from parents about the thoughts and emotions they were experiencing during that interaction. This will help therapists to obtain parents' perspectives during interactions to better understand how the parents are perceiving those interactions. This invitation using an empathic curiosity approach helps parents to share their experiences and thoughts with therapists. I'll demonstrate this in the following example of a parent coaching discussion using reflexive communication and empathic curiosity with Helen and John regarding Helen's attempts to engage John in the activity.

Therapist (showing the video clip of the Ideal World activity): Helen, I noticed you smile here at John when he was standing there by the wall. I'm wondering what you were thinking at that moment?

Helen: I noticed John standing by the wall and he seemed to be having a hard time joining us. He doesn't play much with the girls.

Therapist: What were you feeling at that moment?

Helen: I was worried that he might not want to participate.

Therapist: John, what were you thinking when you were standing by the wall here? I'm wondering what it was like for you in the session?

John: It was weird. I didn't really know what you wanted me to do.

Therapist: It sounds like both of you are unsure how to navigate your relationships with the girls and John and adjust to what has happened? John, how was it for you when Helen smiled at you and encouraged you to join in?

John: That's Helen. She's usually trying to get me to do stuff with the girls.

Therapist: How is that for you that Helen wants you to do stuff with the girls?

John: Fine. I'm just not always sure what to do with them. I have never had daughters before. I only had Thomas before marrying Helen. And, I'm not sure how comfortable Makenzi is with me since Thomas did what he did. I'm not always sure what to do, so I let Helen take the lead with the girls.

Therapist: Helen, I'm curious what that's like for you that John tends to wait to follow your lead?

Helen: I mean, I get it. He's never had daughters and what happened with Thomas makes it hard. I know he feels a lot of guilt that his son did that to Makenzi. He's quiet anyway, so it's just kind of tense at times. Sometimes, I feel responsible to make sure everyone gets along. That's just how it is for now.

Therapist: John, I'm curious what you're thinking about what Helen said?

John: She's right. I feel guilty and I'm not sure how to make that up to Makenzi. I just don't know what to do, so I don't really do anything.

In the first parent coaching session with Helen and John using the video example of the interaction example provided earlier in the chapter, I would highlight Helen's ability to follow the lead of Samantha to engage playfully with Samantha and gently invite Makenzi to join in the activity. I might highlight John's ability to support Helen in the session by helping to structure the session to accomplish the task of creating the Ideal World. As shown in the discussion example with Helen and John, I focused on exploring the relationship dynamics between Helen and John and their ability to work collaboratively to use Family SPACE skills.

From the information gained in the parent coaching session and observing the family interactions during sessions, therapists need to elicit questions from parents to help parents feel empowered in the treatment process. Therapists also want to make sure to address parent questions and concerns in the session to incorporate those concerns into the next phase of Engagement. During the parent coaching session, therapists will provide feedback to parents about what the next four sessions will focus on and enlist parents to provide suggestions as to what they want to make sure to target in those sessions.

In the next four sessions with the Johnson family the Safety and Engagement phase of treatment begins. Helen and John identified that they are not sure how, or if, they should explain to Samantha why Thomas was removed from the home and sent away to a residential treatment center. Helen and

John want to respect Makenzi's privacy and they want to protect Samantha from potential distress after learning what Thomas did to Makenzi. They are also unsure how that information will impact the relationship between Makenzi and Samantha. It was also decided that helping John and Helen to figure out how to effectively co-parent their children will be an important place to start since both Helen's children and John's son have lost their other parent. The death of their spouses created a concern that their children might feel like John and Helen are trying to replace the other parent. Since it would be important to provide some guidance to John and Helen how to address the elephant in the room with Samantha and Makenzi regarding Thomas' sexual abuse of Makenzi, it was decided that the next family session would include only Helen, John, and Makenzi to have a discussion with Makenzi about how and what to communicate to Samantha about the sexual abuse and Thomas' subsequent removal from the home. Samantha had only been told that Thomas was in a residential treatment program because he was not able to be safe due to his anger outbursts at home and aggressiveness toward Samantha and Makenzi.

As the therapist, my focus for the next one to two sessions in the Safety and Engagement phase will be to help Makenzi feel empowered to talk about what she needs regarding respect for her privacy. I would also need to help the parents and Makenzi have an honest and respectful discussion about when and how to tell Samantha about Makenzi's sexual abuse by Thomas and how the family will work to provide a safe home for everyone. In addition to facilitating that discussion for one to two sessions, the next additional two to three sessions will focus on identifying interventions that will help family members to feel safe in the sessions and begin developing more effective communication as well as identifying their emotions and emotional triggers. This will help work toward the ultimate goal of John being able to develop more secure attachment relationships with Makenzi and Samantha. The girls will need experiences with John in a safe manner that will eventually help them accept his structuring skills in the family. Before Samantha's relationship with Makenzi can be repaired, their relationships with parents will need to be strengthened so they can tolerate the challenge of repairing their sibling relationship. Makenzi and Samantha will need to use the support of Helen and John to help them navigate through the likely conflict and mistrust that may occur when challenged to expand their windows of tolerance during the later phases of treatment. Now that a plan is discussed with parents, the Safety and Engagement phase of treatment will begin and parents are on board with the plan.

References

Geller, S. M., & Porges, S. W. (2014). Therapeutic presence: Neurophysiological mechanisms mediating feeling safe in therapeutic relationships. *Journal of Psychotherapy Integration, 24*(3), 178–192. doi:10.1037/a0037511

Gil, E. (1994). *Play in family therapy.* New York, NY: The Guilford Press.

Gil, E. (2006). *Family play therapy: The benefits of using play in family therapy* [DVD and Booklet]. Fairfax, VA: Starbright Training Institute for Family and Child Therapy. Retrieved from https://selfesteemshop.com.

Porges, S. W. (2011). *The polyvagal theory: Neurophysiological foundations of emotions, attachment, communication, self-regulation.* New York, NY: W.W Norton & Company.

Siegel, D. J. (2011). *Mindsight: The new science of personal transformation.* New York, NY: Bantam Books.

Safety and Engagement Phase   **9**

Chapter 9 provides information about the role of therapists during this phase of treatment, and the tasks to be accomplished by the family. Therapists need to maintain attunement with the parents in order to strengthen the therapeutic relationship and provide mirroring to them, so that parents will, in turn, provide mirroring to their children. During this phase of treatment, it's important to teach family members about mindfulness and about coping/calming skills. Clients need to have the ability to tolerate their emotional distress before significant changes can be made, which will require the ability to use the skills to increase their windows of tolerance. This chapter also provides information about types of play and expressive therapy interventions to use during this phase of treatment, based on the knowledge gained in previous chapters about trauma, attachment, and interpersonal neurobiology. Also in this chapter you'll meet the Smith family. Again, as with the Johnson family in the last chapter, for privacy purposes, the Smith family is a fictional family based on clinical issues seen in my experiences working with many similar families. This clinical case example will demonstrate the practical implementation of the model during this phase of treatment.

The Smith family: Paul (age 40) and Julie (age 38) are married and have three children, PJ (age 8), Sara (age 6), and Brendan (age 3). Paul and Julie were separated for six months due to Paul's alcoholism which had led to a domestic violence incident. The children witnessed their parents arguing about Paul's drinking. Paul lost control of his temper, and physically assaulted Julie, hitting her in the face and throwing her up against a wall. Julie had yelled for PJ to call 911, and PJ called the police because he was afraid for his mother's life. Paul was arrested and the children watched their father taken away in handcuffs. Paul entered an inpatient substance abuse program and lived with his parents until he moved back into the family home one month ago.

Julie grew up in a home with an alcoholic father who was abusive to her mother. Her own parents divorced when Julie was 12 due to her father's abuse and addiction. When her father was drunk he would yell at his wife, at Julie, and at her younger brother. When Julie's father physically abused her brother when he was only 7 years old, Julie's mother ended the marriage. Child protective services was called and Julie's father was charged with child abuse. Julie's mother took Julie and her brother to counseling after the incident to address domestic violence in her family. Julie's father moved out of state and she did not have contact with him after her parents divorced. Her mother later remarried and she calls her stepfather her father. Her stepfather eventually adopted Julie and her brother. Paul's own father was an alcoholic until Paul was 14 years old when he went to substance abuse treatment and became active in AA. His father has been sober for 26 years. His parents are still married and a strong support for Paul and Julie.

My working hypothesis for the Smith family includes recognizing relationship patterns and impact of generational addiction and abuse. Mentalizations encoded regarding safety in relationships need to be explored and identified to help family members recognize their interpretations of behaviors and intentions, which will help them to make corrections in their understanding of one another as needed. Julie has a trauma history due to the domestic violence and abuse of her younger brother. Paul and Julie have family histories of addiction, and Paul has an addiction for which he is newly sober. PJ and his siblings observed their parents constantly arguing about Paul's addiction, so their neuroception systems will likely be on high alert and their windows of tolerance for conflict will be low. PJ and his siblings observed significant conflict and emotion dysregulation. Sara tends to emotionally withdraw when conflict occurs. Brendan tends to cry and seek comfort from his mother when conflict in the home occurs. PJ likely feels guilty about calling 911 and has nightmares about his father's arrest. PJ has difficulty regulating his emotions and needs his parents to mirror emotion regulation to him while implementing Family SPACE skills and using the 3 Rs of Relationship. Paul will need to mirror to his children that he can effectively regulate his emotions, and help them to feel secure to use his support when they are distressed. Paul's ability to regulate his emotions effectively and maintain sobriety are critical to establishing safety within the family and mirroring effective emotion regulation to his children. Julie and Paul are also in couples counseling to help them address their marital issues that can undermine their co-parenting ability if not addressed. Their willingness to address their marital issues and having the support of Paul's parents are strengths for this family which can help them when navigating through difficult issues.

Purpose of the Safety and Engagement Phase

During the Safety and Engagement phase of treatment, therapists will continue to build upon establishing safety within sessions to help family members gain stability and safety within their relationships. Since this phase is early in treatment, family members will continue to be guarded. Therapists need to continue creating a foundation of safety within the sessions while introducing skills that will help them during the change process. Frustration needs to be kept to a minimum during the early phase of treatment in order to help family members focus on developing a sense of safety. Therapists need to assess the windows of tolerance of family members, and the parents' ability to co-regulate their children's emotions. The interventions in the family sessions during this phase will focus on helping family members develop coping/calming skills to regulate emotions and begin to communicate their needs. During this phase I like to focus on teaching deep breathing skills and the benefits of practicing mindfulness, labeling emotions in order to develop a *feelings vocabulary*, and helping family members to articulate things that have been bothering them, bringing attention to each person's perception of the issues.

Siegel (2011) advocates for the benefits of mindfulness skills to help provide clients with the ability to be open to new ways of understanding one another, and situations. Mindfulness can be a key skill to help clients improve their mentalizing capacity. Fonagy and Allison (2014) argue that mentalizing is an important component of establishing trust, especially in the therapeutic relationship when working with clients who have personality disorders. The authors view mentalizing as a way to

> help the patient to relinquish the rigidity that characterizes individuals with enduring personality pathology. The relearning of flexibility allows the patients to go on to learn, socially, from new experiences and achieve change in their understanding of their social relationships and their own behavior and actions.
>
> (Fonagy & Allison, 2014, p. 372)

Teaching mindfulness skills to family members early in the treatment process will help them to develop the skills necessary for the change process while also helping to establish trust within the therapy sessions through the use of effective coping skills. Siegel (2011) states that "the brain changes physically in response to experience, and new mental skills can be acquired with intentional effort, with focused awareness and concentration" (p. 84). Mindfulness provides the ability to intentionally pay attention to the *present moment* and be more intentionally aware of what one is experiencing internally. This can be difficult for people who have become disconnected within themselves, using that as a coping strategy to manage emotionally distressing situations. Therapists will need to help clients learn to internally *reconnect* and increase their windows of tolerance using mindfulness skills.

This phase of treatment begins to lay the foundation of safety in order to challenge and replace relationship patterns during the next phase of treatment. A foundation of trust needs to be established in order to help parents and their children increase their ability to tolerate their emotional distress when challenged to make changes that will feel uncomfortable, but are necessary for healing to occur. Crenshaw and Mordock (2007) recommend keeping frustration levels low in the early phase of treatment while helping clients to increase their window of tolerance for emotional distress in order to avoid their regression to using maladaptive coping skills. The authors have worked with traumatized children who manifest maladaptive behaviors of aggression in their fight or flight response to perceived threat. Therapists need to help parents of traumatized children recognize when their children are overwhelmed and avoid responding in punitive ways to correct their child's behavior. Helping parents to recognize the benefit of using a Family SPACE skills framework will result in a more effective parenting approach to address maladaptive behavior.

Therapists will provide psychoeducation to parents during parent coaching sessions which are about the Family SPACE skills framework, and about using the 3 Rs of Relationship skills. The parent coaching sessions focus on helping parents recognize when and how to implement these skills in the sessions and how to use them at home with their children. Therapists need to help parents recognize the need to be aware of, and identify, their mentalizations of family relationships and safety. Wallin (2007) states that

> a mentalizing stance creates the potential for affective, cognitive, and behavioral flexibility, in large part because it allows us to

envision multiple perspectives on any given experience, enhancing the likelihood that pre-existing models can be updated and habitual patterns "deautomatized."

(p. 136)

A high mentalization ability increases the likelihood that parents are able to recognize their separateness from their children to be attuned, aware, and present with their children. Helping parents to adopt a mindfulness practice will help them to strengthen their skills for Family SPACE. Awareness and presence skills of Family SPACE are critical for parents to develop in order to maintain emotion regulation and repair relationship ruptures. Parents who are unable to recognize their own emotional triggers are often unable to effectively regulate their emotions and mirror emotion regulation to their children. This low mentalizing capacity can negatively impact the ability for children to experience positive intersubjectivity necessary for secure attachments and for parents to mirror effective emotion regulation to their children. Fonagy and Allison (2014) stated that mentalizing

is a developmental process that relies on good enough attachment relationships and early attachments in particular, as they reflect the extent to which our subjective experiences were adequately mirrored by a trusted other: that is, the extent to which attachment figures have been able to respond to contingent and marked affective displays of their experience in response to the infant's subjective experience, thus enabling the child to develop second-order representations of its own subjective experiences.

(p. 372)

Paul and Julie both grew up in homes that were not emotionally safe, so it will be important for them to recognize their own emotions and demonstrate healthy intersubjectivity with their children to strengthen their attachment relationships.

Parents with low mentalizing abilities are likely to have significant attachment histories of their own. It is essential for therapists to recognize parents with low mentalizing abilities since this will be an indication that parents will require therapists to assess the windows of tolerance for emotional distress. These parents will require more time in this phase of treatment and will likely need to return to this phase throughout the treatment process to help them remain engaged in the change process and able to use therapist support. Low mentalization capabilities in parents indicates that parents have difficulty recognizing the needs of their children and ability to manage their emotional distress when feeling emotionally threatened. Crenshaw and Mordock (2007) identified several areas that parents may struggle in their parenting that will decrease parenting effectiveness. These include the following: (1) unfulfilled dependency needs, (2) poor self-concept, (3) bonding failures with their child, (4) disturbed identity formation, (5) cognitive immaturity, (6) chaotic lifestyles, (7) denied affects, and (8) socially isolated. These parenting difficulties indicate low mentalizing abilities and will require an empathic, attuned therapist to help parents recognize these issues as barriers to their goal of a healthy, well-functioning family.

Interventions in this phase of treatment will be mildly challenging initially to avoid overwhelming family members too soon. Throughout the treatment process it may be necessary to go back to this phase of treatment to re-establish safety and help family members stay engaged in treatment. Therapists need to be attuned to parents and their children within the sessions in order to read cues of the family and adjust interventions as needed. I like to use the analogy of a dance when helping family members progress through treatment. Therapists sometimes *lead* in the dance and sometimes *follow* the lead of family members. The dance of therapy requires therapists to tune in to their resonance circuits to know when to lead and when to follow with the ultimate goal of helping parents to know how to do this with their children.

Tasks to Accomplish during This Phase and Choosing Interventions

There are essentially four tasks to accomplish during the Safety and Engagement phase (see Figure 9.1) which will help to create the foundation needed before challenging family relationship patterns. These tasks are: (1) psychoeducation with parents attachment repair skills using the 3 Rs of Relationship and the framework of Family SPACE skills, (2) teaching coping/calming skills and mindfulness skills, especially the WiseMind skill to increase windows of tolerance, (3) helping family members to identify their emotions and articulate their concerns safely, and (4) establishing safety within relationships among family members. Figure 9.1 provides an overview of the tasks that need to be accomplished and the

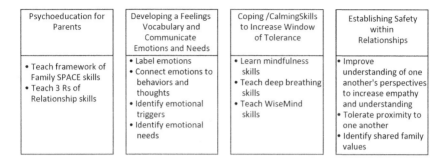

Psychoeducation for Parents	Developing a Feelings Vocabulary and Communicate Emotions and Needs	Coping /CalmingSkills to Increase Window of Tolerance	Establishing Safety within Relationships
• Teach framework of Family SPACE skills • Teach 3 Rs of Relationship skills	• Label emotions • Connect emotions to behaviors and thoughts • Identify emotional triggers • Identify emotional needs	• Learn mindfulness skills • Teach deep breathing skills • Teach WiseMind skills	• Improve understanding of one another's perspectives to increase empathy and understanding • Tolerate proximity to one another • Identify shared family values

Figure 9.1 Skills Focus for Safety and Engagement Phase

focus on the interventions. Therapists need to choose play and expressive arts interventions that will focus on accomplishing these tasks. There are numerous play therapy techniques in a variety of play therapy resources to teach these skills during sessions that are fun and engaging. (See Resources section at the back of the book for a list).

Therapists will use the first two to three sessions during this phase of treatment to provide psychoeducation to parents teach them the Family SPACE skills and the 3 Rs of Relationship skills. It's important to invite parents into the teaching process to help them feel heard and understood. This will help therapists create a strong therapeutic alliance with parents and increase the ability of parents to accept constructive feedback from therapists. Parents and therapists can identify which components of these skills they are more proficient at, and which skills create a struggle for parents. At some point during the treatment process, there may be a rupture in the therapeutic alliance so therapists will need to work through the disruption to help parents regain trust. This is an important part of the treatment process since therapists need to mirror these skills to parents.

In addition to providing psychoeducation about the Family SPACE skills and the 3 Rs of Relationship skills, parents and their children need skills to help them increase their windows of tolerance to manage frustration. Keeping the frustration level low initially in this phase will provide the ability to develop coping/calming and mindfulness skills. This is accomplished by helping family members develop a common feelings vocabulary, learn coping/calming and mindfulness skills, and increasing safety within relationships by increasing intersubjectivity among family members, allowing children to tolerate proximity to one another, and use support. Children will not use support from family members with whom they do not feel safe because their neuroception circuits will activate their threat systems. When this happens, children will not tolerate close proximity to those from whom they experience a threat to their safety. This will be evident in their body language and behavior. It was evident with Paul and his children. The children's experience of Paul was that he was not safe. This created an internal dissonance for the children because they need their father for protection and desire his love, yet his unpredictable and aggressive behavior was frightening to them. PJ would desire to spend time with his father, yet his window of tolerance for emotional distress was low, as seen in his emotional meltdowns when his father was frustrated. Sara was quiet around her father and seemed to be more withdrawn when he was in the room. Brendan tended to stay close to Julie.

Therapists need to choose interventions that will help family members recognize and label emotions so that they have a common language for identifying emotions, communicating their emotions, and experiencing relationships as safe. It is also important to teach coping/calming and mindfulness skills that parents and their children can do together. Paul and his children need to begin to create their feelings vocabulary and increase the children's ability to observe Paul regulating his emotions. Interventions also need to increase a sense of safety and playful intersubjectivity to improve safe proximity with Paul. Developing mindfulness skills as a family can be a wonderful way to increase intersubjectivity experiences and enhance their relationship safety. Parents and children can practice these skills at home in between therapy sessions.

Therapists need to help parents understand that they will be acting as a co-regulator for their children and will need to regulate their own emotions in order to be attuned to their child's needs in the moment of distress to effectively help their child. I love the WiseMind skill taught in Dialectical Behavior Therapy (Linehan, 2015). Parents will benefit from using the Wise-Mind skill to help them regulate their own emotions and tap into their resonance circuits to recognize their child's needs in the moment, and figure out an effective parenting response. WiseMind is essentially a synthesis of two states of mind: emotion mind and logic mind (also known as reasonable mind or rational mind). Emotion mind is essentially when we are experiencing and connected to our emotions and consists only of our emotions. Our emotions add "color" to our experiences in life. Relationships, for example, require that we experience love and closeness in order to have a fully satisfying life. We cannot think logically about a relationship to fully experience the relationship. Thinking logically requires our logic mind, which consists of logic, cause-and-effect, and does not involve emotions. If we allow our emotions to rule our actions, then we end up experiencing difficulties because our emotions can influence the positive and negative quality of our experiences. We need to use logic mind to help us make logical decisions. However, if we are strictly in logic mind then we are disconnected from our emotions and will miss the valuable information that can be gleaned from our emotions. For example, I may be feeling angry if someone is mean toward me or disregards one of my boundaries on a regular basis. My anger provides information to me that something is wrong and needs to be explored. I need to access logic mind when making decisions. For example, if I am planning to buy a car then I need to think about what I can afford and how I need to use my car (i.e. commuting long distances to work each day or transporting multiple children to their various activities). Wise-Mind accesses beneficial information from emotion mind and logic mind to help me navigate through our day. In the example of buying a car, I want to use logic mind to help me decide on the financial and utilitarian aspects of a vehicle and I want to use emotion mind to make sure that I choose a car that I will also enjoy driving.

The WiseMind skill can help parents to regulate their emotions and make parenting decisions from a more integrated and balanced position. If my child is rude or defiant, then I can use the WiseMind skill to help me recognize and label my own emotions to help me understand my own emotional response, then access logic mind to help me effectively identify my child's behavior cues and put their behavior in context. This will help me to make decisions about how to address my child's behavior. Acting from emotion mind in a dysregulated state will result in ineffective parenting and ruptures in my relationships with my children. Likewise, acting from a strictly logic mind will not allow the ability for me to understand the emotional *roots* to my behavior and I may act in an emotionally disconnected manner that will not allow me to use many of the Family SPACE skills such as empathy, presence, awareness, and curiosity. WiseMind can help to provide a framework to engage with children in a more emotionally regulated and wise manner, which ultimately will allow parents to effectively co-regulate their child's emotions when they are emotionally distressed. Accessing WiseMind will require parents to learn mindfulness skills to be more aware of their internal experiences, which will increase their mentalizing capabilities and intersubjectivity experiences with their children.

Case Illustration with Bubbles for Deep Breathing

The following is an example of a family session to teach deep breathing skills and improve safety within relationships. Since the neuroception circuits for the children in the Smith family will be easily activated to perceive threat, it will be important for the family to have access to coping/calming skills and experience playfulness within the sessions to increase their ability to experience family members in a safe way. Also, the children in the Smith family are young and will need interventions that can engage the children in the session. I love using bubbles to teach deep breathing. Bubbles tend to be irresistible for young children, which will increase the playfulness and fun in the session. Since the neuroception circuits that activate the threat response need to be inhibited in order for social engagement to occur, I have found that bubbles are a great way to deactivate threat systems and teach a useful coping skill. The following is an instruction for introducing a play therapy technique that is a great way to teach deep breathing.

Therapist: Today, we're going to learn deep breathing skills to help when you get overwhelmed or angry. It's important to take deep breaths from way down in your belly and breathe in slowly and you can feel your belly button sinking into your belly. Take slow, steady breaths like you are filling up your lungs with your breath and your chest opens up wide with your shoulders back. You're going to practice using bubbles and playing the Bubble Game. When you take slow, steady, deep, belly breaths then slow steady exhales, then you can create big bubbles. The person who makes the biggest bubble wins.

The therapist hands each family member a small bottle of bubbles and demonstrates how to blow a large bubble using the deep breathing technique. Each family member will be provided with a few opportunities to practice before beginning the game. Therapists will observe how each family member engages in the activity. Who engages quickly, who is hesitant to try the bubble blowing, how do family members handle potential frustration if making a big bubble is difficult? Therapists will also observe how parents help their child with frustration, are parents playful with their children, how do they provide coaching with bubble making skills, which parent engages in the activity, and how does each child respond to the parents and each other? Therapists can also engage with family members to help with playfulness and support to parents as needed.

PJ: (Engaging quickly to try his skills with blowing large bubbles) Dad, watch me. I know how to do this. Watch! (PJ takes a deep breath and exhales quickly, so the bubble is small.) Ooops. That was too small.

Paul: Nice try, bud. Try exhaling more slowly. Like this. (Paul demonstrates taking a deep breath and exhaling slowly, but the bubble pops before floating free of the bubble wand. Paul and PJ laugh together.)

Julie: (Notices Brendan spilling bubble liquid on the floor while attempting to blow bubbles) Here Brenny, let Mommy help you.

Brendan: No! I do it! (and he turns away from Julie to continue blowing bubbles and spilling the liquid)

Julie: Brendan, you're spilling the bubbles all over the floor. Let me hold the bottle and you blow the bubbles. (Brendan hands Julie the bottle and keeps the bubble wand. Then he puts the bubble wand in the bottle to get liquid and then attempts to blow bubbles unsuccessfully.)

Paul: (Observes Brendan and Julie and attempts to help Brendan) Here, Brenny, let Daddy show you how to blow the bubbles.

Brendan: No! Mommy helping me! (He turns away from Paul and faces Julie to get help from Julie.)

Julie: Brenny, here, blow with your breath like this. (Julie demonstrates with slow, steady blowing to Brendan. He continues to try blowing bubbles and ends up waving the bubble wand to make bubbles that way.)

Julie: (Observes Sara quietly blowing bubbles) Hey, Sara, how are you doing with bubbles?

Sara: (Quietly blowing bubbles using deep breaths in and slow exhales. She makes a very big bubble) Look! (pointing to the big bubble)

PJ: (Turning to look at what Sara was doing) Wow! How did you do that?

Sara: Like this (She demonstrates her deep breaths in and slow exhales. PJ attempts to blow another big bubble but exhales too quickly which instead creates small bubbles.)

PJ: Hey! (turning to Sara) You're bubbles are better than mine. Let me use your bubbles.

Paul: PJ, Sara can use her bubbles. You can use mine. Let's see how you do. Remember slow inhale and slow exhale.

Sara: Look at my big bubble! (pointing to a very large bubble, laughing. All family members watch Sara's large bubble float away and laugh.)

Julie: That's great honey!

Paul: Nice!

PJ: (successfully makes a large bubble) Look! I did it! (All the family members watch PJ's large bubble float away and laugh.)

Therapist: Okay, everyone has had a chance to practice. Let's see who can blow the biggest bubbles. Ready? Set. Go!

(All the family members blow bubbles, laugh, and seem to enjoy the activity. Julie is still holding the bubble bottle for Brendan and helps him to blow bubbles. Sara blew several large bubbles. PJ was able to blow a few large bubbles. After several minutes, the therapist announces the winner.)

Therapist: Looks like Sara blew most of the biggest bubbles. Yay, Sara!

(Family members congratulate Sara and continue blowing bubbles and enjoying the activity together.)

Usually by the end of the session, family members end up just blowing bubbles for fun. Therapists will observe how parents and their children adjust to the activity and each other. Therapists can give the bubble blowing activity as homework for family members to continue practicing deep breathing and enjoying the activity together.

In this scenario, it is clear that PJ wants to have the attention and approval of his father. Paul provides structuring with PJ to help coach PJ how to blow large bubbles. Paul is able to be flexible and playful with PJ. This intersubjectivity between PJ and Paul will provide positive memories and help Paul make emotional deposits into PJ's emotional bank to help build trust and positive connection between them. Paul attempted to help Brendan, but Brendan is not yet ready to receive help from Paul at this time. Brendan continues to seek support from Julie, who is also not yet ready to fully trust Paul's parenting because she did not intercede to help Brendan use the help offered by Paul. This may be an indication that Julie is still somewhat protective with the children around Paul. Sara seems to continue to be quiet in the family. She does offer to help PJ learn how to blow bubbles, which indicates that she likely feels comfortable with PJ. Paul is able to provide structuring with PJ to allow Sara to keep her own bubbles, while he offers his own bubbles to PJ and continues to help PJ with the task. There is not much interaction between Paul and Julie, which may be an indication that their marital relationship is still somewhat strained, which can undermine their co-parenting if not resolved. Family members did enjoy the playfulness of the session and were able to inhibit their neuroception circuits indicating a sense of safety during the session.

Therapist's Role during Engagement & Safety Phase

The therapist's responses in this session were limited to providing structuring for the session by giving directions for the game, providing time for family members to practice, informing family members when the game would begin, then announcing the winner. The therapist maintained a playful attitude during the session and was aware and present to monitor the family interaction patterns. This allowed the opportunity for parents to take a larger role in engaging with their children rather than engaging more with therapist.

Therapists need to prioritize creating a safe environment for the therapeutic relationship and creating safety for family members during the beginning phase of treatment. Since relationships were unsafe for the Smith family, this is an important focus to help family members begin to repair their relationships. It will be important for the therapist to help Paul make a commitment to his children that he will be committed to his sobriety and manage his anger. The therapist can discuss this with Paul and Julie during the parent coaching session to identify a plan about how Paul can have this conversation with his children. Providing psychoeducation to the children about addiction will be important to help create a common language to discuss addiction and its impact in the Smith family. This will aid family members to have context when discussing their emotions regarding Paul's addiction and help identify boundaries and emotional needs. Therapists can help parents and children to identify safety rules for the home. It's important for parents to communicate with their children in ways that are age appropriate and not overwhelming.

Parent Coaching Session

The parent coaching sessions in this phase of treatment need to prioritize building a therapeutic alliance with parents. When selecting video clips to review with parents, it's important to make sure to have several examples of positive parenting behaviors before and after constructive feedback using the sandwich approach to feedback. Parents need to establish trust with therapists to experience the parent coaching sessions as supportive. They will likely be on the alert for potential judgement and often feel like failures in their parenting. Therefore, it's important to help parents experience the parent coaching sessions as supportive. Look for any and all examples of positive parent behaviors in the video clips, even if there was something negative connected with the interaction. Therapists can highlight the positive parenting behavior and then use curiosity to explore with parents what they were thinking and feeling during the negative part of the interaction. In this way, therapists nonjudgmentally invite parents to explore with them to better understand the interaction. The following is an example of feedback in a coaching session with Paul and Julie using a video clip of the above session to teach deep breathing with bubbles.

Therapist: (showing video clip of the bubble session) How was this session for you guys?

Paul: It was fun. I feel like I lost a lot of time with my kids because of my addiction, so this was nice to spend positive time with them.

Therapist: (looking at Julie) How was it for you, Julie?

Julie: For me, it was a little stressful. I mean, it was nice having fun with them, but I just didn't know what we were supposed to do and Brendan was spilling the bubble liquid all over the floor.

Therapist: Yeah, it's hard sometimes in the beginning because it seems weird to have me sitting there watching. (Smiling at Julie). You did great. I noticed you helping Brendan by holding the bubble bottle and letting him still have control over how he blows the bubbles. That was a great example of structuring and flexibility that we discussed for the Family SPACE skills. I noticed that he was able to take that structuring from you because you can see here (showing the video clip example) where you let him know he was spilling the liquid and you offered to hold the bottle and let him keep the bubble wand. He immediately agreed to that and got back to blowing bubbles and having fun with you. I also noticed that you let him know that he was doing a great job and you were really encouraging with him. I'm curious what you were thinking and feeling at that moment?

Julie: Brendan and I have a good relationship. It was fun and stressful at the same time. I just wish he would let Paul be more involved with him. It gets tiring being the only one who Brendan will go to.

Therapist: Yes, that can be hard. Paul, I'm wondering what that's like for you when Brendan doesn't accept your help?

Paul: It's hard. I feel bad that Julie doesn't get a break with Brendan. I get it, though. He saw me argue with Julie a lot and I think I looked pretty scary to him when I was angry. I try not to think about that too much because I get really upset with myself and I can't change the past. I just have to keep focused on my sobriety.

Therapist: Yes, as a parent, I totally understand. I can get really upset with myself when I blow it with my kids. I just try to work it out with them by apologizing and talking about what happened. Thankfully, we don't have to be perfect parents. We just need to be good enough. I noticed with Brendan that you didn't challenge him when he would not accept your help. You were accepting of the situation with him for now and it sounds like you would like to have a better relationship with Brendan.

Paul: Yeah, I've learned that it only makes things worse with Brendan if I try to make him accept my help right now. I do want things to be better with Brendan, so any help with that would be great.

Therapist: Julie, I'm curious what you're thinking and feeling about what Paul said.

Julie: I'm glad he gets it that he needs to earn trust with the kids.

Therapist: I'm curious about how it is for you to be able to trust Paul with the kids?

Julie: (looking uncomfortable and lowering her eyes to the floor) I mean, it's hard. I know he's trying, but it's just hard. I'm glad he's sober and his parents have been a great support to us.

Therapist: (shifting the discussion to Paul) Paul, I noticed PJ really wanted to engage you in playing with him. You can see here (showing video clip) where he turned right to you and wanted you to watch him and you playfully engaged with him and gave him positive feedback. You can see here on his face that he loved this interaction with you because his face just lights up. When he was struggling to blow big bubbles, he was able to let you show him how to exhale more slowly to get a big bubble. It was awesome to see you laughing together when your bubble popped. I'm curious what you were thinking and feeling at here?

Paul: I love hanging out with my kids. It was fun and it was awesome having that positive time with PJ.

Therapist: So, we'll meet for four sessions with you and the kids together. Is there anything you want to make sure we focus on? How do you feel like you are doing with the Family SPACE skills? Do you have any questions about those? How about the 3 Rs of Relationship skills? Any question about those?

The therapist, Paul, and Julie discussed and identified the focus for the next four sessions to continue to build safety before addressing Paul's addiction with the children. The therapist agreed to identify some interventions that will help Brendan engage in play with Paul. The therapist provided some suggestions for Julie and Paul to allow Paul to give Julie more of a break with Brendan and continue to increase Brendan's sense of safety with Paul. The therapist provided some suggestions to Paul and Julie to use structure and flexibility skills with the children to address misbehavior. The therapist coached Paul about using WiseMind and provided some resources to him regarding where to learn more about WiseMind.

Once therapists have assessed that the parents have developed therapeutic rapport with them, and the children seem to experience the family sessions as safe, it will be time to move into the Realignment phase of treatment. Keep in mind that sometimes it may be necessary to move back to the Engagement and Safety phase of treatment if family members are feeling overwhelmed and distressed. Moving back into the Engagement and Safety phase will help to re-establish a sense of safety and repair and trust in the therapeutic relationship.

References

Crenshaw, D., & Mordock, J. (2007). *Understanding and treating the aggression of children: Fawns in gorilla suits*. Lanham, MD: Jason Aronson.

Fonagy, P., & Allison, E. (2014). The role of mentalizing and epistemic trust in the therapeutic relationship. *Psychotherapy, 51*(3), 372–380. doi:10.1037/a0036505

Linehan, M. M. (2015). *DBT skills training manual* (2nd ed.). New York, NY: The Guilford Press.

Siegel, D. J. (2011). *Mindsight: The new science of personal transformation*. New York, NY: Bantam Books.

Wallin, D. J. (2007). *Attachment in psychotherapy*. New York, NY: The Guilford Press.

Realignment Phase   10

The Realignment phase of treatment is essentially the restructuring and change phase and takes up the majority of the treatment process. It's not uncommon during this phase that family members will need to go back to tasks of the Safety and Engagement phase to re-establish trust and stability when issues become emotionally overwhelming, especially during the early part of this phase.

The Safety and Engagement phase provides the foundation for building safety and trust that will allow for the change process to occur. The Realignment phase focuses on helping parents develop skills to make changes within the parent–child relationship to increase secure attachments. This phase also focuses on helping the children to use their parents and siblings for support, as well as tolerating attachment ruptures and repairing those attachment ruptures. This chapter provides information about the tasks to be achieved by the family and the role of the therapist. Therapists learn the types of play, and expressive arts therapy interventions, to use during this phase of treatment.

In this chapter, we'll examine how to apply the Family SPACE and the 3 Rs of Relationship skills with the Johnson family, whom you met in Chapter 8. During the Safety and Engagement phase of treatment, Helen and John were provided with psychoeducation about Family SPACE and the 3 Rs of Relationship skills framework. John struggled with awareness and presence since he struggled with significant emotional disconnection due to his own history of childhood sexual abuse. In the beginning, he occasionally dissociated during the sessions when his own trauma memories were activated. It was recommended that he seek individual therapy to address his unresolved trauma while he was also participating in the family play therapy sessions. Family members learned coping/calming and mindfulness skills to better manage their emotions and emotional distress. They also began to talk about the trauma that happened to Makenzi to help family members open up a developmentally appropriate communication process. John worked on developing skills to be more emotionally present in the sessions. The relationship between Samantha and Makenzi is still distant entering into the Realignment phase, and Makenzi struggles to use support from her mother and John. She is aloof and moody most of the time. She is easily upset and angry with Samantha. Samantha tends to stay away from Makenzi to avoid her anger. John and Helen still experience significant guilt and shame about the sexual abuse. They are unsure how to address Makenzi's anger toward Samantha and her moodiness. Helen feels caught between her desire to support her husband, and her feeling of guilt over the fact that John's son sexually abused her daughter, which undermines her confidence when she addresses issues of concern with Makenzi regarding Makenzi's unhealthy behavior.

During the Safety and Engagement phase of treatment, Makenzi, Helen, and John identified a plan to explain to Samantha what happened to Makenzi and why Thomas was sent to a residential treatment center. Makenzi decided to use some of her artwork from her individual therapy to explain to Samantha how the sexual abuse impacted her. Using the artwork would help Makenzi talk about the sexual abuse in a way that was emotionally comfortable for her and not overwhelm Makenzi and Samantha. Makenzi and her parents decided that Helen and John would explain to Samantha at home, with Makenzi present, the day before the family therapy session in which Samantha would be told what happened to Makenzi. It was decided that John and Helen would tell Samantha that Thomas acted in unsafe ways toward Makenzi and that he sexually abused Makenzi. Helen and John met with the therapist during a parent coaching session to help them prepare to witness Makenzi's telling of the impact of the sexual abuse on her. It's important to help family members prepare to hear the impact of the trauma so that they can effectively help support the traumatized child and aide in the healing process. It can be difficult to *bear witness* to the trauma story of the traumatized child. After Helen, John, and Makenzi informed Samantha about the sexual abuse, Makenzi shared her trauma story with her family members during their therapy session the next day with all four family members. Then, all four family members processed their thoughts and emotions. The following three family sessions focused on helping family members explore their emotions and concerns about the trauma and learn coping/calming skills. John and Helen practiced using Family SPACE skills during those sessions to help process the impact of the trauma within the family.

Family members learned coping/calming and mindfulness skills, identified emotions, and increased their comfort level in family therapy sessions during the Safety and Engagement phase of treatment that would allow them to progress to the Realignment phase. During this phase, family members will continue to build trust and safety within their relationships while also changing relationship interaction patterns. Makenzi will continue to work on using family relationships for support and overcoming the negative impact of the sexual abuse on her core beliefs (discussed in Chapter 4) and her ability to engage in healthy relationships.

Purpose of the Realignment Phase

The Realignment phase of treatment is the heart of the change phase because family members will be challenged to learn, and implement, new skills within their relationships. Parents will likely experience emotional distress during this phase when challenged to explore and identify their own emotional triggers, increase their awareness of factors contributing to those emotional triggers, and challenge ineffective parenting behaviors. Therapists need to monitor and adjust the pacing of the change process to maintain their therapeutic relationship during this phase. Parents are the foundation to attachment security, so they are the key to helping their traumatized child learn to use their parental support, regulate their emotions, communicate their needs, and recognize healthy relationship boundaries to learn to trust others. One of my favorite frameworks to use with clients is the dialectic of Acceptance and Change from Dialectical Behavior Therapy. This dialectic views clients as doing the best that they can at any moment in time (Acceptance) while also believing clients can make the necessary changes to improve their lives (Change) (Linehan, 1993). I love this Acceptance and Change concept because it affirms clients to help reduce shame and increase self-acceptance while also challenging them to make important changes that are outside of their comfort zone, which will require them to increase their window of tolerance to make the necessary changes.

Role of Therapists

This therapeutic dance of creating safety (Acceptance) while also challenging clients (Change) requires therapists to be attuned with family members during sessions. Therapists working with traumatized clients need to have the capacity to therapeutically hold a tremendous amount of emotional content as they help guide family members through the treatment process. Parents and therapists work collaboratively in this therapeutic relationship to help family members navigate through the healing process. This requires therapists to tune into their resonance circuits to effectively use themselves therapeutically. This can be emotionally exhausting and overwhelming for therapists, so it is critical that they have their own support system and access to consultation to help them recognize when they have gotten pulled into reenacting unhealthy family relationship patterns. Any therapist who has worked with families will know that it is not a matter of *if* they get pulled into unhealthy family patterns, but *when* and *how often* they get pulled into these family patterns. If therapists can use the same self-compassion and curiosity they encourage parents to use, then therapists can use this curiosity mindset to explore and examine how they got pulled into the unhealthy relationship patterns and identify information about the family dynamics to help them better understand the family. Transference and countertransference information can provide valuable information to therapists and help them identify intervention targets.

During this phase of treatment, therapists monitor and assess the parents' ability to implement Family SPACE and the 3 Rs of Relationship skills and provide ongoing coaching as needed. This requires therapists to continue to maintain a safe environment for therapeutic relationships with family members, so that parents and their children can receive constructive feedback as needed to make necessary changes. It's not uncommon for relationship ruptures to occur within the therapeutic relationships since this phase of treatment is the heart of the change process and challenges family members' windows of tolerance for distress. Therefore, therapists need to assess when the neuroception circuits have been activated and help family members work through the relationship repair process. This will require therapists to mirror the 3 Rs of Relationship and emotion regulation skills. When possible, therapists need to monitor pacing of the interventions during sessions in order to stay within family members' windows of tolerance without significantly overwhelming family members. This pacing of interventions also allows parents the opportunity to practice using the Family SPACE skills during the sessions when their children become distressed.

Helping family members engage in safe, healthy relationship patterns is a central focus during this phase of treatment. Therapists provide ongoing psychoeducation about the neurobiology of trauma and attachment to help parents and family members understand how their brain directs their behavior when their neuroception circuits are activated. I believe helping family members understand the neurobiology of their behavior helps them to become curious about learning about their behavior and what it's communicating, rather than increasing their shame and mistrust. Therapists need to help family members become more attuned within themselves and with one another. This helps to increase safety within family relationships as family members increase their mentalization abilities to more accurately understand the intentions of family members and increase positive intersubjectivity experiences.

Tasks to Accomplish in This Phase of Treatment

Parents need to tap into their own internal experiences to recognize when their neuroception circuits have been activated to potential threat. This requires parents to first use awareness and presence within themselves in order to recognize and name what has activated their heightened sense of threat. John will need to recognize when his neuroception circuits have been activated and resulted in either emotional withdrawal or irritability, as well as those times when he dissociates. Using curiosity and a nonjudgmental mindset, he can challenge himself to face these activating situations to recognize and label these triggers so that he can learn from them. For example, when John overhears Makenzi talking with Helen about her fears of Thomas returning to the home because he said that he would kill her if she ever told anyone, then John is taken back in time to his own experience of sexual abuse by a family member who said the same thing to him. His body becomes tense, his heart rate increases, and he feels an overwhelming sense of fear and helplessness. He is no longer present in the moment and his fear circuits have been activated. John's ability to be aware and present will require him to tolerate his emotional distress in the moment so that he can allow himself to be curious about what his body is communicating to him—he felt alone and scared at that moment when he was being sexually abused as a child. His ability to allow himself to name these emotions and identify his need at that moment, which was for someone to protect him and help him. John can identify that he felt powerless and unable to use his voice to seek help and protection.

With a nonjudgmental and accepting mindset (Acceptance), John can begin to allow himself to be compassionate toward himself. He can recognize that his dissociation became his protective cover to help him remain safe at that moment. With a new understanding of his dissociation, and the wisdom that he gains from allowing himself to be curious enough to explore his dissociation, John can begin to recognize his trauma triggers and how his neuroception circuits become activated. This information will help John understand that he is not feeling safe in the moment and begin to use skills to help him feel safe in the moment (Change). This self-compassionate view of himself will allow his neuroception circuits to be deactivated when he is able to recognize perceived threat versus real threat in the moment.

This is important work for parents with their own trauma histories because they are unable to engage their resonance circuits to be attuned to their children if their neuroception circuits have been activated. Traumatized children need their parents to be strong and wise for them to help them feel safe while they work through the same process that John himself needs to work through, as described above. This facilitates increasing a sense of safety and security within family relationships at home. In traumatized families, neuroception circuits will be activated since relationships have not been experienced in a safe manner. In the case of Makenzi, she tends to isolate herself from family members and project her anger onto Samantha. Makenzi and Samantha need their parents to accurately read their behavior cues using WiseMind to help them effectively implement Family SPACE skills. To do this, John and Helen have to be able to tolerate their children's emotional distress without becoming emotionally dysregulated themselves. In the early stage of this phase of treatment, therapists may need to provide interventions that help family members re-establish safety to reduce their emotional distress before proceeding again to interventions focused on the change process.

Figure 10.1 provides an overview of the tasks to accomplish in this part of treatment. During the Realignment phase, parents need to use the support of therapists to help them implement the Family SPACE skills in the moment and effectively repair relationship ruptures with their children. This phase can be tenuous if parents become overly reactive and unable to recognize their own emotional triggers and engage in unhealthy projection. This will be discussed in more depth in Chapter 12. Therapists may need to slow down the treatment process to re-establish trust with parents and return to interventions geared toward Safety and Engagement.

Parents need to:

- Recognize their own emotional triggers
- Tune into their own neuroception circuits and resonance circuits to gain wisdom through the use of WiseMind
- Recognize their children's cues and respond effectively
- Implement Family SPACE and the 3 Rs of Relationship skills

Family members need to:

- Experience relationships safely and develop healthy relationship skills:
  - *Tolerate proximity with family members and improve intersubjectivity experiences*
  - *Communicate needs and resolve conflict effectively*
  - *Children use parent and sibling support*
- Tolerate emotional distress and regulate emotions:
  - *Use coping/calming skills when necessary*

Figure 10.1 Tasks to Accomplish in the Realignment Phase

Family members need to work toward experiencing relationships safely and develop healthy relationship skills. Traumatized children often struggle with close proximity to others due to the nature of their traumatic experience. In the case of the Johnson family, Makenzi often projects her anger and shame onto Samantha, which results in Samantha feeling uncomfortable around Makenzi. Samantha and Makenzi struggle with tolerating close proximity and do not experience positive intersubjectivity in their relationship. Siblings can be a great source of support throughout their lives. It will be important for Makenzi and Samantha to create a sense of safety and support within their relationship. This can help Makenzi to decrease her sense of isolation and mistrust. Makenzi also needs to learn to use support from Helen and John to manage her stressors. John will need to manage his own trauma triggers to initiate healthy attachment behaviors with his two stepdaughters.

Family members also need to learn to effectively communicate needs and resolve conflict. In traumatized families, children often struggle with communicating their needs to parents. It's difficult for children to know how to assert and communicate their needs if they do not feel safe within their relationships. Trauma disempowers people, so learning to recognize and ask for what they need can be challenging. Learning skills to recognize when their neuroception circuits are activated helps traumatized children and their parents communicate their needs and seek support. It's also important for family members to learn to effectively resolve conflict and repair their relationship ruptures. To do this, family members need to increase their ability to tolerate emotional distress and use coping/calming skills while they are working through their conflict. Interventions during this phase of treatment focus on parents using the 3 Rs of Relationship skills to help their children resolve conflict and repair their relationships when conflict occurs. Unresolved conflict can undermine the ability for family members to experience safety and support within their relationships.

Choosing Interventions

Therapists need to choose interventions that teach new skills for communication, resolving conflict, repairing relationships, and regulating emotions. Therapists continue to help family members process the impact of the trauma and develop resiliency. Using play and expressive arts interventions incorporates playfulness into the sessions to help reduce potential tension and provide the ability to create safety within the sessions. Neuroception circuits must be disinhibited before PLAY circuits can be accessed. Therefore, interventions have to take into consideration different family personalities, developmental stages, and windows of tolerance of family members.

Since the Johnson family needed to help Makenzi increase her willingness to use their support and help her to increase her mentalization abilities regarding relationships, using interventions in the sessions that focus on helping her to engage collaboratively and cooperatively are a good place to start. Makenzi's neuroception circuits are activated most of the time during family sessions, so using interventions that integrate the sand tray tend to work best with her. She is also creative and enjoys writing poetry. Samantha engages easily during the sessions and tends to acquiesce to anything that will allow Makenzi to engage in the activity. John tends to be quiet and more peripheral, so I chose to use an expressive arts activity with the sand tray that would allow each family member to use the figures to help them communicate. In this session, I chose to focus on helping family members to understand one another's perspectives of the family, and their place in the family, as a way to examine the impact of Makenzie's trauma within the family relationships.

This sand tray activity involves having each family member pick a sand figure and place their figures in the sand tray in response to the following questions: (1) How do you think your family members see you?, (2) How do you see yourself in your family?, (3) How would you like your family to be?, and, (4) How would you like your family to see you? Family members are given the following rules for the activity:

> Each person chooses figures to answer each of the four questions. Everyone is allowed to pick their figures and other family members cannot make negative comments about figures chosen by another family. If you did not put the figure in the sand tray, then you cannot take it out of the sand tray. It's important for each person to be respected in the session and allow their perspectives to be heard by other family members.

Therapists silently observe how family members choose their figures, how they interact with one another, how they manage the space in the sand tray, and what types of figures are chosen. This provides information about relationship dynamics, how family members adjust to one another's differences, ability to tolerate proximity, and quality of intersubjectivity within their relationships. Once all family members have chosen their figures and placed them in the sand tray, therapists invite family members to share, one at a time, which figures they picked for each question. Therapists invite each family member to share as much or as little as they would like about the figures chosen for each question. It's important that therapists create a safe therapeutic *space* in the session for family members to inhibit the neuroception circuits and allow family members to participate fully in the sessions.

Expressive arts interventions allow family members to use metaphors to express themselves. Metaphors through the use of symbolism via sand tray figures allow clients to access nonverbal memory and bring those memories into consciousness, and to verbally process the memories and examine mentalizations. Buk (2009) linked the mirror neuron systems (MNS) and the ability to create metaphor. The author states "MNS is intimately linked to the construction of the mental models that make up the implicit memory system" (Buk, 2009, p. 65), which includes the sensory information of emotions stored nonverbally. This supports Gantt and Tinnin's (2009) view in which they conceptualize trauma as a nonverbal problem. The authors discuss the connection between *alexithymia*, the difficulty identifying and labeling emotional states, and trauma. Symbolism through the use of expressive arts provides an avenue to inaccessible traumatic memories and disintegrated understanding of events to more effectively process the impact of the trauma (Buk, 2009; Gantt & Tinnin, 2009; Gantt & Tripp, 2016; Steele & Raider, 2001). Regarding the processing of traumatic memories, Steele and Raider (2001) state:

> when that memory cannot be linked linguistically in a contextual framework it remains at a symbolic level for which there are no words to describe it. In order to retrieve that memory so it can be "encoded" and given a language and then integrated into consciousness, it must be retrieved and externalized in its symbolic perceptual (iconic) form.
>
> (pp. 33–34)

Traumatized children need to learn how to reconnect with family members after a traumatic experience. They need a way to process difficult information, such as the trauma and the impact within their relationships, in a way that creates a sense of safety. Client metaphors allow the ability to use symbolism in a way that provides safe psychological distance for emotional content in order to process clinical issues within their windows of tolerance, and avoid activating neuroception circuits. For example, children can choose a family of animals and display them separated in various parts of the sand tray scene to reveal their feelings of disconnection with family members. They don't need to use words to describe their pain of emotional disconnection because children don't have the ability to cognitively articulate these concepts. Therapists can stay in the metaphor to explore the child's perceptions in a way that allows the child to feel safe by referring to the animals' feelings and perceptions rather than the child's.

In the following example, a child has chosen a baby bear and a momma bear (child's labeling of the animals) for the sand tray and the momma bear is not in the same area as the baby bear during a family sand tray activity. The therapist can explore the child's mentalization of the mother–child relationship using the metaphor of momma bear and baby bear and include the child's mother in the metaphor dialogue to restructure the relationship perceptions.

Therapist (to the child): I'm wondering what the baby bear thinks about its mother being over there? (pointing to the momma bear on the other side of the sand tray)

Child: The baby is scared and wants his momma.

Therapist (to the child): I wonder what the baby bear is afraid of?

Child: The baby got lost and can't find his mother. He's worried that his mother left him.

Therapist (to the child): Oh, that does sound scary. I wonder if we can ask the momma bear if she knows how to help the baby bear?

Child: Okay. (then looks at mother)

Therapist (to mother): I'm wondering what the momma bear is thinking about the baby bear being so far away?

Mother: The momma bear is wondering where the baby bear went. She wants to find the baby bear to make sure the baby bear is safe.

Therapist (to mother): Does the momma bear want to look for the baby bear now?

Mother (playing along, she moves the momma bear figure to begin looking for baby bear): Baby bear! Where are you? (moving momma bear figure to baby bear figure) Oh, there you are! I was worried about you. Are you okay?

Child (moving baby bear figure close to momma bear figure): I'm scared.

Mother (momma bear figure to child's baby bear figure): I'm here now. Why are you scared?

Child (to mother's figure): I was afraid you would leave without me. I got lost.

Mother (to child's figure): I'm here. I wouldn't leave without you. I'll keep you safe. You're okay now.

Child (to mother's figure): Okay.

In this example, mother is able to use playfulness, empathy, curiosity, and presence during the session via the metaphor with her child to help the child experience mother in a protective and supportive manner. This can help to verbalize underlying fears and allow the child to use mother as a secure figure to increase a sense of safety.

Therapists can use metaphors to help family members process their experiences about family relationships with one another using safe psychological distance. The sand tray therapy activity focused on helping family members share the reason they picked each figure. This provided an opportunity for family members to share their perceptions of themselves in their family, their family relationships, and how they would like things to be in their family. The ability to explore their mentalizations about their family provides valuable information to assess the intersubjectivity within family relationships. Intersubjectivity will be hindered if family relationships are perceived as unsafe because neuroception circuits will be active and social engagement will be inhibited. Using the metaphors of the figures chosen, therapists can facilitate metaphoric dialogue between family members using their sand tray figures to increase communication and improve perceptions within their relationships.

Parent Coaching Sessions

During this phase of treatment, the parent coaching sessions continue to teach attachment repair skills and Family SPACE skills to change family relationship patterns. Therapists continue to video each family session and then choose which video clips to present in the parent coaching session. It's important to continue showing video clips of positive examples of using Family SPACE skills as well as using clips of challenging interactions to elicit self-exploration and increase self-awareness for parents.

In the following example, the therapist shows a video clip of an interaction between family members during the sand tray activity. In this clip, Makenzi was sullen and emotionally withdrawn during the activity. Makenzi reluctantly participated in the activity to choose figures for each of the questions and grumbled about the activity being "stupid." At that point, Helen tried to engage with Makenzi to help her choose figures, but Makenzi became more irritable and physically withdrew. Helen directed an irritated facial expression at Makenzi and asked her why she was having a "bad attitude." At that point, Makenzi responded curtly that she wasn't as perfect as Samantha. With that remark, Samantha looked at her mother with a frustrated facial expression, and Helen mouthed the words "don't take it personal" to Samantha. John engaged in the discussion telling Makenzi not to be rude to Samantha.

Therapist: Helen, I'm wondering what you are thinking as you're watching this video clip? (Curiosity)

Helen: I remember feeling really embarrassed by Makenzi's behavior because she was being so rude and irritable. She's that way a lot at home and it bothers me how she blames Samantha.

Therapist: Not that I don't get it, and I'm wondering specifically for you, what was embarrassing about Makenzi's behavior?

Helen: I just feel like a failure with her. I feel guilty about the abuse and feel like I should have protected her better. So, I just don't know what to do when she behaves that way. I feel bad for Samantha because she takes the brunt of Makenzi's anger. I feel like I'm failing Samantha because Makenzi is so rude to her. It's exhausting and I feel like I should know what to do. I don't always feel like being curious or empathic to Makenzi when she's been rude all day long.

Therapist: That makes a lot of sense. It's really hard not to feel like you failed her as a mother because you didn't protect her. (Empathy and Acceptance) I remember your talking about your relationship with your older sister in one of our other parent sessions. I'm wondering if Makenzi's behavior reminded you about the way your sister used to treat you and how you felt like your mom never intervened to help you. What are your thoughts about that?

Helen: Hmmm. I didn't really think about that. I guess that's true. I feel so bad for Makenzi and then I feel bad for Samantha and I'm their mother. I should know what to do to protect them. That's what mothers do. But then I just feel so guilty and like I'm not doing a good job as a mother.

Therapist: I'm wondering, John, what do you think about what Helen is saying? How do you think she's doing as a mother? (Curiosity and Reflexive Communication)

John: I think she's doing a great job. Makenzi is really exhausting some days with her attitude. Helen is so patient with her. She spends time with Makenzi and they work on puzzles together. I get frustrated and walk away because Makenzi's behavior is so irritating sometimes and then I feel guilty because Thomas is my son and he did that to Makenzi.

Therapist: Yes, it sounds like you have a lot of guilt about what happened and then it's hard to know what to do when Makenzi is irritable. (Empathy and Acceptance)

John: Yeah, I really don't know what to do. I feel like I'm failing Helen because I'm not really helpful with the skills you taught us when I'm irritated.

Therapist: It sounds like both of you feel really guilty and feel like you are failing as a parent. Trauma changes everything and brings up a lot of feelings of powerlessness and hopelessness. Sounds like there is a lot of shame as well. It can be really exhausting some days and you guys are doing such a good job of hanging in there and trying hard to help your children. (Empathy and Acceptance) What's the hard part about using the Family SPACE skills when Makenzi is having a really hard day? (Curiosity and Reflexive Communication)

Helen: My guilt and I don't know when to hold limits with her because I feel guilty. Then I just go downhill from there.

Therapist: That makes sense. How do you think you are doing reading her cues?

Helen: I think I'm doing a little better with that. I'll try to check in with her and use curiosity and reflexive communication to find out what is going on. That usually helps and eventually she'll open up to me about what is bothering her. Right now she's been really worried about where Thomas will live when he's finished with treatment. She feels guilty because he can't move back into the home with us, at least not right away. I try to reassure her that we still love Thomas and we love her and Samantha, but we need to make sure the home is safe and Thomas can be safe before he can move back home with us. John has a brother who lives about three hours away. His children are grown. We think Thomas will stay with John's brother and his wife for a while until we can figure out if Thomas can move back into the home with us. Right now, we just want to get through this with Makenzi and Samantha. Thomas still has another 6–8 months where he is, so we have time to figure that out.

John, Helen, and the therapist continue to explore factors interfering with Helen's and John's confidence in using the Family SPACE and relationship repair skills. The therapist helps Helen and John to use Wise-Mind to increase their awareness and presence skills to figure out how they can hold boundaries (Structuring and Flexibility) with Makenzi regarding her treatment of Samantha. When focusing on Structuring and Flexibility skills to hold firm boundaries with Makenzi, the therapist helps John and Helen use reflexive communication skills when addressing their concern with Makenzi about why she is taking out her anger on Samantha. Parents need to hold healthy boundaries with their children, but they also want to help their children recognize the *why* of their behavior so it will help them learn to match their behaviors with their values. In this case, Makenzi values treating others with respect. She also believes people should feel safe, which is important to Makenzi because she did not feel safe when the sexual abuse was happening to her. Helping Makenzi realize that her behavior toward Samantha does not match her values, and is due to her shame and resentment toward Samantha, will pave the way for Makenzi to make healthier choices about her behavior in the future toward Samantha. The therapist, Helen, and John also explore ways to help Samantha become more assertive with Makenzi and let Makenzi know how her behavior is affecting Samantha. The therapist, Helen, and John discuss when and how to help both Makenzi and Samantha use relationship repair skills to improve their relationship. It's important not to force repair onto children while also helping them learn the importance of repairing their relationships.

In this parent coaching session, the therapist continues to mirror many of these skills to the parents. Helen is able to reflect on her own emotional triggers such as her guilt and shame as well as a past history of unhealthy family dynamics in her childhood. John also reflects on his difficulty regulating his emotions when Makenzi engages in irritable behavior. Since Helen and John have established therapeutic rapport with their therapist, this allows them to use that therapeutic relationship to explore and identify their emotional triggers. It also allows John and Helen to be vulnerable with their therapist to use her support and feedback. The ability of John and Helen to be vulnerable with their therapist is an indication that their neuroception circuits are inhibited, which allows their social engagement circuits to use support. Remember, therapists want to mirror healthy attachment behaviors to parents in order to help parents use these skills with their children. This becomes challenging for therapists when working with parents whose neuroception circuits do not allow for a strong therapeutic alliance with therapists. This will be discussed more in Chapter 12. In the next chapter, we'll discuss the final phase of treatment with the Smith family.

References

Buk, A. (2009). The mirror neuron-system and embodied simulation: Clinical implications for art therapists working with trauma survivors. *The Arts in Psychotherapy, 36,* 61–74.

Gantt, L., & Tinnin, L. W. (2009). Support for a neurobiological view of trauma and implications for art therapy. *The Arts in Psychotherapy, 36,* 148–153.

Gantt, L., & Tripp, T. (2016). The image comes first: Treating preverbal trauma with art therapy. In J. L. King (Ed.), *Art therapy, trauma, and neuroscience: Theoretical and practical perspectives* (pp. 67–99). New York, NY: Routledge.

Linehan, M. M. (1993). *Cognitive-behavioral treatment of borderline personality disorder.* New York, NY: The Guilford Press.

Steele, W., & Raider, M. (2001). *Structured sensory intervention for traumatized children, adolescents, and parents: Strategies to alleviate trauma.* Lewiston, NY: The Edwin Mellen Press.

Attunement Phase and Termination   **11**

By the time families reach this phase of the treatment process, they have started to demonstrate their ability to tolerate close proximity to one another, work through difficult issues while making progress tolerating emotional distress, and feel safe within their family relationships. This chapter will focus on the implementation of the Attunement phase of treatment to help parents strengthen and maintain changes within the parent–child relationship and to continue increasing secure attachments. We'll explore the progress made by the Smith family and the tasks to be achieved by the family in this phase of treatment. Play and expressive arts therapy interventions will focus on helping family members continue to increase safety and support within their relationships and strengthen their relationship skills. Therapists will assist parents to take a more prominent role during therapy sessions which should help them increase their confidence in implementing Family SPACE and the 3 Rs of Relationship skills. This is the final phase of treatment and a major transition point for families as they prepare for discharge. Termination of treatment can activate unresolved issues of loss in clients, and therapists will need to facilitate sessions with an understanding that termination may trigger those unresolved issues.

Purpose of the Attunement Phase

The Realignment phase tends to be a challenging part of the treatment process because family members will be learning skills in order to resolve issues that are emotionally distressing and activate their neuroception circuits. Many parents will not be able to tolerate the increased emotional distress that often manifests during this phase and may prematurely terminate treatment to avoid the emotional pain. The Realignment phase can be anxiety-producing for parents. Therapists will need to therapeutic-ally hold this turmoil while mirroring to parents how to do this with their children to help them advance to the Attunement phase of treat-ment. Families enter into the Attunement phase when parents demon-strate the ability to tolerate their own emotional distress effectively and increase their skillfulness at helping their children resolve conflict and communicate their needs. Therapists will help parents to increase their confidence, reduce their dependence on therapists, and help them skill-fully navigate "emotional storms" with their children. The key focus in the Attunement phase will be helping parents to feel confident in their ability to implement Family SPACE and the 3 Rs of Relationships skills to prepare them for their eventual discharge.

At the heart of the Attunement phase will be strengthening the attach-ment relationships within the family, and helping parents to feel confident in their ability to use the skills necessary for creating safety and resiliency within their family relationships. During this phase of treatment, parents will demonstrate the ability to implement Family SPACE and the 3 Rs of Relationship skills with special emphasis on the ability to be attuned to their children. Parents will be able to recognize their own internal emo-tional states so they can maintain the ability to use wise decision-making as they navigate through relationship distress with their children, and help them to repair relationship ruptures.

During the Realignment phase, the Smith family worked on improving their ability to tolerate emotional distress and create a sense of safety within their relationships. Due to the history of addiction and domestic violence within the Smith family, this was an important clinical focus during the family and parent coaching sessions. The Smith children would not be able to develop secure attachments with their parents, espe-cially with Paul, if they could not feel safe, and feeling safe was heavily dependent on the parents' demonstration of appropriate emotion regula-tion, and on Paul's sobriety. Paul attended AA meetings regularly and worked with his AA sponsor to maintain his sobriety which was essential for Paul to earn the trust of his family and provide a sense of safety within the family relationships. Staying sober was also crucial in enabling him to regulate his emotions and improve the quality of his attachment with his children. Paul and Julie continued to work on their marital rela-tionship since this relationship provides the foundation for family stability and affects parents' ability to effectively co-parent.

Due to the high level of conflict and emotional chaos within the family, the Smith children needed their parents to demonstrate the ability to provide flexibility and structuring, as well as the other Family SPACE skills. It's been my experience with families who have experienced domestic violence and addiction that the threat of violence can create unhealthy structure and disorder within the family system. In the case of the Smiths, the children often felt like they had to "walk on eggshells" around Paul, and they focused on pleasing him with their good behavior in order to avoid his angry outbursts that had at one time resulted in heated verbal and physical conflict between Paul and Julie. When the threat of violence is removed, it can be difficult for family members to reorganize their relationships in a new, healthy way. During the Attunement phase, Paul and Julie will need to continue to work on using Family SPACE skills to strengthen the sense of safety within the family, and provide them with the parenting tools they'll need in order to successfully transition to termination.

Since Paul was a teenager when his father stopped drinking, he had not experienced his father mirroring to him healthy emotion regulation and relationship repair. Julie also grew up in a home with limited healthy relationship mirroring by her parents. During the Realignment phase, both Julie and Paul worked hard to learn Family SPACE and the 3 Rs of Relationship skills. Paul and Julie were receptive to both positive and constructive feedback during the parent coaching sessions. They developed a trusting relationship with their therapist and relied on her to help them increase self-awareness and learn to be more emotionally present with their children.

Developing a strong therapeutic alliance with their therapist was an important step for Paul and Julie since they needed a trusted support person to help them increase their internal emotional awareness and mentalization capabilities to improve their ability to read the cues of their children. Their therapist mirrored to Paul and Julie how to be attuned to their needs and use reflexive communication with curiosity to explore with them what activated their threat systems during distressing situations with their children, each other, and the therapist. Therapists will need to model to parents how to be attuned and work through difficult relationship issues.

Affectively attuned parents are able to communicate in a manner that will demonstrate "receptivity and responsiveness to the affective signals of others" (Wallin, 2007, p. 106), which relies heavily on right brain processing between individuals. As discussed in Chapter 3, these right brain circuits are critical for reading the nonverbal social cues of others, such as facial expressions, body language, and voice prosody. According to Wallin (2007), "communication that is collaborative, contingent, and affectively attuned is at the heart of the prescription to parents who would provide for the children the experience of a secure attachment" (p. 106).

Tasks to Accomplish

As Paul improved his ability to regulate his own emotions, he was more able to use Family SPACE skills with his children to create a greater sense of safety within the family relationships. During the Attunement phase, parents will continue to create a sense of safety for their children and help them feel that they can use the parents for support. Parents in this phase of treatment focus on creating resiliency through improved attachment with their children and creating safety. Post-traumatic growth is a concept that recognizes a traumatized person's movement from viewing themselves as victims who are helpless and powerless to people who are thriving because they have overcome the negative impact of trauma. Post-traumatic growth focuses on helping trauma survivors move toward the ability to utilize the traumatic experience to catapult themselves to a more rewarding and fulfilling life. A life that gives them meaning and the ability to find gratefulness rather than sorrow and shame. Parents will be the key to moving their family into post-traumatic growth as they improve their ability to implement Family SPACE and the 3 Rs of Relationship skills.

So what exactly do therapists want to see from families in this phase of treatment? Therapists will want to observe more confidence by parents in their ability to be attuned to the needs of their children. Parents will be able to help their children repair relationship ruptures and show that their children are comfortable using the parents for emotional support. How do parents demonstrate attunement? Parents will be able to identify the emotional needs of their children because they are attuned to them. With an increased self-awareness, parents will be able to recognize their own emotional triggers, regulate their emotions effectively, and tap into their resonance circuits to understand how to best help their children. This will help parents to meet their children's emotional needs appropriately. Children will be able to *feel felt* by parents and one another because their parents are attuned to them, which will help to increase empathy and understanding within relationships and aide in the relationship repair process. With increased empathy and understanding within the family, family members will continue to improve intersubjectivity experiences with the traumatized child. Figure 11.1 highlights the reciprocal nature of the skills parents and their children need to accomplish during this final phase of treatment.

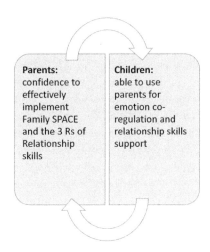

Figure 11.1 Tasks to Accomplish in the Attunement Phase

In the Smith family, Paul and Julie worked to rebuild trust within their marital relationship and support each other while parenting their children. As Paul and Julie were able to work collaboratively together, they increased their ability to use each other for support when making parenting decisions and manage the stressors of raising young children. Julie would often become overwhelmed with Brendan's clingy behavior when he was emotionally distressed. In the past, she felt like she could not use Paul for support because she thought he was too harsh with their children. Paul and Julie discussed ways for Paul to work more effectively with Brendan when Brendan was upset so that Julie could take some breaks for her own emotional self-care. This not only helped reduce Julie's stress level, but also helped to improve Paul's relationship with Brendan.

As Paul and Julie were able to use each other in more supportive ways, they were also able to increase their self-awareness for their own emotional triggers which helped them to be more attuned to their children's needs. Julie recognized subtle ways in which she struggled to allow Paul to take a more active parenting role with the children because she was afraid he might let her down again by drinking, which activated her mentalizations about fathers' inabilities to be a good parent. Her own biological father was an alcoholic and unreliable, and Paul was unreliable when his addiction with alcohol was dominating their family life. Since Julie's threat systems were activated about fathers, she was unable to recognize the negative impact on her children if they did not develop a healthy relationship with Paul. Julie began to slowly relinquish excessive control and allow Paul to take a more active role in parenting. She began to recognize jealousy emotions that welled up in her at times when Brendan went to Paul instead of her for comfort as their relationship improved. This was an important milestone for Paul and Julie.

Parents provide the foundation for attachment changes during the Attunement phase. Family members will continue to build upon the healthy changes made in the previous phase to strengthen and maintain these changes. They will continue to nurture secure attachment interactions that will improve intersubjectivity experiences and increase a sense of safety and security. Conflict is a fact of life within relationships, so parents will need to be able to help their children resolve conflict and communicate effectively to maintain healthy relationships. Parents will need to tolerate their own emotional distress and regulate their own emotions so they can work through the relationship repair process. Parents will continue to develop the ability to co-regulate their child's emotions effectively so that children can use their parents to help them manage their strong emotions. This will be important because eventually therapists will no longer be part of their support system after discharge from treatment, and family members will need to demonstrate the ability to regulate their emotions even when conflict occurs.

Helping Families Terminate Treatment

I have always told my clients that my job is to work myself out of a job. Working through the termination process can be difficult for both clients and therapists since it tends to activate attachment responses to loss. As discussed throughout this book, the brain dictates responses to perceived threat. Experiences of loss may trigger unresolved trauma and grief memories, and thus activate the neuroception circuits resulting in the resurfacing of fight, flight, or freeze behaviors that may have been previously addressed in treatment. Parents with dismissing and preoccupied attachment styles will likely struggle with the termination process (Marmarosh, 2017; Wallin, 2007). Therapists will need to be able to help parents through this part of the treatment process because endings and transitions are a part of life.

From the start of treatment, therapists work toward ending treatment, and in between therapists work toward creating emotional safety and encourage vulnerability. The therapeutic relationship is weird in many ways because it is a relationship cultivated to create emotional safety and authenticity within a framework of professional boundaries and ethics. It's not a friendship, and yet attachment therapists work toward creating a strong therapeutic alliance with their clients that often involves various levels of self-disclosure within professional boundaries. Wallin (2007) states:

> it can be deeply affecting—painful and bittersweet—to experience the prospect of ending the new attachment relationship that therapy has provided. As such, termination provides an extended opportunity to revisit and further resolve the patient's past and present issues around attachment and loss. Needless to say, termination involves not only an emotionally charged backward look, but also the possibility of saying good-bye in a way that is a complete and fully felt as possible.
>
> (p. 206)

The termination process in treatment will vary based on each family's unique needs and attachment styles. The truth is that all families will need to terminate treatment, and that is a cause for celebration. Saidon, Shafran, and Rafaeli (2018) state "as psychotherapy is both an intrapersonal growth process and an interpersonal relationship, its ending is a formidable and multifaceted task, requiring attention to both therapy goals and the therapeutic relationship" (p. 385). I like to view the termination process as a celebration for graduation from treatment. It's important to celebrate the accomplishments of family members (treatment goals), while also taking time to review the family's experience of the therapeutic relationship. This treatment model views the therapeutic relationship as a mirroring of healthy attachment interactions to parents and their children. The termination phase will allow therapists and clients to resolve unidentified relationship ruptures for repair prior to ending their therapeutic time together.

Most families will need reassurance that their therapist will be available at a later time if needed. I often find that clients will finish a course of treatment with me and return to treatment at times of high stress to seek assistance working through those difficult times more successfully. When I was young, my father would work on our cars to fix the mechanical problems that caused them to break down, or he would do some maintenance work, such as an oil change, or change the brakes. When I would ask him what he was doing, his initial response was usually, "I'm tweaking it" and then he'd smile at me. He would "tweak" the car when it needed some repair or maintenance. We all need tweaking at times to help us continue the journey of life. The same is true with therapy. Clients will often return to treatment when a tweaking is needed, either for preventative work or for repair work when life gets difficult. This can be difficult to navigate if you work in an agency setting because you may or may not be with that agency if the family needs to return to services. It will be important to be honest with clients about your availability at a later date as well as ensuring agency policies are followed.

Sometimes clients will terminate treatment prematurely, and avoid a productive termination process due to their own unresolved attachment wounds. It will be important for the therapist to use the Family SPACE skill of awareness to recognize their own experiences of loss so they do not engage in negative countertransference with clients. This subject will be discussed more in Chapter 12.

Therapist's Role

During this phase of treatment, therapists will begin to "turn over the reins," so to speak, to parents so they can take more of a leadership role in the change process. Therapists will continue to coach parents to become skillful when using Family SPACE and the 3 Rs of Relationship skills. It will be important for therapists to shift to more of a consultant role in this phase of treatment so that parents can increase their confidence in their ability to effectively implement the strategies they learned in treatment. Therapists will continue to provide feedback to parents during parent coaching sessions to help parents identify their family's growth and encourage resiliency.

Parents will need ongoing support through the Attunement phase, and therapists will need to continue to maintain a safe, nonjudgmental, therapeutic environment to support families as they work toward termination. Therapists will need to choose activities for the family sessions that will enhance emotional connection between parents and their children. These activities will focus on strengthening family relationships and increase family members' ability to communicate while tolerating emotional distress.

Assessing the family's readiness for termination is a collaborative process between therapists and parents. Therapists will need to elicit feedback from parents during the parent coaching sessions to identify the family strengths and areas of weakness. Parents and their therapist will identify milestones to be achieved that will indicate when the family is ready to discharge from treatment. When assessing a family's readiness for discharge, I typically look at how well parents are able to tolerate their own emotional distress, read their child's cues, and work through the conflicts with their children. When parents are able to demonstrate these abilities, they will be able to provide a more secure foundation for post-traumatic growth. This will be a huge milestone for traumatized families because it means family members have developed resiliency to tolerate life's stressors without destroying healthy attachments.

Choosing Interventions in the Attunement Phase

Therapists and parents will choose clinical targets for interventions during this phase of treatment based on the unique needs of the family. It will be important for therapists to include parents in the decision-making process to choose interventions because this will help parents use their wisdom to know what their family needs, and how to help meet those needs. Parents possess wisdom and understanding of the nuances within the family dynamics that therapists don't possess since we don't live with the family. This collaborative process with parents helps them to feel *seen* and *heard* during the treatment process. If therapists want parents to see and hear their children, then we therapists need to mirror this to parents.

During this phase of treatment with the Smith family, the interventions focused on improving a sense of safety, especially between Paul and his children. The earlier intense conflict between Paul and Julie had created significant uncertainty and fearfulness for their children, especially after watching their father being taken away by the police in handcuffs following a heated argument. To improve safety within their relationships, Paul and Julie needed to increase playfulness in their relationship so that family members could feel joy during their intersubjective experiences. Since the Smith children were young, it was decided to integrate simple children's games during some of the family sessions. The following example was based on playing a common children's game of *Duck, Duck, Goose*. Family members decided to change some of the rules of the game to strengthen a focus on love and connection. One of the rules that was changed was the use of the terminology of Stew Pot when someone was caught. The terminology was changed to Happy Place, and the focus changed to helping *caught* family members feel loved even when tagged out. During the following example, PJ became frustrated when he was tagged out by Sara. Paul and Julie use their Family SPACE skills to help PJ remain in the game.

Sara: I got you PJ!

PJ: No you didn't! You missed me!

Sara: No, I got you, PJ! Mommmm, PJ's cheating!

Julie (to PJ): You're really disappointed about being out. I know that's hard because you like to run really fast and stay in the game.

PJ: She's lying!

Paul (to PJ): Come here, buddy. We'll sit in the Happy Place together. We can see how fast everybody runs while we're in the Happy Place.

PJ (to Paul): I don't want to sit in the Happy Place. I want to play the game.

Paul (to PJ): I know, buddy, you like to run. It's disappointing when you get out. I'll sit with you. We can sit in there together.

PJ: But I don't want to.

Paul: I know, buddy. We can't keep playing, though, if you can't follow the rules so we can all have fun together.

Julie (to PJ): You're doing such a good job playing nicely with us. We really like playing with you. You can sit in the Happy Place with Daddy. You like hanging out with Daddy.

PJ (half-heartedly and with resignation): Okay, fine. I'll sit in there with Daddy. How long will I have to stay there?

Paul: Awesome, buddy! You can keep Daddy company until the next person gets tagged. We'll watch how fast everyone runs.

PJ (without enthusiasm): Fine.

In this example, you'll notice that Julie reflected back to PJ his emotions to validate that he was disappointed about getting tagged out. Julie and Paul did not respond to PJ's blaming behavior because they knew PJ was disappointed and having a hard time accepting that he was tagged out. Paul and Julie were fully present during the game to share a fun, intersubjective experience with their children, which helped PJ stay motivated to remain in the game. Paul offered to go into the Happy Place with PJ to reinforce their shared positive experience during the game because

Paul knew that PJ enjoyed spending time with his father. Paul and Julie remained calm during their discussion with PJ to co-regulate emotions with him and help PJ learn to regulate his emotions when he was distressed. Paul and Julie also accepted that PJ was struggling with disappointment and did not want to go into the Happy Place because he liked the excitement of chasing and being chased. They knew he was an active boy and recognized this aspect of his personality while they helped him respond to their structuring with him so that he could accept the rules of the game. Paul and Julie knew that PJ's ability to play within the rules of the game would be important for him to be successful within his social relationships. Other children would not want to play with him if he could not respect the give and take of the rules of the game, which in turn would negatively impact his self-concept.

Paul and Julie were able to support each other and collaboratively parent PJ even when he was struggling to accept the rules of the game. This was a big step for their relationship because Julie had begun to trust Paul to regulate his emotions and make wise decisions when PJ became emotionally distressed. In the past, Paul would have yelled at PJ to stop cheating and blaming his sister. PJ would have gotten angrier, and the conflict between PJ and Paul would have resulted in a power struggle between them. Julie was able to witness Paul's implementing the Family SPACE skills more successfully, which increased her trust in Paul. This was important since all parents struggle at times to be effective. With improved trust, Julie would be able to maintain trust in Paul's parenting even when he struggled occasionally. In those instances, it would be important for Julie to step in and help with the parenting in a supportive way rather than increasing her mistrust of Paul.

Parent Coaching Sessions

The parent coaching sessions in the Attunement phase of treatment will focus on helping parents increase their confidence and skill using Family SPACE and the 3 Rs of Relationship skills. The relationship between the therapist and parents will need to shift to more of a consultant–parent relationship and move away from the expert–parent type of relationship. Therapists will need to help parents feel more like experts to help them feel more confident in their decision-making process with their children. During this phase, parents and their therapist will explore and identify when the family is ready to successfully end their time in treatment. In

my experience, this can increase anxiety in parents because they worry
that they will not be able to maintain their progress without the help of
their therapist. The therapist will need to take on an encourager/cheer-
leader role to remind parents of the progress they have made and the
wisdom they have gained.

In the following example, the therapist reviewed a video clip of the
above family session. The therapist pointed out the positive changes Paul
and Julie made in treatment, which resulted in PJ's ability to use his parents to help him regulate his emotions when he was distressed during the
game.

Therapist (to Julie and Paul): I'm wondering how you guys thought the
  session went and how things went in this video clip?
Julie: I thought it went really well. It's nice to have fun family time.
  We didn't have that before because we were always fighting.
  I noticed the kids really like when we have family time together
  doing fun things.
Therapist (to Paul): How about you, Paul? What are your thoughts?
Paul: Yeah, it's nice having positive time with the kids. I missed a lot of
  their lives because I was drinking so much. I want my kids to remem-
  ber me in a positive way. I still feel guilty about my drinking, but
  I can't focus on that because it just makes me go to a dark place.
  I want to be there for my kids and I want them to know how much
  I love them.
Therapist: You've worked hard on your sobriety. Your love for your
  family is a strong motivator for you. Your love for your kids is awe-
  some to see. They love you. Your sobriety is a gift to them from you.
  Julie, I'm wondering what your thoughts were in this session when
  Paul stepped in to help with PJ?
Julie: It was nice to see Paul helping PJ to play the game and stay calm. In
  the past, Paul would have just started yelling and then left to go out
  drinking because he was mad. I can see how much PJ responds in
  a good way when Paul spends time with him.
Therapist: You guys have worked hard to learn the skills. Parenting is hard
  and you guys have been through a lot. I can see how much you love
  each other. What skills do you think you used here?
Paul: Well, I kept thinking in my head to use empathy and acceptance
  with PJ. I remember when I was his age. I would get so intense when
  I played games and had a hard time losing. My dad was drunk all the
  time, so I didn't have him to help me back then. Now that he's sober,

he's been really supportive. That helps a lot when I'm struggling, so I want to be able to do that with my kids.

Therapist (to Paul): Any other skills?

Paul: Well, I think I used awareness and presence to help me recognize my own emotions so I could use WiseMind to help me figure out that it might be helpful to PJ if I sat in the Happy Place with him. I know he likes to hang out with me, so I thought that might help him to accept the rule to sit in the Happy Place.

Therapist (to Julie): How about you, Julie? Do you think you used any skills?

Julie: I definitely used awareness and presence to help me stay calm.
I could feel my frustration starting to come up because I was afraid there would be a big meltdown and ruin our fun time together. Once I could see that Paul was doing a good job with PJ, I could relax more. (Julie turned to Paul) Paul, I saw you use structuring with PJ when you reminded him that he needed to follow the rules. I think you used empathy with him first and offered to have him sit with you in the Happy Place, then he was willing to follow the rules.

Therapist (to Julie): How was that for you to see Paul doing such a good job with PJ?

Julie: It helps me to trust Paul when I see him staying calm and using the skills you taught us. Paul and I are doing much better working together with the kids. That takes a lot of pressure and worry off me. Paul is working really hard on his sobriety.

Paul: Yeah, Julie and I have been doing much better together. We don't argue over the kids like we used to. I want to show Julie that she can trust me. I know I have to keep working on my sobriety. When I get frustrated with the kids, Julie is great about stepping in so I can cool down. I think I'm doing better staying calm.

Therapist (to Julie): How is that for you when you see Paul gets frustrated? It sounds like you are starting to trust him more and you guys are working more collaboratively together. As a mom myself, I know that sometimes I need to tag team with my husband so he can take over when I'm having a bad day. It's nice to have that support because parenting is not for the "faint of heart."

Julie: That's for sure. I think Paul and I are working much better together. He gives me breaks with the kids and I feel more comfortable leaving the kids with him so I can take a break. It's been really nice.

In this example, the therapist helped Paul and Julie recognize the skills they were using so they could feel more confident in their abilities to use them. The therapists used the Family SPACE skill of curiosity to help Paul and Julie identify their progress rather than simply telling them what she has noticed. It's important for parents to recognize how well they are doing because it will increase their confidence when they gain that awareness. The therapist reinforced their progress working collaboratively and highlighted their love for their children. Paul and Julie identified that their ability to work together has made a difference and has enabled PJ to use Paul's support. Paul and Julie were able to identify the skills they used, recognize the importance of self-awareness to help them co-regulate their children's emotions, and use WiseMind to help them make effective parenting decisions.

As the family continues to progress in treatment, the therapist, Paul, and Julie will begin to explore and identify when they are ready to discharge. This will be an important part of the treatment process for the family because it will demonstrate their resiliency and post-traumatic growth. The therapist will continue to help Paul and Julie recognize their progress using Family SPACE and the 3 Rs of Relationship so they can feel more confident in their abilities. Paul and Julie will be ready to discharge from treatment when they recognize their consistent ability to implement the skills they learned in treatment, and their children are able to feel safe in their relationship with Paul. Since children need to feel safe in order to engage playfully, their ability to engage playfully with Paul will be a strong indicator of their improved relationships. Paul and Julie will need to demonstrate their ability to use each other for support, and repair their relationship ruptures in order to maintain trust in their relationship. They will be the foundation for secure attachments with their children. Remember, parents don't need to be perfect, they just need to be good enough more often than not in order to provide a secure foundation for their children.

References

Marmarosh, C. L. (2017). Fostering engagement during termination: Applying attachment theory and research. *Psychotherapy*, *54*(1), 4–9. doi:10.1037/pst0000087

Saidon, H. S., Shafran, N., & Rafaeli, E. (2018). Teach them how to say goodbye: The CMRA model for treatment endings. *Journal of Psychotherapy Integration*, *28*(3), 385–400. doi:10.1037/int0000127

Wallin, D. J. (2007). *Attachment in psychotherapy*. New York, NY: The Guilford Press.

Clinical Considerations When Working with Traumatized Families **12**

All families are different and unique based on their individual personalities, culture, life experiences, and generational histories. As discussed in Chapter 7, families are complex. Working with traumatized families is a multifaceted process requiring therapists to have an understanding of trauma, attachment, and the nuances of each family system, as well as the communities and organizations in which they interact. In my experience, the likelihood of working with a difficult family system when there are multiple agencies involved is high, and therapists will need to make a commitment to these families if they are accepted as clients. Working with challenging families within a multisystemic and multicultural framework will require therapists to remain focused on the importance of improving attachment security within the family and advocate for the implementation of a trauma and attachment lens by the various systems involved with the family. This chapter will discuss an overview of several areas of special consideration when working with families. It is beyond the scope of this book to address these areas in depth.

Traumatized families may need to utilize additional services to support the family, such as social services and court personnel. Therapists working with children in foster care will require them to work collaboratively with foster care workers and court personnel. Families involved with Child Protective Services (CPS) often have a high level of mistrust due to the nature of trauma and neglect, having a child removed from parental care, and the possibility of legal ramifications for parents. Parents with mental health issues can also create challenges for the family's ability to make progress in treatment. Therapists need to recognize and assess the severity of the mental health issues, and the parent's ability to create stability and safety within the family to determine when additional resources may be needed to address the impact of trauma. Cultural considerations will be discussed to ensure that therapists implement the treatment model with sensitivity to the nuances of the family's culture in order to help them heal. Therapists will need to help parents and their children successfully navigate these issues to help parents and their children maintain healthy relationships.

Working with Challenging Families

Working with challenging families can be exhausting for therapists due to the intensity of the emotions activated within the family system, as well as the emotions that get stirred up by the addition of the new therapeutic relationship. Therapists enter into the therapeutic relationship with their own attachment histories and ability to regulate their emotions when their own neuroception circuits become activated, so they will need to actively monitor their own countertransference in order to help family members co-regulate and effectively work through relationship disruptions. Therapists will need to act as an attachment figure for families while parents are increasing their attachment skills in order to fulfill that role with their children and overcome the negative impact of trauma. This can be difficult when working with challenging families, so it will be important for therapists to seek consultation and support to maintain clinical clarity and stability.

Families with generational trauma, attachment, and/or addiction problems tend to have an increased risk of maladaptive psychological functioning within family relationships. In my experience working with parents who demonstrated significant personality psychopathology, parental sensitivity to their child's social and emotional needs was significantly limited due to low mentalizing abilities and limited sensitivity to their child's needs. These parents often demonstrated a high level of neuroception activation and difficulty regulating their emotions when their threat systems were activated. Their ability to use the Family SPACE skills, especially awareness and presence, was significantly impaired. I've found when the therapist was able to use the Family SPACE skills effectively with challenging parents this greatly increased the likelihood of gaining therapeutic trust with the parents. The treatment process generally took longer in order to slow the pace of change to an acceptable and safe level for parents to avoid overwhelming their ability to allow activation of their social engagement systems. Issues that are common in challenging family systems include high conflict divorce dynamics, personality psychopathology, dissociative parents, disengaged foster parents, ongoing substance misuse in the family, low cognitive capacity of parents, high crisis oriented clients, and/or parents with low mentalizing abilities. These issues can create significant challenges during the treatment process, and therapists must be able to assess parental capacities and adjust expectations as needed throughout treatment.

Sometimes, despite our best efforts, clients will choose to terminate treatment prematurely. This is usually hard for me because in my heart I want the family to be able to experience the benefits of healing. However, parents may not be able to tolerate the emotional distress of the change process. There may be other reasons families prematurely discontinue treatment, such as insurance payment denials, financial hardships, or relocation to another town or state. This is a reality that I have come to understand in my clinical work with families, and, when appropriate, I use it as an opportunity to self-reflect on my effectiveness with the family so that I can continue to grow professionally and personally. Rodriguez-Seijas, Morgan, and Zimmerman (2019) reviewed the literature regarding client premature treatment termination and found that about one in five clients will end treatment early. Premature termination tends to result in negative outcomes for those clients, and therapeutic orientation does not correlate with better or worse results for completion of treatment. The authors explored the correlation between premature termination from treatment and the presence of personality psychopathology in adults who participated in a partial hospitalization program. Their results indicated "that individuals who prematurely terminated treatment reported higher levels on all maladaptive personality domains when compared with those who completed treatment" (Rodriguez-Seijas, et al., p. 6). Since I know that some families may terminate treatment prematurely for various reasons, I try to "plant seeds" of knowledge and expectation as much as possible so that the next time the family seeks treatment they may resonate with information repeated by the next therapist to help them stay engaged in the change process.

When Additional Services Are Needed

Sometimes traumatized families will need more support than weekly therapy sessions to help them in the healing process, and therapists can help family members recognize the need for additional assistance. Creating a support network for families can reduce stressors for families, and increase their ability to engage in the change process. This is especially true for children who have experienced ongoing developmental trauma. Their neuroception circuits will be easily triggered, including during school, daycare, community activities, and sports activities. Crenshaw and Mordock (2005) coined the term *fawns in gorilla suits* to describe aggressive children who have often been the victims of developmental trauma. Caregivers of these children are often overwhelmed by the magnitude of helping their traumatized child heal from the impact of their emotional wounds. The authors state "any caregiver working with children in gorilla suits needs a backup person. Rather than a sign of defeat or failure, it is a sign of strength to know when help is needed" (Crenshaw & Mordock, 2005, p. 159).

Therapists can be an advocate for families to get additional assistance, and help them access those resources. Oftentimes, traumatized children may require additional support at school to help them when the school setting has become overwhelming. Helping parents identify and access those resources will be invaluable so they can support their traumatized child's ability to succeed at school. In addition to obtaining aid at their child's school, parents may need assistance in identifying which local resources are needed and how to access those resources. These additional support systems and resources can include engaging religious and community organizations to aid with emotional support and practical needs, such as financial assistance, childcare, and mentoring.

Working collaboratively with additional agencies, such as foster care workers, guardian *ad litems*, and court personnel can present many obstacles since these systems are not always supportive to traumatized families. Continuity of care across multiple agencies can be quite overwhelming for families, and parents need assistance to navigate through these agencies to ensure their needs are met and their rights are respected. Therapists can help parents access resources and learn to be assertive to get their needs met within these systems. Silberg (2013) recommended that therapists become champions for the needs of traumatized children when multiple bureaucracies are involved in the child's life, such as court systems, social services, and insurance companies. According to Silberg (2013), "no matter what treatment model one uses, systems dilemmas will arise that require a thoughtful, child-focused, and trauma-sensitive response" (p. 207). It will be important for therapists to work with parents to assess their needs and the effectiveness of the systems involved with their family to figure out where and how to advocate when necessary.

Therapists will need to monitor safety risks in families in which one or more of the family members struggles with suicidal ideation and/or self-harm. Families with a strong history of abuse and neglect, parental personality psychopathology, and substance abuse will need to be monitored for parental capacity to maintain safety and address challenging behaviors in a safe and appropriate manner. If there is a concern that a family member is a high risk of harm to self or others, then the therapist will need to provide coaching to parents about when to seek inpatient hospitalization for stabilization of safety risks. At times, therapists will be required to contact Child Protective Services when there is a threat to a child's safety. These are difficult issues to navigate with families that will require therapists to be attuned to the family dynamics, and be clear about their role as mandated reporters in their local jurisdiction.

There will be times when therapists need to recommend a child be placed in a residential treatment facility due to the severity of the child's unhealthy behaviors and inability to use their parents for emotion regulation and attachment security. Sometimes, parents are unable to help their traumatized child heal at home, and therapists need to help parents recognize and access residential treatment for their child. Seeking residential treatment for a traumatized child will be a difficult and heart-wrenching process for parents. Parents often feel like failures when their child requires more long-term 24-hour treatment. In my experience working at adolescent treatment facilities, families of the traumatized child are overwhelmed and emotionally exhausted by the traumatized child's unsafe and aggressive behavior within the home and the community. Placing the child in a residential treatment facility is often necessary and a last resort for parents to help their traumatized child heal. Therapists will need to provide guidance to parents regarding how to access an appropriate treatment facility for their child that is experienced and knowledgeable about working with children who have trauma and attachment issues, and to ensure their child's needs are met in the residential program.

Cultural Considerations

Working with families will require therapists to have a framework for understanding cultural contexts for racial and ethnic minority families in treatment. When working with immigrant families, I have found it helpful to use a framework of assessing acculturation within families and helping family members to navigate their differing acculturation levels.

Acculturation is generally understood as a bidirectional process of navigating two distinct cultures in which one's culture from their country of origin and that of the host country intersect across various dimensions of one's daily living, for example, family and home life, school, work, and social domains (Lawton, Gerdes, & Kapke, 2018; Yoon et al., 2013). According to Tikhonov, Espinosa, and Huynh (2019), racial and ethnic minority (REM) immigrants that maintain their ethnic identity while also adopting the national identity of the host country "is associated with better mental health outcomes than endorsing either cultural identity exclusively" (p. 495).

Children of immigrant parents tend to acculturate more quickly and globally than their adult family members since they tend to attend school where they are immersed in the host country culture. Parents will likely vary in their acculturation levels depending on their immersion into the host country's culture. More isolated family members may have a lesser degree of acculturation and maintain the beliefs and customs of their country of origin. Therapists can assist parents and their children to successfully navigate cultural diversity issues by helping them to identify their values and customs that are important to maintain within their family. I have found it helpful to invite family members to teach me about their culture and customs to better understand them, and help them work through conflict when culture clashes occur between parents and their children. Ultimately, family members will need to work to better understand one another, which will aid them in establishing healthy relationships while respecting their heritage.

Families who have immigrated to the United States from countries with high incidences of trauma will require therapists to understand a more global impact of trauma within a community or country. In countries with high crime and violence, the trauma becomes more integrated into the culture rather than individual or family specific. It will be important for therapists to explore with parents during coaching sessions the extent and nature of cultural influences within the family relationships and how trauma is perceived within a cultural lens. This will require therapists to recognize differences among parenting practices in other cultures, and help parents to understand what may or may not be acceptable in American culture, especially as it relates to corporal punishment. Therapists may need to provide psychoeducation about mental health, trauma, and attachment with sensitivity to the cultural practices of a parent's country of origin. Ultimately, therapists will focus on helping parents and their children to develop strong relationships while helping them to maintain a healthy cultural identity to support post-traumatic growth and resiliency.

Not all minority families in the United States are considered to be immigrants and yet they have a minority status in our culture. African American families and Native American families will require Caucasian therapists to be knowledgeable about the values, beliefs, and customs of these communities. As with immigrant families, therapists need to recognize the need to view African American and Native American families with a racial and ethnic minority lens to ensure sensitivity to their cultures. When working with African American families, Hinds (2005) encouraged therapists to understand the role of spirituality, racism, and values within the African American community which she refers to as the African American "village." Hinds (2005) stated that therapists need to

> step into the African American "village" in order to gain insight into the role of play as influenced by slavery, religion, socioeconomic status (SES) and gender differences. By gaining this information, the therapist will be better able to form a stronger bond with the "villagers".
>
> (p. 115)

Glover (2005) asserted that working with Native American families will require therapists to recognize that there are tribal differences within the Native American community, and, therefore, therapists will need to become familiar with the specific values and customs of the tribes from which their families are connected. As with other cultures, there will be varying levels of acculturation among tribal members.

The vast majority of cultures share a common value of collectivism rather than individualism. In the United States, individualism is dominant, which views the needs of the individual as greater than the needs of the family and community. Collectivism is the prevailing value within racial and ethnic minority communities. This value of collectivism believes the family and community needs are more important than the needs of the individual. The influence of collectivism is seen in the values evident within family relationships and connection to their communities. Therapists should check their own personal biases to work effectively with racial and ethnic minority families who have experienced trauma. It will be important for therapists to explore views of play, mental health, therapy, and expectations within family relationships. Therapists will likely need to provide psychoeducation about mental illness, impact of trauma, and the benefit of therapy, and will require therapists to be culturally sensitive when providing psychoeducation. In my experience, when family members have been able to experience the therapist as respectful and genuine, then that will increase the ability to build a "bridge" of trust across the cultural divide and allow the therapist to establish therapeutic rapport.

Since a primary focus of this model is to integrate play and expressive arts into the treatment process, therapists need to ensure there are culturally diverse materials available for use. Art materials need to include multicultural art supplies, such as crayons, markers, paint, and construction paper. Therapists will need to integrate multicultural games, books, and toys when working with families. Sand tray figures from different cultures are important to have in your collection to allow family members to access symbols that represent them. Integrating culturally diverse toys and art materials in the therapy sessions will allow therapists to provide a therapeutic environment that is respectful to culturally diverse families. Drewes (2005) recommended that "materials that are highly structured, are stereotyped, or promote antisocial or competitive behavior should be avoided" (p. 195). She recommended that therapists invite racial and ethnic minority parents into the playroom office prior to beginning sessions to view what supplies are present and give feedback to the therapist. Drewes (2005) further recommended that "sensitivity to the images in the playroom is essential, as well as those in the waiting area and office; no therapist will want to offend clients by inadvertently including something viewed as taboo, or considered bad luck or evil" (p. 195).

References

Crenshaw, D., & Mordock, J. (2005). *Understanding and treating the aggression of children: Fawns in gorilla suits*. Lanham, MD: Jason Aronson.

Drewes, A. (2005). Multicultural play therapy resources. In E. Gil & A. Drewes (Eds.), *Cultural issues in play therapy* (pp. 195–205). New York, NY: The Guilford Press.

Glover, G. (2005). Musings on working with Native American children in play therapy. In E. Gil & A. Drewes (Eds.), *Cultural issues in play therapy* (pp. 168–179). New York, NY: The Guilford Press.

Hinds, S. (2005). Play in the African American "village". In E. Gil & A. Drewes (Eds.), *Cultural issues in play therapy* (pp. 115–147). New York, NY: The Guilford Press.

Lawton, K. E., Gerdes, A. C., & Kapke, T. (2018). The role of acculturation differences and acculturation conflict in Latino family mental health. *Journal of Latino/a Psychology*, 6(2), 94–114. doi:10.1037/lat0000084

Rodriguez-Seijas, C., Morgan, T. A., & Zimmerman, M. (2019). Associations between maladaptive personality domains and premature treatment termination in an acute clinical setting. *Personality Disorders: Theory, Research, and Treatment.* Advanced online publication. doi:10.1037/per0000387

Silberg, J. L. (2013). *The child survivor: Healing developmental trauma and dissociation.* New York, NY: Routledge.

Tikhonov, A. A., Espinosa, A., & Huynh, Q. (2019). Bicultural identity harmony and American identity are associated with positive mental health in U.S. racial and ethnic minority immigrants. *Cultural Diversity and Ethnic Minority Psychology, 25*(4), 494–504. doi:10.1037/cdp0000268

Yoon, E., Chang, C.-T., Kim, S., Clawson, A., Cleary, S. E., Hansen, M., Bruner, J. P., Chan, T. K., & Gomes, A. M. (2013). A meta-analysis of acculturation/enculturation and mental health. *Journal of Counseling Psychology, 60*(1), 15–30. doi:10.1037/a0030652

Resources for Play and Expressive Arts Family Play Therapy Interventions

Buchalter, S. I. (2013). *Mandala symbolism and techniques: Innovative approaches for professionals*. London, UK: Jessica Kingsley Publishers.

Cohen, B. M., Barnes, M., & Rankin, A. B. (1995). *Managing traumatic stress through art: Drawing from the center*. Baltimore, MD: The Sidran Press.

Crisci, G., Lay, M., & Lowenstein, L. (1998). *Paper dolls and paper airplanes: Therapeutic exercises for sexually traumatized children*. Indianapolis, IN: Kidsrights.

Gil, E. (1994). *Play in family therapy*. New York, NY: The Guilford Press.

Gil, E. (2006) *Family play therapy: The benefits of using play in family therapy* [DVD and Booklet]. Fairfax, VA: Starbright Training Institute for Family and Child Therapy. Retrieved from https://selfesteemshop.com.

Holmes, M. M. (2000). *A terrible thing happened*. Washington, DC: Magination Press.

Kaduson, H. G., & Schaefer, C. E. (Eds.). (2001). *101 more favorite play therapy techniques*. Northvale, NJ: Jason Aronson Inc.

Lowenstein, L. (2006). *Creative interventions for bereaved children*. Toronto, Ontario: Champion Press.

Lowenstein, L. (Ed.). (2010). *Creative family therapy techniques: Play, art, and expressive activities to engage children in family sessions*. Toronto, Ontario: Champion Press.

Manasco, H. (2012). *An exceptional children's guide to touch: Teaching social and physical boundaries to kids*. London, UK: Jessica Kingsley Publishers.

Schaefer, C. E., & Cangelosi, D. M. (Eds.). (1993). *Play therapy techniques*. Northvale, NJ: Jason Aronson Inc.

Sheppard, C. H. (1998). *Brave Bart: A story for traumatized and grieving children*. Clinton Township, MI: The National Institute for Trauma and Loss in Children. Retrieved from www.starrtraining.org/tlc.

Index

attention deficit hyperactivity disorder
(ADHD) 15
attunement 41, 54; Attunement phase 22,
121–122, 186–199; empathic 87–89,
143–144; flexibility 98; innate drive for
129; intersubjectivity 70, 72; mirror
neurons 37; Safety and Engagement
phase 155
autonomic nervous system (ANS) 30, 39,
45, 58
avoidant attachment 10, 64, 66, 68
awareness: Attunement phase 198; emotion
regulation 112, 133; Family SPACE skills
103, 106–107, 163; mindfulness approach
143–144; Realignment phase 175, 184;
termination of treatment 193; *see also*
self-awareness

Badenoch, B. A. 34
Balbernie, R. 70
Barbosa, M. 54
bearing witness 172
Becker-Weidman, A. 19
Beeghly, M. 54
behaviors: Attachment-based Family Play
Therapy Framework 126; core beliefs
77–78; empathy and acceptance 110;
mentalization 90; reading cues 90,
91–92
belonging 20, 129, 132
Biringen, Z. 64, 66
Blank, A. 111–112
Blatz, William 20
blended families 127, 137, 141, 150
Borelli, J. L. 79, 128, 134
Borg, M. 111–112
boundaries 97, 99, 122–123, 125, 131–132;
Realignment phase 173, 184; Safety and
Engagement phase 167; structure 126; *see
also* limit setting
Bowlby, John 10
brain 6–7, 20, 26–45; brain development 6,
47, 55, 84; danger alerts 134; plasticity
136; PLAY system 17; sense of self 12–13;
threat system 115; *see also* neurobiology;
neuroception
brainstem 4, 27–28, 37, 40–41, 44, 75
Bratton, S. C. 14
breathing skills 164–166
Broday, R. 79
Brown, Brené 73, 89
bubbles activity 164–166, 168–169
Buk, A. 179
bullying 41

Burkhart, M. L. 79, 90
Byng-Hall, J. 11

Cadvar, A. 14
Camp, A. C. 14
CARE system 43, 66
challenging families 201–202
change 173
Child-Centered Play Therapy (CCPT) 14
Child Protective Services (CPS) 200, 204
cingulate gyrus 29
co-regulation 10–11, 22, 44, 55, 66;
Attunement phase 190, 191, 196, 199;
Safety and Engagement phase 157, 162;
see also emotion regulation
coaching: Attunement phase 193, 196–199;
cultural issues 205; Observational
Assessment phase 150–153; Realignment
phase 174, 182–185; Safety and
Engagement phase 158, 167–170
collectivism 206
communication 11–12, 69; Attunement
phase 191, 193; babies 135; empathic
attunement 88–89; of needs 177–178;
Observational Assessment phase 144;
parental 167; play 15; reflexive 110–112,
151, 183, 184, 188; Safety and
Engagement phase 153
Compare, A. 128
compassion 89, 123
conflict: Attunement phase 191; blended
families 127; case example 156, 194;
challenging families 201–202; divorced
families 127–128; Family SPACE skills
112; Realignment phase 177, 178; repair
of relationship ruptures 114; Safety and
Engagement phase 153
consultation 123
containment 70
Cooper, G. 65, 133
coping skills 160–161; Realignment phase
173, 177, 178; Safety and Engagement
phase 155, 157
core beliefs 73, 76–78
Cornett, N. 14
corpus callosum 29, 34, 35
cortex 26, 32–34
Cortina, M. 71–72
countertransference 38, 144, 174, 193, 201
Crenshaw, D. 158, 160, 203
cues 28–29, 31, 47, 64; flexibility 98;
nonverbal 188; reading 72, 84, 89–92
cultural issues 201, 204–207
Cummings, E. M. 131

self-care 85, 95, 190
self-compassion 174, 176
self-concept 10, 144, 160, 196
self-control 131–132
self-harm 204
self-soothing 41, 54
senses 6, 29, 49–50
sexual abuse 9, 32, 53, 79; case example
137–138, 140–142, 149–150, 153, 171–173,
175, 184; dissociation 59; empathic
responding 93; mentalization 128, 134;
nightmares 50; siblings 78, 118, 130–131,
139, 149–150
Shafran, N. 192
shame 73, 82, 83, 89, 110, 124; Acceptance and
Change 173; Realignment phase 177, 183,
185; sexual abuse 150, 172; siblings 131
Shapiro, Francine 52
shared attention 72–73
siblings 20–21, 56, 116, 126, 129–131;
intersubjectivity 72; Observational
Assessment phase 142, 144, 151;
perceptions 5; Realignment phase 177;
repair of relationship ruptures 84; Safety
and Engagement phase 153; sexual abuse
78, 118, 130–131, 139, 149–150
Siegel, Daniel J.: attachment 9–10, 11;
cortical areas 32; mind maps 35, 36;
mindfulness skills 157, 158; preoccupied
attachment 68–69; presence and acceptance
123, 124; relational mind 5; resonance
circuits 37, 75, 79, 92; self-awareness 133;
therapeutic presence 143
Silberg, Joyanna 60, 75–76, 203
single parents 127
Snavely, J. E. 128
social and emotional development 74, 131
social brain 35–36, 52, 53
social engagement system 17–18, 26, 39–41,
45, 130, 144, 185, 201
Solomon, E. P. 49, 50
Solomon, Judith 10
Sommer, M. 111–112
SPACE skills 103–104, 105–110, 112, 114;
Attunement phase 186, 187, 188, 189,
190, 195, 196, 199; challenging families
201; Observational Assessment phase
138, 140, 142, 145, 152; Realignment
phase 172, 174, 176, 177, 182, 184;
Safety and Engagement phase 156, 158,
159, 161, 163, 168, 171; termination of
treatment 193
Steele, W. 15, 16, 180
Strange Situation 42, 65
stress 7, 30, 31, 45, 54, 81, 83

structure 41, 95–97, 126, 133, 170, 187–188;
Attunement phase 198; blended families
150; emotion regulation 86; Family
SPACE skills 103, 105, 106, 168;
Observational Assessment phase 145;
Realignment phase 184
substance use 9, 13, 116, 122, 128, 202, 204;
see also addiction
suicidal ideation 204
sympathetic nervous system (SNS) 30, 39,
40, 50, 58

target points 142–143
termination of treatment 121–122, 186, 188,
191–193, 194, 199, 202
Terr, Lenore 31
Tetherball analogy 56, 61, 86
thalamus 29
therapeutic alliance 125, 161, 167, 185,
188, 192
therapeutic relationship 65, 122, 150, 174,
185; Attunement phase 192; challenging
families 201; empathic responding 95;
Observational Assessment phase 143,
144; presence and acceptance 123;
Realignment phase 173; Safety and
Engagement phase 155, 167, 170;
termination of treatment 192
therapist, role of 123–125, 143–144, 167,
173–175, 193–194
threats 7, 12–13, 28; activation of threat
system 115; amygdala 29–30; dissociation
58, 61; hypervigilance 90; limbic system
92; memories and threat response 52, 55;
neuroception 17, 39–40, 43, 48, 51, 162,
164, 175; play 17–18; Realignment
phase 176
Three Rs of Relationship 104, 110–114;
Attunement phase 186, 187, 188, 189,
190, 193, 196, 199; Realignment phase
171, 174, 177, 178; Safety and
Engagement phase 156, 158, 161
Tikhonov, A. A. 205
Tinnin, L. W. 179–180
tone of voice 11–12, 49–50, 52–53, 55; FFSF
experiment 54; intention 85;
mentalization 75; neural circuits 44, 51;
Observational Assessment phase 149;
parental engagement 132–133
transference 144, 174
trauma 7–8, 47–63; art therapy 15;
attachment-based interventions 18;
attachment patterns 11; bearing witness
172; clinical considerations 200–207;
corpus callosum 35; dissociation 59, 60,

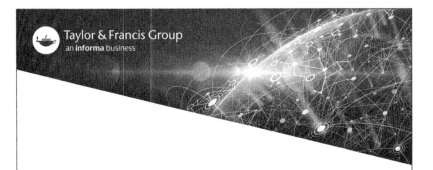